THE
EVERYTHING®
PARENT'S GUIDE TO
CHILDREN
WITH
ADD/ADHD

A reassuring guide to getting the
right diagnosis, understanding treatments,
and h... ...l focus

Li... ...D.

Welcome to

THE
EVERYTHING®
PARENT'S GUIDES

As a parent, you're swamped with conflicting advice and parenting techniques that tell you what is best for your child. THE EVERYTHING® PARENT'S GUIDES get right to the point about specific issues. They give you the most recent, up-to-date information on parenting trends, behavior issues, and health concerns—providing you with a detailed resource to help you ease your parenting anxieties.

THE EVERYTHING® PARENT'S GUIDES are an extension of the bestselling Everything® series in the parenting category. These family-friendly books are designed to be a one-stop guide for parents. If you want authoritative information on specific topics not fully covered in other books, THE EVERYTHING® PARENT'S GUIDES are the perfect resource to ensure that you raise a healthy, confident child.

Visit the entire Everything® series at *www.everything.com*

THE
EVERYTHING®
PARENT'S GUIDE TO
Children with ADD/ADHD

Dear Reader,

Perhaps I devoted so much of my life to studying ADD/ADHD because I have all of the symptoms. Since I grew up before this diagnosis existed, I thought of myself as different, not disordered. After working for a quarter century with so many children diagnosed with ADD/ADHD, I became convinced that whether our "problem behaviors" are disorders or aspects of personality, they can have real value.

I prize my incredibly high energy level, wearing as it is for others. I like being able to tune out everything and concentrate for hours when something holds my interest, though it frustrates those who want my attention. I do wish I weren't so impulsive and could remember to look before I leap. Still, I am proud when a fast decision lands me on soft turf. When I crash land, I tend to my bruises and carry on. I can't stand that faint sounds, scents, and movements distract me so, and wish that crowds and clutter didn't set my nerves on edge. But I've learned to control my environment when I can and cope when I cannot.

I hope your children can overcome or accept their weaknesses, develop their talents, use their strengths, and appreciate themselves for who they are. Then their ADD/ADHD battle will have been won.

Dr. *[signature]*

THE
EVERYTHING

PARENT'S GUIDE TO

CHILDREN WITH
ADD/ADHD

A reassuring guide to getting the right
diagnosis, understanding treatments,
and helping your child focus

Linda Sonna, Ph.D.

Adams Media
Avon, Massachusetts

To Lois Mark, a one-of-a-kind mom.

Publishing Director: Gary M. Krebs
Managing Editor: Kate McBride
Copy Chief: Laura M. Daly
Acquisitions Editor: Kate Burgo
Development Editor: Karen Johnson Jacot
Production Editors: Jamie Wielgus,
Bridget Brace

Production Director: Susan Beale
Production Manager: Michelle Roy Kelly
Cover Design: Paul Beatrice, Matt LeBlanc
Layout and Graphics: Colleen Cunningham,
Rachael Eiben, John Paulhus,
Daria Perreault, Monica Rhines, Erin Ring

• • •

An Everything® Series Book.
Everything® and everything.com® are registered trademarks of F+W Publications, Inc.

Published by Adams Media, an F+W Publications Company
57 Littlefield Street, Avon, MA 02322 U.S.A.
www.adamsmedia.com
ISBN 13: 978-1-59337-308-5
ISBN 10: 1-59337-308-2

Printed in Canada.

J I H G F E D

Library of Congress Cataloging-in-Publication Data
Sonna, Linda
The everything parent's guide to children with ADD/ADHD / Linda Sonna.
p.   cm. — (An everything series book)
ISBN 1-59337-308-2
1. Attention-deficit hyperactivity disorder—Popular works.
I. Title. II. Series: Everything series.

RJ506.H9S658 2005
649'.154—dc22
                    2004026354

This publication is designed to provide accurate and authoritative information with regard to the subject matter covered. It is sold with the understanding that the publisher is not engaged in rendering legal, accounting, or other professional advice. If legal advice or other expert assistance is required, the services of a competent professional person should be sought.

—From a *Declaration of Principles* jointly adopted by a Committee of the American Bar Association and a Committee of Publishers and Associations

Many of the designations used by manufacturers and sellers to distinguish their products are claimed as trademarks. Where those designations appear in this book and Adams Media was aware of a trademark claim, the designations have been printed with initial capital letters.

The information contained in this book is designed for educational purposes only and is not intended to provide medical advice or other professional services. The information should not be used for diagnosis, treatment, or as a substitute for professional care. If your child has a medical or behavioral problem, or you suspect such a possibility, consult your health-care provider. All case studies are composites designed to reflect common behaviors and situations. Information has been changed to protect parents' and children's identities.

All the examples and dialogues used in this book are fictional, and have been created by the author to illustrate disciplinary situations.

Attention-Deficit Disorder (ADD) n. An individual who is markedly inattentive, disorganized, distracted, and forgetful. Low self-esteem and academic underachievement are common.

Attention-Deficit/Hyperactivity Disorder (ADHD) n. An individual who is exceptionally active, restless, and/or impulsive. Difficulties learning in traditional academic environments and defiance are common.

Acknowledgments

For their advice, contributions, and support,
I am grateful to Lois Mark, Jack Carpenter, Michele Potter,
Dr. Larry Sonna, Dr. Jonathan O'Leary, Tina Hahn of Taos Herb,
Dr. Jonathan Walker of Neurotherapy Associates of Dallas, Laurie
Boucke, Chyna Dixon, Phaedra Greenwood, Diane Gilliard, Laura
Stevens, Ted Nero, Tobin Herold, Henry Herold, Jim Malloy, Margie
Henzel, Dr. Brotman, Jessica Quintana, and Mark Sonna.

Special thanks to research assistants Lyn Bleiler; Jan Abeita,
and Kathleen Knoth; copy editors Lois Mark, Elizabeth
Cunningham, Jack Carpenter, Jack Derby, Debi Gutierrez,
and Lyn Bleiler; and the many children who taught me so much,
especially Michele and Zion Gia, Timmy and Shéa White,
Christine Archuleta, and Ruben Martinez.

. . .

Contents

CHAPTER 1

What Is ADHD?

In the past, children were diagnosed with attention deficit disorder (ADD) because they didn't pay attention, had poor organizational skills, and did poorly on tasks requiring sustained mental activity, such as schoolwork. Children were diagnosed with hyperactivity (ADHD) if they were constantly on the go and behaved impulsively. Now the two diagnoses have been combined into attention-deficit/hyperactivity disorder (ADD/ADHD), and the definitions have been expanded. Today almost any misbehaving child can be diagnosed ADD or ADHD. That includes youngsters with a low energy level and a tendency to daydream.

Life with an ADD/ADHD Child

James's father smiled as he watched his small son run in circles around the coffee table. "He certainly is all boy, isn't he?" he asked his wife. His wife frowned. She wondered if all little boys were such bundles of energy. Her friends said their toddlers had acted like little perpetual motion machines at his age, so maybe James's behavior was normal and he would outgrow it. Still, she thought it strange that he showed no signs of tiring after running for ten minutes as fast as his legs could carry him. Actually, he was running faster than his legs could carry him. "Slow down, honey," his mother said. James gave no sign of having heard her. A moment later he tripped and fell. His head hit the coffee table and made an alarming thud.

Alert!

Hyperactivity and problems getting babies to pay attention and mind typically appear when they begin to crawl and walk. Because normal tots are so active, inattentive, and independent, doctors used to be reluctant to medicate children under age three. However, this has become a popular practice.

James's mother kissed his latest boo-boo. "You need to be careful," she said. But as soon as his wails subsided, he was off and running again. He widened his circle and spread chaos throughout the house as his mother trailed after him, issuing "no-no's." When she turned her back, he pulled an entire row of books off the shelf. While she was putting them away, he dumped out his toy box and scattered blocks across the room. While she was picking up the toys, he somehow scaled the dining room hutch and emptied an entire drawer. If she sent him to his room for a time-out, he would wreak havoc there, too.

James's mother put on a video and bribed him with a snack to sit down and watch. Even while his eyes were glued to the screen, he continued to fidget and squirm. The pediatrician said that was because James was hyperactive, and he didn't listen because he had an attention deficit. The doctor wanted to prescribe medication, but her husband was strongly opposed. James's mother didn't like the idea of medicating a tot, either, but she herself had started taking pills to help her cope. Maybe James would benefit from medicine, too.

Current Definitions

The Diagnostic and Statistical Manual of Mental Disorders, Fourth Edition, Text Revision (DSM-IV-TR), which was published by the American Psychiatric Association in 2000, lists all of the mental and behavioral disorders currently recognized by U.S. doctors. The standard attention-deficit/hyperactivity disorder diagnosis is divided into three types. The "predominantly inattentive type" is for children with attention deficits but no problems with hyperactivity. The "predominantly hyperactive/impulsive type" diagnosis is used for hyperactive children, who may also be impulsive. The "combined type" is for children with both inattentive and hyperactive/impulsive behaviors.

 **Fact**

An estimated seven percent of U.S. children are diagnosed with ADD/ADHD. In some counties, ten percent of children are being medicated. In a region of Virginia, twenty percent of all students were taking amphetamines or Ritalin for ADD/ADHD.

Adolescents and adults may outgrow or overcome their symptoms. If so, they are diagnosed as being "In Partial Remission." This reflects the new view that people do not outgrow the disorder but may learn to compensate so that the symptoms are not disabling. There is also a catch-all diagnosis for children who don't meet the standard criteria. If they don't have enough symptoms or their symptoms aren't severe enough, they can be diagnosed with an atypical form of ADHD called "Attention-Deficit/Hyperactivity Disorder Not Otherwise Specified" or "ADHD-NOS."

ADD Symptoms

Most people refer to the "predominantly inattentive type" of Attention-Deficit/Hyperactivity Disorder simply as "ADD."

- Difficulties listening, even when being directly addressed
- Difficulties continuing to pay attention to activities involving either work or play
- Difficulties paying attention to details and avoiding careless mistakes

- Difficulties completing tasks, chores, and assignments
- Difficulties organizing activities and tasks
- Difficulties doing tasks that require sustained mental effort, like that required for schoolwork
- Difficulties keeping track of possessions and materials, such as toys, clothes, homework papers, and school supplies
- Being easily distracted
- Difficulties remembering

In order to be considered bona fide symptoms, it should be clear that a child cannot sustain attention and cannot concentrate on mental tasks for extended periods. Problems stemming from boredom, disinterest, lack of motivation, and defiance are not supposed to be counted as ADD symptoms—though they often are. It is easy to see why attention deficits create problems in school. Students with short attention spans cannot concentrate on schoolwork for long periods as is required to do their work. Being easily distracted poses a major problem in crowded classrooms, which are filled with continuous rustles and murmurs. If students' attention wanders at unpredictable moments, they miss portions of lectures and don't hear explanations about assignments and tests.

Alert!

Combine all of the ADD symptoms, and what emerges is a description of an absent-minded professor. If your child has his head in the clouds and can't keep his feet on the ground, an ivory tower might be just what the doctor ordered. When he's scaled the academic heights, losing mittens and wearing mismatched socks won't seem like such major problems.

Lapses of attention when a parent gives directions and instructions can result in considerable frustration and upset at home. A parent might send a child to clean up his room and later discover him playing with baseball cards instead of doing his chore. If the child's attention strayed while the parent was giving instructions, the youngster might have understood that he was to go to his room but missed what he was expected to do when he arrived. Or, after going to his room to clean it, he might see his box of baseball cards and spend an hour going through them without giving another thought to what he was supposed to do.

Poor organizational skills can cause a host of problems in school and at home. Many children get confused during projects and tasks to the point that they don't know how to proceed. Some youngsters become upset and cry over seemingly simple homework assignments and chores, claiming they don't know how to do them. If parents and teachers are convinced that a youngster is bright enough and possesses the skills needed to do the work, they may conclude that the child is overly emotional. Other youngsters don tough-guy masks and display an "I couldn't care less" attitude, so it is hard for adults to recognize that poor organization is at the heart of many of their problems. The solution may be to break long assignments and projects into a number of small steps and have students complete them one at a time.

Poor organization can also lead children to make many careless mistakes when completing assignments and chores. Unless students are methodical and focused while doing schoolwork and checking their answers, they may end up overlooking some items altogether. They misnumber problems so that all of their answers are counted as errors or make many small mistakes that lower their grades. Again, if carelessness stems from indifference, laziness, or an unwillingness to put forth the effort required to line up numbers and check work, the problem should not be considered a symptom of ADD.

ADHD Symptoms

The second type of Attention-Deficit/Hyperactivity Disorder, which includes hyperactivity and impulsiveness, is technically known as the "predominantly hyperactive type." Most people refer to it simply as "ADHD." For this type, children's difficulties must stem from hyperactivity or from a combination of hyperactive and impulsive behaviors. Altogether, the DSM-IV lists six symptoms of hyperactive behavior and three symptoms of impulsive behavior. A child must have six out of the nine symptoms to be diagnosed with the predominantly hyperactive type.

Symptoms of Hyperactivity

Hyperactive children have an energy level that their parents and teachers consider excessive. They must appear to be driven by a motor, so that they continue to wiggle even when at rest.

- Squirming and fidgeting even when seated
- Getting up when expected to remain seated
- Running excessively and climbing in inappropriate situations
- Difficulty playing quietly
- Being always on the go
- Talking excessively

Some youngsters squirm and fidget while sitting at their school desks, while watching television at home, and while listening to bedtime stories. Hyperactive adolescents may swing their legs, tap their feet, drum their fingers on their desk, pop their chewing gum, or chew their fingernails. Few teenagers keep getting up from their desks to wander through the classroom, run through the house, or climb every tall object in sight. They are more likely to report that they feel restless much of the time. Some say that when they must remain seated for more than a few minutes, they feel as though they're about to jump out of their skin.

Despite their short attention spans and inability to pay attention in school, they can concentrate on a video game or television program so well that they don't even notice when someone is standing two feet away, yelling for their attention. Most parents find this extremely irritating. They think their child is defiant, pointing out that he concentrates and sits still well enough "when he wants to."

Professionals believe that both ADHD and ADD sufferers share a common problem: they require much more stimulation to remain attentive than the average youngster. As anyone who has sat through a long sermon or attempted to read a book they find boring knows, the mind must have enough stimulation to remain attentive. Too little, and the mind begins to wander. The natural physical response is to become fidgety and restless, as if the mind were trying to create some additional stimulation in order to stay awake. When children diagnosed with ADD and ADHD are fully engaged in a highly stimulating activity such as a television program or interactive game, they become so attentive that they cannot readily shift their attention away from it. Do the minds of children diagnosed with ADD/ADHD move at the same speed as a fast-action video game and rock video? This seems to be a possibility.

 **Fact**

Any misbehaving child can be diagnosed with ADD/ADHD. Ten million children have been diagnosed with it, and ninety percent of Ritalin is sold in the U.S. Many believe that the real problem is cultural. Life has become so stressful that most adults feel overwhelmed by normal children.

Impulsiveness

In addition to hyperactive behavior, children diagnosed with ADHD may also behave impulsively. Impulsive children have difficulty inhibiting the urge to act or speak and often seem unable to contain themselves. There are three main signs doctors look for.

- Blurting answers before the teacher or parent has finished asking the question
- Not waiting his or her turn
- Interrupting conversations or intruding into other's activities

Impulsive children reach for fragile objects despite repeated reminders not to touch. They grab other children's toys without asking permission. At school, they get up to sharpen their pencils the moment they determine their tip is dull or broken without waiting to ask permission. Parents and teachers spend a good deal of time and effort admonishing impulsive youngsters to slow down and think before they do or say something, but they seem incapable of remembering. Many parents come to doubt the intelligence of children who don't anticipate the consequences of their actions. But for those diagnosed with ADHD, the problem is not lack of intelligence or willful misbehavior. Their minds simply work differently.

Alert!

Peers dislike having other students disrupt the classroom, interrupt their conversations, and intrude in their games, so impulsive children often have social difficulties. Some impulsive children alienate others because they have hair-trigger tempers and are quick to take affront.

The knee-jerk reactions of impulsive children may occur because they are actually wired differently. Scientists hypothesize that the part of the brain controlling automatic reactions propels them to react before the part that handles conscious thought can process and evaluate information (see Chapter 11, Cutting-Edge Treatments).

Other Diagnostic Requirements

Although every child could qualify for a diagnosis of atypical ADD/ADHD, the requirements for a standard ADD or ADHD diagnosis are quite stringent. Besides having enough symptoms of attention deficits, hyperactivity, and/or impulsiveness, signs of these problems must have been present early in childhood—at least before age seven. While a child might not have been evaluated by a professional until after that age, the developmental history must indicate that the behaviors were present early in life. In addition, the current troublesome behaviors must have been present for at least six months. Behavior problems that have been going on for shorter periods are more likely to be reactions to a specific trauma or life change, such as the birth of a sibling or a family move. To be considered symptoms of ADD or ADHD, the behaviors in question must be more frequent as well as more severe than is typical for youngsters at the same level of development. Children must have serious behavioral problems in two or more important settings for a standard ADD/ADHD diagnosis.

- At home
- In school
- With peers
- On the playground
- At work

Question?

My child keeps getting in trouble at school. Could she have ADHD?
If she is doing well in other settings, the first step is to find out if there is a problem at school that needs attention. Everything from being bullied to having an especially strict or permissive teacher can cause children to act up. Sit in the classroom to observe.

Behavior problems that are limited to home are more likely to stem from family stress, poor parenting, or difficult family dynamics. If students have problems at school but get along well in other environments, this usually suggests they are struggling with teaching or learning difficulties. Only having problems getting along with peers is usually due to poor social skills. Problems that are confined to the playground, including unsupervised playtime in the neighborhood, suggest problems coping with unstructured situations or having a personality trait known as risk-taking or thrill-seeking. People with this trait require more stimulation to avoid boredom, and they are drawn to activities that most youngsters would view as overly dangerous or frightening. Problems getting along at work can develop when children are old enough to hold down jobs. If teenagers are having difficulties at work but get along in other settings, there's a good chance that simply changing jobs or employers will solve the problem. Hence, a standard ADD/ADHD diagnosis should not be made when a child only has significant problems in one setting.

Alert!

A child with a low energy level can be diagnosed with atypical ADD/ADHD. So can a daydreamer. In fact, a youngster with *any* combination of problematic behaviors can be diagnosed with atypical ADD/ADHD. The technical name is Attention-Deficit/Hyperactivity Disorder Not Otherwise Specified (ADD/ADHD-NOS).

In addition to having serious difficulties managing in several environments, the standard Attention-Deficit/Hyperactivity Disorder diagnosis requires "clear evidence" of "significant impairment in social, academic, or occupational functioning," according to the DSM-IV-TR. Impaired social functioning might mean that the child cannot make or keep friends because of his off-putting behavior. The way to determine that a child's academic functioning is impaired is to compare scores on standardized achievement tests with IQ test scores. If achievement test scores are much lower, students are assumed to have a problem since they are not progressing as would be expected based on their intellectual potential. In the absence of a specific learning disability, the problems may be attributed to ADD/ADHD. In fact, large percentages of children with ADD/ADHD also have learning disabilities. Impaired occupational functioning can become a problem during middle or late adolescence. The typical manifestation is getting fired from jobs because of problems with attention, hyperactivity, and impulsivity.

For the standard (as opposed to "atypical") ADD/ADHD diagnosis, a child must have many specific symptoms reflecting difficulties with attention, hyperactivity, and impulsivity. In addition, the problems must have started before age seven, and they must be pervasive, and severe. However, a child can be diagnosed with Attention-Deficit/ Hyperactivity Disorder Not Otherwise Specified (ADHD-NOS) with just a few symptoms that only create problems in one setting and that started later in life. The DSM-IV-TR indicates that this diagnosis is even appropriate for children with "a behavioral pattern marked by sluggishness, daydreaming, and hypoactivity" or low energy level. Any combination of problematic behaviors can now be diagnosed as ADD or ADHD.

Few experts now believe it is necessary for all of the criteria to be met before ADD/ADHD is diagnosed. Since academic success is so important for a child's current and future happiness and well-being, most doctors diagnose and treat it even if the behavior problems only occur at school. Be that as it may, it really does not make sense to say that symptoms must have been present early in life. Hyperactivity and inattention can stem from head injuries or lead poisoning that happen after age seven.

Rethinking ADD/ADHD

James's parents realized that all of their "no-no's" were not helping their tot to settle down. Instead, he seemed to become crankier and less cooperative. After consulting a child guidance counselor, they decided to change the environment to accommodate James's need for so much active play. They moved the sofa and television into James's bedroom and turned it into a small sitting room. What had been the living room became a giant playroom. They set up James's bed and dresser at one end and hung a curtain around it to create a small sleeping area for him. They left the center of the room empty so James could run and play. He could even ride his Big Wheel inside.

In the past James's parents had constantly urged him to slow down and be careful. After learning that attention improves when children are engaged in highly stimulating activities, his parents searched for a new approach to getting their son to concentrate. They ended up inventing a game called "Hurry, Hurry" that made a world of difference in his behavior. When they wanted James to put on his socks, help set the table, go to the potty, buckle his seatbelt, or do other small chores, they would say, "How fast can you do it? Let's see! Hurry, hurry!" For tasks like carrying a glass of juice to the table or pouring cereal, they added, "How fast can you do it without spilling it?"

 **Fact**

An exceptionally high activity level, inattentiveness, and impulsiveness are all part of being a toddler. Little people are very reactive to stress, which can make them hyperactive. Inattentiveness is often due to their poor language abilities. Research indicates that parents think they understand far more than they actually do.

Amazingly, James had fewer mishaps when he was hurrying, perhaps because he was so focused. When he was thoroughly engrossed in what he was doing, he wasn't so easily distracted. His father turned the chore of picking up toys into the "Daddy's gonna catch you!" game, and they played it each day. James scurried about picking up toys, trying to get them all into his toy box before his father could catch and tickle him. The game usually ended in peals of laughter and a fairly tidy room. Cutting back on the "no-no's" and making the house conform to James's needs instead of the other way around made for a much happier child. And that made for a happier family all around.

CHAPTER 2

ADD/ADHD Evaluations

O btaining the kind of comprehensive evaluation required to identify what is causing a youngster's ADD/ADHD symptoms is surprisingly difficult. Insurance companies and managed care organizations discourage physicians from running the medical tests that are required to rule out likely causes, and many doctors believe that tests probably would not reveal anything anyway. Yet identifying the cause is critical for pinpointing the type of treatment that is needed. You may need to nudge the doctor and lobby third-party payers to ensure that your child has the proper tests.

Diagnostic Dilemmas

Angelica couldn't afford to miss work, but once again she was going to have to leave early. For the third time in a month, the director of her daughter's preschool had telephoned to say that she had to leave the center immediately. Since turning three Valerie had been feisty, headstrong, and readily moved to tantrums and tears whenever she didn't get her way. Since Valerie's parents had separated and she had moved with her mother into an apartment a month ago, Valerie's behavior had worsened. She lashed out at her little classmates when they did something as innocent as humming a tune Valerie didn't like. "Stop making that noise!" she had ordered a classmate last week. Then Valerie had punched him so hard that he fell, bit his lip, and ended up having stitches. Angelica didn't know what her daughter's latest crime was, but during the brief telephone call, the director had issued an ultimatum: get Valerie on medication or find another preschool.

Alert!

Pediatricians commonly diagnose ADD/ADHD and write prescriptions during a thirty-minute office visit. Thereafter, they see youngsters for fifteen-minute follow-up appointments. Specialists say this is completely irresponsible. They also say it happens all the time.

When Angelica finished pouring out her troubles to Valerie's pediatrician, he said, "Let me guess. This lovely little girl is a handful at home as well?" Angelica nodded. "I see this kind of problem all the time," he said kindly. "Not to worry. This prescription should help. Give her one dose before school each morning. My nurse will explain the rest." After he left, the nurse glanced at the chart and reassured Angelica that Valerie wasn't being naughty on purpose. She wasn't misbehaving because of anything that Angelica was doing wrong. Valerie was suffering from ADHD. She couldn't control herself. The doctor would want to see her for a follow-up appointment in three months.

Angelica's initial relief that her daughter's problem had a name and a simple solution soon vanished beneath a cloud of troubling doubts. How had the doctor diagnosed Valerie without running any tests? How did the nurse know that Valerie's problems weren't because of Angelica? She tried to be a good mom, but her temper had been short since she had separated from Valerie's father. Angelica suddenly remembered that she had meant to mention the separation to the doctor and ask whether three-year-olds could get depressed. She had been so upset, it had completely slipped her mind. Maybe she should get a second opinion. But where should she take Valerie? How could she make sure the next doctor checked her thoroughly?

Alert!

Give the doctor a chance to see what your child's behavior is really like by arriving half an hour early for the appointment. Once the novelty of the new environment wears off and boredom sets in, the office staff will get to see your youngster's typical behavior.

Qualified Evaluators

Today, anyone and everyone seems to feel qualified to diagnose ADD/ADHD. Relatives, friends, and even grocery store clerks offer opinions about rowdy youngsters, suggesting that they are hyperactive or have an attention deficit. School-aged children do the same, referring to disruptive classmates as "hyper." In truth, almost anyone can recognize ADD/ADHD symptoms and make a diagnosis in a matter of moments, but that does not address the real question: what is causing the behavior problems?

Teacher Evaluations

Classroom teachers are usually the first to urge parents to seek an ADD/ADHD evaluation. Because they work with so many students, teachers have a better basis than parents for judging whether behavior is typical. Because teachers are less emotionally involved, they also tend to be more objective than parents. If a teacher says that a child has ADD/ADHD and needs to take Ritalin, parents usually respond by scheduling a doctor's appointment immediately. But many teachers are anxious to eliminate behavior problems and think that medication is fine if it makes the class easier to manage. And most parents do not realize that doctors consider a teacher's reports of problems and recommendations sufficient to warrant an

ADD/ADHD diagnosis and to write a prescription. This is a dangerous practice.

Alert!

Many school psychologists do educational testing, as do educational diagnosticians working in public school settings. If parents demand an educational evaluation and the school agrees that it is warranted, they are spared the expense of a private educational evaluation.

Connecticut legislators became alarmed by the large numbers of students in their state that were taking mind-altering drugs. An investigation revealed that parents of disruptive students were being told by school officials that their children would be expelled unless they started taking Ritalin or another psychotropic ("mind altering") drug to eliminate disruptive behavior! Although only doctors can legally make a medical diagnosis (teachers cannot even diagnose learning disabilities), legislators decided to take a stronger stand. They passed a law specifically prohibiting school personnel from suggesting a diagnosis or recommending medication. Connecticut educators can only recommend that parents seek a medical evaluation. Legislatures in half a dozen states are considering similar legislation. Because teachers are key players not just in referring youngsters for evaluations but in sharing their opinions with doctors regarding a child's diagnosis and need for treatment, it is unlikely that these laws alone will make much difference in the numbers of children being medicated.

Qualified Diagnosticians
The best way to locate a specialist to do an ADD/ADHD evaluation is to contact your child's pediatrician or a child guidance clinic for a referral. Ask if there are any clinics specializing in ADD/ADHD in your area. The tests your child needs cut across a number of specialties, and a clinic is likely to house most of the professionals under one

roof. Clinics specifically designed to evaluate and treat ADD/ADHD are few and far between, so most families use their child's physician, a psychologist, or a psychiatrist to coordinate the referrals to various specialists, compile all of the test results, pull together the recommendations, and conduct checkups after treatment has begun. For a comprehensive evaluation, many professionals need to be involved.

- MD (Medical Doctor) or DO (Doctor of Osteopathic Medicine)
- Child Psychologist
- Child Psychiatrist
- Neurologist
- Audiologist
- Educational Diagnostician
- Allergist
- Clinical Nutritionist (licensed by the Clinical Nutrition Certification Board)

Any state-licensed physician or psychologist can legally diagnose and treat ADD/ADHD. Psychiatrists are physicians and can prescribe medication. Psychologists specialize in psychological testing. (Both may also provide counseling and psychotherapy.) They do not prescribe medication in most states, although this is changing. Licensed educational diagnosticians can diagnose disorders and make treatment recommendations if they have a doctorate degree, but they do not usually provide treatment.

If you are in need of a new physician, a doctor of osteopathic medicine (DO) may be a good choice. Like other physicians, DOs attend medical school, but their curriculum places more emphasis on preventative, family, and community medicine. DOs prescribe medication and perform surgeries but tend to be broader in their approach and more concerned with holistic healing. They are listed in the yellow pages after "Physicians and Surgeons (MD)" under the heading "Physicians and Surgeons—Osteopathic." Be sure to ask if the doctor works with children before scheduling an appointment.

Medical Tests

Children with ADD/ADHD symptoms should undergo a number of medical tests. Testing for lead poisoning is essential. It is a good idea to run tests for other heavy metals as well. A neurological evaluation is important, since petit mal seizures can cause spaciness and lapses of attention. Thyroid problems can cause children's activity level to be abnormally high or low, and can cause inattentiveness. Deficiencies of zinc, magnesium, B vitamins, and iron produce hyperactivity and attention problems. Since dietary imbalances can cause ADD/ADHD symptoms, a nutritional evaluation is in order. All children should be tested for allergies and sensitivities, since they produce symptoms that are routinely mistaken for ADD/ADHD. Children should have their hearing checked. Middle ear infections can be so minor that there is no fever, but the combination of muffled sounds and feeling under the weather can make children distracted, inattentive, and irritable. An audiologist should investigate the possibility of language processing problems. If all of those tests are passed, it is time for a psychological evaluation and educational testing.

Alert!

Stimulant medications dramatically increase heart rate and affect other organs and body systems. Medications for other psychological disorders also have profound physical effects. Children should have a thorough physical before taking psychotropic medications and be monitored as long as they continue.

Evaluation Procedures

Methods of evaluating children for ADD/ADHD are not as scientific as most people assume. In fact, they are not scientific at all. There are no tests for this condition. Because children's behavior typically improves in unfamiliar environments such as waiting rooms and examining offices, doctors do not expect to personally witness the behavior problems that are of concern. Many rely exclusively on information provided by a parent or teacher.

Parent Interviews

The typical first step in the evaluation process is to collect background information and take a detailed developmental history. The goal is to ascertain the exact nature of the behavior problems, determine that they have been present for at least six months, establish that they occur in multiple settings, identify any special stresses the child has been under, find out what has been done at school and at home to try to help, and ensure that another diagnosis does not better explain the difficulties. To prepare for the interview, collect your youngster's medical and school records and take them with you to the appointment unless your doctor requests them in advance. If you have recorded information in a baby book about the age at which your child first sat up alone, walked, talked, etc., be sure to have it with you as well.

The parent interview usually takes about an hour. Some physicians spend only fifteen to thirty minutes obtaining basic information about the problems and then refer the child to a psychologist or psychiatrist to take the developmental history, screen the child for emotional problems, and determine whether other psychological and educational testing is needed.

Behavior Checklists

The parent completes a checklist of problem behaviors, and a similar checklist is sent to the child's teachers so they can indicate which they have observed. Often the checklists are mailed to the school before the first appointment so the doctor can review the information in advance. If teachers do not respond, most doctors attempt to talk to them on the telephone. Although parents and teachers tend to report different problems on the behavior checklists, they usually agree that the youngster's behavior is difficult, trying, and frustrating.

Many doctors consider teacher reports of behavior problems relayed by an upset parent sufficient for an ADD/ADHD diagnosis and a prescription for amphetamines.

Mental Health Screening

Children should be screened for other emotional and mental disorders before a diagnosis is made. Depression, anxiety, and stress reactions from psychological trauma ("posttraumatic stress disorder") cause difficulties with sustaining attention and produce agitation that can look so much like hyperactivity, even seasoned professionals cannot tell them apart. Moreover, almost two-thirds of children diagnosed with ADD/ADHD also have another psychological, behavioral, or learning disorder. Some pediatricians, family practice doctors, internists, and neurologists regularly perform mental status evaluations, so they have a good deal of solid experience screening youngsters for mental health problems. But most family physicians refer young patients to a child psychologist or psychiatrist rather than trying to conduct this type of screening themselves.

 **Essential**

Adolescents should be screened for alcohol and drug use before psychotropic medication is prescribed since the combination can be lethal. A 2001 Department of Health and Human Services survey found that nineteen percent of teens consumed five drinks during a single sitting in the previous month.

Psychological Evaluations

If mental health screening suggests that a youngster has another psychological problem in addition to or instead of ADD/ADHD, further evaluation by a psychologist, psychiatrist, or another credentialed mental health provider is in order. A psychological evaluation involves taking a psychosocial history by interviewing parents in order to identify current and past individual, family, and social problems. Trauma from parental divorce, abandonment, alcoholism, abuse, domestic violence, and stress from chronic family tension can cause ADD/ADHD symptoms and other psychological, behavioral, and learning problems. Older children are then interviewed at length and younger children are observed in a playroom. Children age six to twelve typically undergo a combination of interviews and playroom observations. If the interviews and observations suggest a need for further evaluation, the next step is likely to be psychological testing. A complete psychological evaluation includes personality, intelligence, neuropsychological, and educational testing. A school psychologist or educational diagnostician employed by the school district may be legally obligated to administer some or even all of the tests, which relieves the family of this financial burden.

 **Fact**

A test to measure how quickly and accurately a child responds to images flashed on a computer screen can be used to assess impulsiveness. However, this test is usually administered in laboratories during research investigations and is rarely used in clinical settings.

Educational Testing

Students diagnosed with ADD/ADHD should undergo educational and intelligence testing. The required tests can be administered by the psychologist during the psychological evaluation or by a qualified educational diagnostician, either through the school or privately. Learning disabilities are rampant among children with ADD/ADHD, so there is a good chance that special education services will be helpful. Moreover, students with severe learning problems often misbehave in school or simply stop paying attention because they are frustrated and overwhelmed by the work. They act up at home because they are so upset about their inability to succeed academically. Their ADD/ADHD symptoms disappear once they receive instruction targeted to their particular learning style and needs. The same applies to students who are especially academically advanced, except that their inattention, frustration, and classroom behavior problems are more likely to stem from boredom. They settle down and their concentration improves when they are given more challenging work. Educational testing can often pinpoint issues that are causing children to misbehave.

Impediments to Evaluation

The insurance and pharmaceutical industries have shaped the way ADD/ADHD is evaluated and treated. The result is that parents may have a hard time getting the psychological and medical tests needed to determine what is causing ADD/ADHD symptoms. Too many end up being medicated for years on end when a change in diet is all that is needed.

 Essential

During an ADHD evaluation, the doctor should ask whether there have been any recent changes in circumstances or special stresses that might be affecting your child. To diagnose ADHD, the current behavioral symptoms must have been present for at least six months.

Thirty percent of all outpatient visits to doctors' offices and clinics for youngsters from ages three to eighteen are for services related to a single diagnosis: ADD/ADHD. Insurance companies, managed care organizations, and other third parties who pay medical costs are understandably concerned about the tremendous expense. They save money by severely limiting reimbursements to doctors for their work with this disorder, and doctors report that the payments they receive are grossly inadequate. Psychiatrists in New Mexico received fifteen dollars for a follow-up appointment with an ADD/ADHD Medicaid patient in 2000. Because appointments are so brief, doctors cannot do more than ask how the child is doing and write a prescription for a refill. Providing the children with therapy and advising the parents are not possible under these circumstances.

Since the practice of paying bonuses to doctors for not recommending expensive medical procedures was outlawed, many insurance companies and managed care organizations have taken another approach to containing costs. When doctors apply to join a network of authorized health service providers, a representative from the company or organization conducts an interview to learn how they evaluate and treat ADD/ADHD. Expressing the belief that children should undergo psychological, neurological, and allergy testing or that they would be likely to benefit from parent counseling or individual therapy raises red flags for cost-conscious companies. By not adding such doctors to their provider list, companies require their insured clients to bear a greater share of the cost if they wish to utilize their services or pay for it themselves. Few physicians have any psychiatric background or training. The pharmaceutical companies are the main source of information for most doctors. Most are convinced that they can arrive at an accurate diagnosis by conducting a parent interview and reviewing a teacher checklist of behavior problems. Most have been convinced that ADD/ADHD is a genetic disorder that does not respond to other types of treatment, amphetamines are effective, and the listed side effects are rare and not a real cause for concern. The practice of providing an on-the-spot prescription is commonplace.

Getting a Second Opinion

Three-year-old Valerie's behavior improved dramatically when she took the medication the pediatrician had prescribed. When the doctor was checking her during a follow-up appointment, her mother asked how long she would need to keep taking it. "Most likely through adolescence," the doctor replied, "Quite possibly for the rest of her life." When he saw Angelica's shocked expression, he added, "ADD/ADHD is inherited. This is not something she is likely to outgrow."

After Angelica learned about the many things that could cause Valerie's type of behavior problems, she took her to a psychologist for an evaluation. The psychologist determined that Valerie was still grieving for her father, whom she saw infrequently. Since the deterioration in her behavior coincided with the family breakup and move, he believed that diagnosing her with ADD/ADHD had been an error. The psychologist also expressed concern about her daycare center. He talked to Valerie's teacher on the phone and heard some disturbing conversations in the background. "The workers sounded impatient and were yelling at the children and ordering them around. Valerie may order other children around because she is copying their behavior. In any case, children her age must be taught how to get along with peers. Punishment makes some youngsters more aggressive without teaching them what to do." The psychologist recommended moving Valerie to a different daycare center, increasing visitation with her father, and having a child psychiatrist evaluate her need for medication. The psychologist personally thought that grief counseling would probably make medication unnecessary. If those measures were not enough, he would recommend additional testing to rule out other medical problems. That made much more sense to Angelica than medicating Valerie for years on end.

CHAPTER 3

The ADD/ADHD Diet

Research indicates that most children's ADD/ADHD symptoms, and often their learning problems, are caused by nutritional imbalances, deficiencies, excesses, allergies, and sensitivities. Studies show that improved nutrition is as effective as Ritalin for three-fourths of the children diagnosed with hyperactivity and attention deficits! Amazingly, most physicians recommend medication for symptom control over dietary changes. While cleaning up your child's diet requires some effort on your part, your youngster's health should be a priority. Clean up your own eating habits, and your behavior and mood are likely to improve, too!

Kids and Food

Carol's parents were not happy that their daughter consumed more candy bars and cookies than apples and asparagus, more pizza and potato chips than bananas and broccoli. But her diet didn't seem much different from her friends', and they were unsure how to improve it. They knew they could not control what Carol ate when she was at school or with friends, and they understood that food struggles could set the stage for an eating disorder during adolescence. Her parents gave her a multivitamin tablet each day and insisted she drink milk with meals so she would get enough of that all important bone-builder, calcium. Because she ate plenty of peanut butter sandwiches, they knew she was getting enough protein.

They never really worried about her diet until she was diagnosed with ADD/ADHD. Her mother asked the doctor about the Feingold diet, which had worked wonders for her nephew's hyperactivity and attention deficit.

 **Fact**

When it comes to food allergies, cow's milk leads the pack. Infants produce the enzyme needed to digest their mother's milk; then, production slows. In most cultures, only babies drink milk. Youngsters can get enough calcium from vegetables, including cabbage, broccoli, parsley, okra, beets, carrots, celery, and greens.

Carol's pediatrician had very strong opinions about the importance of good nutrition for physical health. She delivered an impassioned lecture about the sorry state of most children's diets. "Obesity and exploding cholesterol levels are expected to translate into an epidemic of heart attacks in the coming decades," she said. Nevertheless, she said that diet did not cause behavior problems, and the best diet in the world would not clear up ADD/ADHD. "Think of it this way," she said. "Most kids have terrible eating habits, but only a small percentage is hyperactive with attention deficits." That made sense to Carol's parents, and they dropped the subject. They were surprised when they later learned that the pediatrician was seriously misinformed.

The Food Controversy

When parents ask if nutritional problems could be contributing to their youngster's ADD/ADHD symptoms or if a change in diet could relieve them, most doctors give the same answer: the notion of a connection between ADD/ADHD and food is an unfortunate myth, according to a national survey investigating pediatricians' knowledge and attitudes concerning diagnosis and treatment of ADD/ADHD published in the Archives of Pediatric Medicine in 1995. Many health care professionals feel strongly about this subject—as strongly as the many researchers who say that poor nutrition can cause ADD/ADHD symptoms and good nutrition can cure them.

 Essential

Most children know a lot about nutrition but like adults, they lack self-control. To keep your youngsters from eating sugary, high-fat snacks at home simply do not buy or make them. Or say they are for "adults only" and keep them under lock and key!

The Feingold Diet

Most doctors warn patients away from dietary cures because of a controversy that began in the 1970s. A research investigation found that removing dyes, additives, and salicylates from the diets of a group of children diagnosed with ADD/ADHD reduced their hyperactivity and problems with inattention. The news made headlines and caused untold numbers of parents to embrace a diet formulated by Dr. Benjamin Feingold that would relieve ADD/ADHD symptoms. Following the Feingold diet is a major undertaking. Anything containing salicylates is forbidden, and they are in a wide range of fruits and vegetables. They are the main ingredients in aspirin, as well as in countless over-the-counter medications and cosmetics. Salicylates can be absorbed through the skin, so parents even have to be careful about the shampoos and skin lotions their child uses. Feingold diet chapters across the country provide support meetings and offer parents the opportunity to share advice and recipes.

Food Fanatics

Parents were alarmed by the news that children could be harmed by the artificial colors, sweeteners, preservatives, and texturizers that companies add to packaged foods. Public concern about the widespread contamination of the food supply intensified when it was realized that the residue from the pesticides used on crops and the hormones fed to farm animals was building up in people's systems. The concentrations of chemicals in mother's milk were so high, some officials joked that if Congress passed some proposed legislation making it illegal to transport pesticides across state lines, a nursing mother could be arrested for vacationing in another state. The Federal Food and Drug Association eventually banned a few chemicals and required manufacturers to affix labels to food items listing the ingredients. Food processing companies and agribusinesses complied but continued to insist that their chemical additives were harmless. Suddenly the Feingold diet proponents found themselves being attacked as frauds, and the diet was declared a hoax.

Alert!

Many parents are lobbying to oust soda, sugary juice, candy, and chips from school vending machines and for more nutritious cafeteria meals. A simple telephone call to the principal, school board member, or PTA president may be enough to set the wheels in motion. Start dialing!

In the heated debate over food additives and impurities, people with an interest in ADD/ADHD split into two factions with equally extremist views. The Feingold fanatics (mostly parents, nutritionists, dieticians, naturopaths, and holistic healers) maintained that better diet was the solution for every child with hyperactivity or attention deficits, even though many youngsters on the diet did not improve and it was obvious that other problems can cause ADD/ADHD. The Feingold bashers (mostly physicians) declared that food affects the body but not the brain, even though it is obvious that the brain is an organ like any other and that people cannot think clearly when they are hungry or ill. Most ADD/ADHD research dollars went to investigating medications, but a handful of scientists continued to study nutrition and found links between certain dietary problems and ADD/ADHD. Emotions on the subject clouded all reason, and most parents and professions twisted the findings to fit their personal beliefs.

Alert!

The Feingold diet may be more than your child needs. Eliminating just one or two chemicals may be enough for your youngster's thinking to clear, her mood to stabilize, and her behavior to normalize. For optimal health, serve only fresh, organic foods, and avoid all artificial ingredients.

The Food Connection

Research on the food/behavior connection is unequivocal: nutrition affects the functioning of the brain, but particular ingredients affect children differently. For instance, caffeine is a stimulant that energizes most children, creates a sense of well-being, and boosts concentration. But some youngsters react by becoming distracted, nervous, cranky or weepy, and so jittery that their hands shake and they cannot sit still. How a particular child reacts to an ingredient can change over time. A sugar feast typically induces feelings of contentment, but most preschool children crash when the sugar hits the bloodstream, and their mood, thinking, and physical coordination deteriorate. Wender and Solanto found significant decreases in performance on a continuous performance task among hyperactive children after they ingested sugar, according to a 1991 research report in *Pediatrics*. Older children and adults are not usually so strongly affected.

Artificial food colorings and preservatives have a significant impact on hyperactivity levels in very young children, according to research conducted at the University of Southampton in the United

Kingdom and reported in the *Archives of Disease in Childhood*. Nearly 300 three-year-olds were screened for hyperactivity and allergies. During the first week, the children ate only foods free of the preservative sodium benzoate and artificial colorings such as tartrazine, sunset yellow, and carmoisine. During the second and fourth weeks, they were given a daily dose of fruit juice, with or without colorings and preservatives. The children became significantly less hyperactive during the period when the additives were removed and more hyperactive when they were put back into the diet.

Question?

How do I protect my child from salicylates?
They are found in tea, peanuts, mint, and many fruits—to name a few. Lists of foods that contain them are available at ✒*www.feingold.org*. See ✒*www.nlm.nih.gov* for a list of over-the-counter medications.

In 2003 a group of researchers undertook the massive task of reviewing all of the studies on ADD/ADHD. They concluded that there are eight main risk factors for this disorder.

- Allergies to foods and additives
- Toxicity from heavy metals and other environmental pollutants
- Low-protein/high-carbohydrate diets
- Mineral imbalances
- Deficiencies of essential fatty acids and phospholipids
- Amino acid deficiencies
- Thyroid disorders
- B-vitamin deficiencies

The researchers concluded that for children with ADD/ADHD, "These findings support the effectiveness of food supplement treatment in improving attention and self-control." An additional finding was that food supplement treatment was often as effective as Ritalin! Yet a study published in the *Archives of Pediatric Adolescent Medicine* reported that most pediatricians continue to believe that nutrition does not affect ADD/ADHD. In fact, one-fifth of the pediatricians surveyed said that parents of children with ADD/ADHD suffer from the "common misperception" that diet can cause it.

The finding that nutritional problems can cause ADD/ADHD symptoms does not mean that the Feingold diet can cure them. Many youngsters are allergic or sensitive to a food or ingredient that this diet allows. In that case, eliminating additives and salicylates may not be enough to overcome problems with hyperactivity and/or inattention.

Food Allergies and Sensitivities

An estimated ten to twenty percent of children have food allergies. Besides causing the behavioral symptoms associated with ADD/ADHD, common physical symptoms include dry, scaly skin or eczema, a stuffy or runny nose, watery or red eyes, and asthma. One telling sign is dark shadows under the eyes that give them a sunken appearance. Adverse reactions to foods and food additives (as well as to ragweed, pollen, animal dander, dust, etc.) are called "allergies" if the immune system identifies them as harmful and produces antibodies to try to fight them off. Elevated blood levels of immunoglobulin E (IgE) indicate that a youngster has recently been exposed to something she is allergic to. Many specific allergies can be identified by an allergist via a skin prick test. Allergists can prescribe medications to suppress the physical symptoms, but the medication may not help with the behavioral symptoms. In fact, some allergy medications worsen ADD/ADHD symptoms. The only solution is to eliminate allergens from your child's environment altogether.

Adverse reactions to foods and additives (as well as to pollutants) are called "intolerances" or "sensitivities" if no antibodies are produced. Intolerances and sensitivities do not show up on skin or blood tests, but they cause a wide range of neurological reactions, from hyperkinesis to seizures, from minor headaches to migraines, from difficulties focusing attention to fainting. Food sensitivities also cause a wide range of physical reactions, including upper respiratory problems (sneezing and runny nose), digestive problems (especially upset stomachs and diarrhea), diffuse pains (achy legs), skin ailments (flaking and eczema), and hives.

Identifying ingredients your child is sensitive to and eliminating them from his diet can be difficult, but it is definitely worth the trouble. This has been shown to stabilize children's brain waves on EEG tests and improve their behavior as effectively as Ritalin.

Identifying which foods and additives a child is sensitive to (the "offending substances") can be difficult. Allergic reactions tend to occur within minutes of exposure to an allergen, but up to 48 hours can elapse before symptoms of sensitivity appear. To further complicate matters, when a youngster is exposed to a variety of mildly offending substances faster than the body can detoxify itself, toxic overload may develop. That means that even though a child does not have a problem with individual ingredients, certain combinations trigger an adverse reaction.

The Food-and-Mood Journal

The first step to identifying allergies and sensitivities is to keep a food-and-mood journal for one or two weeks to establish a baseline. Keep track of everything your youngster eats and note all of his emotional and behavioral changes. Involve your school-age child in the process of creating and keeping the journal. If he turns out to be sensitive to some foods, you can refrain from serving them at home, but it will be up to him to refrain from eating them at other times. He will be more likely to just say no if he understands the consequences. Do not criticize what your child eats or attempt to improve his diet during the baseline period, as he may decide not to admit to everything he eats.

Monday, April 10		
Food: Breakfast: Orange juice, wheat cereal, wheat toast, milk, butter		
Time	**Mood**	**Notes**
7:30	Happy	In a good mood
8:00	Sad	Tearful
8:30	Mad	Tantrum
9:00	Silly	Disrupting class
9:30	Hyper	Out of seat 3 times
10:00	Confused	On the wrong page
10:30	Spacey	Daydreaming
11:00	Sleepy	Yawning

All mental, emotional, and behavioral changes should be recorded. It is a good idea to record all physical changes as well. A hiccup can indicate digestive problems. Stumbling or spilling something can indicate that coordination has been adversely affected. Needing to have a question or comment repeated might mean that fluid in the ears is muffling incoming sounds. Watch for a sneeze, the scratching of an itch, the rubbing of an eye, a yawn, and ask your child to report all physical sensations: a knee ache, numbness or tingling of the feet or hands, feeling sleepy, etc. Be particularly alert to the behaviors that have been problematic.

- **Mood swings**—Bouts of tearfulness, whining, worrying, nervousness, fearfulness, frustration, irritation, depression, and crankiness as well as feelings of well-being and contentment.
- **Behaviors**—Restlessness, impulsiveness, aggression, hyperactivity, sluggishness, defiance, calm, cooperative, able to delay gratification, able to tolerate frustration, disorganized.

- **Thinking**—Confusion, forgetfulness, spaciness, disorganization, difficulties concentrating, difficulties shifting attention, slow to respond, clouded thinking.

After keeping a journal for a week or two, review all of the entries and see if you can discern any patterns. If restlessness, hyperactivity, and fidgeting increase after eating a burrito, a sandwich, a bowl of cereal, spaghetti, and a piece of cake, wheat might be a problem. Whether or not patterns emerge, the next step is to begin an elimination diet.

The Elimination Diet

An elimination diet involves methodically removing specific foods from your child's diet and looking for changes in mood and behavior to determine which ingredients are having adverse effects. Because school-age children trade lunches, buy items in the cafeteria to supplement lunches from home, purchase snacks from school vending machines, and eat at class parties and afterschool programs, it may be best to put your youngster on an elimination diet during a school vacation. There are several types of elimination diets. One of the least complicated is a "hypoallergenic" diet. That involves avoiding the foods that are the most problematic for the largest number of children.

- Milk
- Wheat
- Rye
- Barley
- Oats
- Eggs
- Soy
- Corn
- Citrus fruits
- Nuts
- Chocolate
- Coffee
- Food additives

To eliminate corn you must also eliminate corn syrup and cornstarch. To eliminate milk you must check food labels for milk solids and whey. Wheat is in an amazing number of processed foods.

To avoid all the dyes, preservatives, and flavor enhancers means avoiding restaurants, take-out dinners, and most frozen, canned, and packaged meals. There are various opinions about which foods and beverages are the least likely to cause adverse behavioral reactions and are therefore safest for children on an elimination diet. Besides mineral water, vitamins without sweeteners and artificial colorings, and sunflower oil, some allergists allow lamb, chicken (free-range, without chemical additives), potatoes, rice, banana, and apple. Some also allow brassicas, which include broccoli, spinach, cabbage, cauliflower, Brussels sprouts, kale, collard greens, bok choi, and kohlrabi.

For one study, a group of young children diagnosed with ADD/ADHD were restricted to rice, turkey, pear, and lettuce for two weeks. Sixty-two percent showed a fifty percent improvement on both the Connor's and the ADD/ADHD Rating Scales. Keep track of your youngster's diet and reactions by entering information into the food-and-mood journal. Do not be surprised if your youngster's behavior deteriorates before it improves. Lots of children become very cranky during the first week, as if going through withdrawal. Mother Nature seems a bit perverse, because people have a tendency to crave the food items they are most allergic to. Provide extra doses of TLC—but do not pamper your child with food!

Phasing in Ingredients

If your child's ADD/ADHD symptoms improve while on the elimination diet, that means she is allergic to one or more ingredients. The next step is to begin adding various foods back into her diet one at a time. If the food-and-mood journal indicates a setback within 72 hours after eating a particular ingredient, eliminate it again and see if her behavior improves. In actuality, adverse reactions can appear within minutes or take longer than a week; the average is two to three days.

If your youngster turns out to be sensitive to a wide range of very common ingredients, as is often the case, do not despair! After completely abstaining from an ingredient that is causing problems for a time (some doctors say four to six months; some say for six months to a year), there is a good chance that your youngster will be able to tolerate it in moderate doses. Exceptions are allergies to peanuts and shellfish, which tend to last a lifetime.

Anemia and ADD/ADHD

Several nutritional deficiencies cause anemia, which can cause ADD/ADHD symptoms. Anemic children lack enough healthy red blood cells in the bone marrow. Blood tests can determine whether a youngster is anemic. Across the globe, insufficient iron is the most common nutritional deficiency. Common symptoms include inattention, behavior problems, learning difficulties, and poor school performance. The main symptoms that doctors look for are paleness, fatigue, and irritability, and in children they can be easy to miss. Detecting paleness requires knowing what the skin color would be if the child were healthy. Many youngsters are chronically sleep deprived, and young people tend to become more wound up when they are very tired. Since even exhausted children commonly resist taking naps and going to bed at night, parents may report that hyperactivity is a problem, not fatigue. They may not report irritability, either, since some children become weepy rather than short-tempered when they are not feeling up to par.

Essential

Fried foods, starches, and sweets have lots of calories but little nutritional value. Food loses a lot or even most of its value during processing. Buy fresh fruits and vegetables, not canned or frozen! Buy whole grain cereals and breads.

A tendency toward anemia may be inherited, but the condition usually develops from improper diet. Some toddlers fill up on milk instead of eating other foods. Since meat is one of the best sources of iron, vegetarians are at risk. So are picky eaters, who fill up on starches and other processed foods. A physician can rule out iron deficiency with a simple blood test. Organ meats such as liver are the best source of iron but may contain heavy concentrations of chemical pollutants unless they are organic. Prepare food in iron cookware, since the iron leaches into the food.

Iron-Rich Foods	
Meat and Seafood	**Other**
Clams	Fortified breakfast cereal
Liver	Dried peas, beans, lentils
Mussels	Whole grains
Oysters	Dried fruit
Beef	Blackstrap molasses
Shrimp	Wheat germ
Turkey	Baked potato with skin

Iron is more readily absorbed into the system if a food containing vitamin C is eaten at the same time, so serve citrus fruit with iron-rich foods.

Vitamin B Deficiency

The B vitamins are important for a healthy nervous system, and youngsters do not have to be deficient to have problems. Being at the low end of the normal range can cause disturbances in memory, attention, mood, and behavior. The B vitamins work together, and because these vitamins are not stored in the body, they must be replenished each day. Good nutrition is a must. Factors associated with deficiencies of B vitamins include consuming a lot of sugar, white flour, and processed foods; following a vegan or vegetarian diet; taking antibiotics; and excessive urination.

Problems with memory, irritability, depression, and learning problems have been associated with insufficient vitamin B_1 (thiamin). Vitamin B_3 (niacin) facilitates the metabolism of carbohydrates, fats, and proteins, and has been used to treat schizophrenia and other mental illnesses. Behavioral symptoms of deficiency include depression, insomnia, loss of appetite, low blood sugar, and muscular weakness. Vitamin B_6 (pyridoxine) is essential for brain development, and deficiencies are extremely common among children with ADD/ADHD symptoms. Vitamin B_6 has been found to be as effective as Ritalin for lessening hyperactivity in B_6 deficient children. Folic acid (vitamin B_9) deficiency is associated with depression. In fact, up to a third of depressed individuals are low in this vitamin, and the most depressed tend to have the lowest levels. Poor balance, confusion, depression, and feelings of dread and impending doom are signs of vitamin B_{12} (cobalamin) deficiency. Fortified breakfast cereals, trout, salmon, and beef are good sources of B vitamins.

 **Essential**

Scientists continue to discover new phytochemicals, so do not assume vitamin and mineral supplements can take the place of a healthy diet. For that, your youngster needs to eat a wide variety of fresh foods. And if you do give vitamin pills, remember that more does not mean better!

Mineral Imbalances

Deficiencies of certain essential minerals, especially zinc, magnesium, copper, and calcium, are common among children diagnosed with ADD/ADHD. These deficiencies are associated with hyperactivity and inattention, as well as with bedwetting, stuttering, disruptive behavior, and separation anxiety. Supplementing the diets of deficient children with zinc sulfate significantly reduced hyperactivity, impulsiveness, and social problems in research studies. Similarly, hyperactivity decreased significantly after magnesium-deficient ADD/ADHD sufferers were given magnesium supplements for six months. In both cases, research shows that correcting the deficiencies is as effective as Ritalin for most children! Have your child undergo testing to check for mineral imbalances.

Omega-3 Fatty Acids

Boys with low blood levels of essential omega-3 fatty acids (EFAs) are more likely to be diagnosed with ADD/ADHD and to have assorted learning and health problems. EFAs cannot be manufactured by the body and must be consumed each day. The best sources are fish in general and salmon, tuna, mollusks, and shellfish in particular. Following some encouraging research showing that EFAs were powerful mood stabilizers, many psychiatrists began encouraging patients suffering from bipolar disorder (also known as manic-depression) to eat fish at least three times a week or to supplement their diet with a teaspoon or two of fish oil, flaxseed oil, or primrose oil each day. This treatment was later found to be effective for relieving depression, and in Europe, EFA supplements are more widely prescribed than Prozac. More recently, EFA deficiencies have been linked to violence and learning disorders, and now these deficiencies have been linked to ADD/ADHD symptoms as well. One study found that most youngsters diagnosed with ADD/ADHD were severely deficient. It is now understood that nerve and brain cells need EFAs to function properly. Laura Stevens, author of *12 Effective Ways to Help Your ADD/ADHD Child*, says, "In our studies at Purdue University, we found that about 40 percent of children with ADD/ADHD had many of the following symptoms of EFA deficiencies as reported by parents: excessive thirst, frequent urination, dry skin, dry hair, dandruff, brittle nails and/or tiny hard bumps on the backs of the arms or thighs. If you want your child to look sharp, feel sharp, act sharp, and enjoy good health, make sure he gets adequate amounts of essential fatty acids, especially omega-3 oils." Children can take EFAs capsules, or the oil can be purchased and stirred into salad dressings or other foods. Docosahexaenoic Acid (DHA) was found to be effective for treating ADD/ADHD but can interact with certain over-the-counter and prescription medications. Consult a nutritionist or other health care professional before giving it to your child.

Food Additives

A number of food additives have been found to cause adverse reactions in many children. Even small quantities of monosodium glutamate (MSG) can cause dramatic behavior changes. Most people associate MSG with Chinese food, but this flavor enhancer is added to a range of foods during processing. Aspartame, a popular artificial sweetener that is in everything from diet sodas to flavored yogurt, has been linked to brain tumors, movement disorders, and seizures. It apparently affects the neurotransmitters, especially dopamine, and can trigger depression in susceptible individuals. Some children are extremely sensitive to small doses and display dramatic behavioral reactions. A 1998 study published in *Life Sciences* concluded that "Aspartame consumption may constitute a hazard because of its contribution to the formation of formaldehyde adducts." It has been suggested that phosphate, an additive to carbonated drinks, may contribute to hyperkinesis by producing exaggerated muscle activity. The combination of high levels of phosphorous and low calcium and magnesium levels creates a potential for hyperactivity and seizures.

The High Carbohydrate/Low Protein Diet

Carol's parents began researching nutritional treatments for ADD/ADHD, and learned that a high carbohydrate/low protein diet could cause symptoms. They suspected that might be the problem, but did not realize until they started keeping a food-and-mood journal how poor her diet really was. Too often, her breakfast consisted of donuts, a fruit pie, or frozen waffles soaked in maple-flavored syrup and a glass of juice. She usually had a peanut butter sandwich and chocolate milk for lunch, and often bought French fries in the cafeteria.

She usually snacked on potato chips and a soda after school, and it was hard to get her to do more than taste green vegetables at dinner. If she did not like the main dish her mother served, as was often the case, she filled up on rolls and potatoes. Nevertheless, she always had room for dessert.

Improving Diet

To improve Carol's diet, her parents decided to stop eating out, since that usually meant she ate fried foods. They stopped buying chips, sodas, candy, and pastries and bought a B-vitamin complex, magnesium supplements, and flaxseed and primrose oil. They started a food-and-mood journal, hoping it would help them to spot sensitivities to foods or additives that might be contributing to Carol's inattentiveness, hyperactivity, impulsiveness, and learning problems. The first day Carol was on her new-and-improved diet, she had a fit because she couldn't have buttered popcorn—Carol's proposed solution to the lack of potato chips in the house. But the next night she accepted her mother's offer of yogurt, and the food battles that her parents had anticipated never materialized. In general there were fewer confrontations with Carol than before, perhaps because she was in a generally sunnier mood. Her mood suddenly turned stormy after soccer practice one Saturday afternoon, and her food-and-mood journal suggested the sport drink she used to quench her thirst during the break might have been responsible. Her parents later determined that she was sensitive to the yellow dye, and they were shocked to learn that all kinds of foods contained it. Feeding her was definitely more challenging than in the days when they grocery shopped without giving much thought to more than satisfying her appetite. But having a happier child who was doing better in school made their lives easier in other ways. They never doubted for a moment that the trade-off was worth it.

CHAPTER 4

The Heavy Metal Connection

I t may be the best kept secret in America: lead poisoning affects children from all social and economic groups. The Center for Disease Control is aware that the problem is widespread and recommends testing for *every* child. Most people have heard that impoverished babies living in dilapidated tenements get lead poisoning from eating chips of paint that are peeling from the walls. Even many professionals who treat children diagnosed with ADD/ADHD do not know that the problem is so pervasive. You need to have your child tested! Other heavy metals can cause behavioral problems, too.

Warning Signs

Kyle was an easy-going, happy tot. Both of his parents worked out of their new, custom-built home and were able to give their only child a lot of attention. Perhaps too much attention, they decided. They had been spared terrible two's, but shortly after Kyle turned three he became willful and demanding. Thinking that he would benefit from having playmates his own age, they enrolled him in a nearby preschool. It was expensive but had many advantages, such as swimming lessons and lots of interesting craft activities.

First Symptoms

Kyle's mood improved. He came home from preschool singing songs in Spanish as well as English, and after a month the refrigerator was cluttered with his drawings. He had never been fond of baths, but the swimming lessons turned him into a regular little fish. Each evening he played in the tub until his fingers pruned. He had always been a picky eater but was better about finishing his milk and vegetables when they were served in the ceramic cup and bowl he had painted at school.

Alert!

Nervous system damage from exposure to elemental mercury vapor results in tremors and mood and personality alterations, and is commonly diagnosed as ADD/ADHD. So are the attention problems, hyperactivity, and impulsiveness caused by PCBs, a pollutant found in the Great Lakes area.

Shortly before turning four, Kyle began complaining of tummy aches. He had been a bit constipated, and his parents had him drink more of his favorite brand of juice. Since he also seemed a bit low on energy, they took him to the doctor for a checkup. A blood test showed him to be slightly anemic. The doctor said he needed more iron, and more vitamin C to increase iron absorption. His parents fed Kyle more organ meat and encouraged him to drink more juice. Kyle's next checkup showed he was not anemic, but his parents were very alarmed by his behavior, which was worse than before he had entered preschool. He was stubborn and uncooperative and sometimes responded to small frustrations by becoming unreasonably angry. His moods changed swiftly, and they never knew what might set him off. His mother feared that Kyle might have manic-depression like one of his aunts.

The next six months were miserable for Kyle and his parents. There were many small problems—Kyle kept losing hats and mittens, which frustrated them, and pictures he made at school, which upset Kyle. There were medium-sized problems—Kyle left his toys on the floor, carelessly walked on them, and then got upset if something was lost or broken. There were big problems—he wandered about the classroom during crafts activities, story time, and lunch, insisting that he wanted to play outside. But he seemed joyless, tense, and unfocused even on the playground. They took him to a psychiatrist, who diagnosed ADD/ADHD and prescribed Ritalin. The Ritalin definitely helped but was not enough. After antidepressants were added, Kyle started acting so strangely, his parents called the psychiatrist in alarm. The psychiatrist stopped the antidepressants and prescribed a new medication to treat a condition she called "bipolar disorder." That turned out to be the new name for manic-depression! His mother's worst fear had come true.

 **Fact**

Babies spend a lot of time with their hands in their mouths, so touching objects containing lead is dangerous for them. Plastic mini blinds imported from China, Taiwan, and Mexico contain lead. They should be replaced with blinds manufactured in America.

The Silent Scourge

Professionals have long known that lead poisoning causes all of the typical ADD/ADHD symptoms. Many do not realize, however, the extent of the problem. Lead has so permeated the environment and so many youngsters are being poisoned that the Center for Disease Control and the Association for Retarded Citizens call lead poisoning the most widespread children's health problem. Medicaid's federal guidelines require testing for *all* young recipients. The Environmental Protection Agency (EPA) recommends that all babies be tested at age twelve months and again at twenty-four months. Six-month-olds should be tested if there is any reason to suspect that they might have been exposed to lead. Decisions about further testing should be based on previous test results and on the risk of further lead exposure.

The protective guidelines are in place, yet children continue to pour through the medical cracks due to lack of public awareness.

Even a slightly elevated level of lead in the body produces ADD/ADHD symptoms ranging from mild to severe. Because brain development is so rapid before birth and during the baby years, the effects of lead on unborn children, infants, toddlers, and preschoolers are especially great. Because their livers are less efficient at ridding the body of toxins, they have stronger reactions to very low levels of lead. A number of behavioral problems commonly result from lead poisoning.

- Attention deficits
- Distractibility
- Hyperactivity
- Restlessness
- Aggression
- Hostility
- Violence
- Anti-social behavior
- Anxiety
- Irritability
- Lethargy

 **Fact**

Acute cases of lead poisoning do occur, but chronic, low-level exposure to lead is by far the most common. Symptoms usually disappear once lead has been cleared from a child's system. IQ test scores then increase an average of nine points.

Intellectual problems from lead poisoning range from learning difficulties and reduced scores on IQ tests to serious developmental delays and severe mental retardation. Because the liver and kidneys

are especially effected, common physical problems include mild anemia, loss of appetite, constipation, and diarrhea. Visual and motor disturbances affect children's fine and gross motor skills. In mild cases,
the results are clumsiness, poor handwriting, and various learning
difficulties; tremor, paralysis, and seizures result from more serious
poisoning. Damage from prenatal exposure to lead does not seem to
be reversible. The severity of the symptoms from postnatal exposure
and the extent to which they can be reversed depends on how much
lead was absorbed and the duration of the exposure. Ingesting large
quantities can cause permanent brain damage and can be fatal.

 **Fact**

Deteriorated lead paint on walls cannot easily be removed. Because
lead dust is stirred up in the process, the building itself becomes too
toxic. The EPA can provide guidance to consumers about how to stabilize the paint or locate a professional contractor.

Lead Poisoning from Paint

Lead paint was used in most homes and apartments built prior to
1978. Covering it with several layers of non-leaded paint is no guarantee of safety. Family members inhale it when breathing the dust
that is in the air, and crawling babies ingest minute flakes while suck-
ing on their hands and toys. Antique toys and furniture painted with
lead paint are other sources of poisoning. The lead content of paint
manufactured before 1960 is especially toxic, with concentrations as
high as 50 percent. Toddlers standing by rocking chairs, at windows,
or in cribs ingest lead as they mouth wooden arms, sills, and railings.
Even if a youngster's home is free of lead, his daycare center, and the
homes of babysitters, relatives, and friends, may be contaminated.
In 1998, almost every school tested in California contained lead.
Seventy-eight percent exceeded the lead levels deemed safe and had

to be repaired. Although babies are the most susceptible to harm since lead concentrations build up faster in their small systems, children of all ages can be poisoned by lead, as can adults.

Lead Poisoning from Food

Amazingly, thirteen to twenty-two percent of the lead children absorb from food comes from canned goods! U.S. canners agreed to stop using lead solder to seal food cans in 1995. Nevertheless, the Federal Drug Administration estimates that ten percent of the canned goods coming in from other countries are sealed with lead solder. A popular brand of fruit juice imported from Mexico and available at many health food stores comes in a can sealed with lead solder. Look for a slender silver-gray strip and small indentations running along the seam of the can. Lead-free cans have no seam, or else the seam is a thin blue-black line. The Center for Disease Control recommends that after opening a can containing lead solder, the food should be removed and placed in a different container and should never be stored in the can. It would seem that a safer solution is not to buy food packaged in cans sealed with lead!

Leaded crystal contains lead, so food should not be stored in it. Glazed pottery and ceramic ware may contain lead. The glaze eventually cracks and the lead can seep into food. If there appears to be a dusty or chalky gray residue on the glaze after washing, do not use the pottery for food. Pottery manufactured in the U.S. with lead glaze must bear a label that says "Not for Food Use," but small crafters working from home do not always provide consumer warnings.

Beware of imported herbal products that come from countries where lead is an even more serious problem than in the U.S. A popular Mexican remedy that is used to treat children for symptoms resembling colic is ninety percent lead. It is known by various names: Azarcon, Luisa, Liga, Greta, Coral, and Rueda. Similarly, a popular fever remedy from Indochina called Pay-loo-ah has been found to contain up to ninety percent lead.

Lead Poisoning from Water

Scientists have known since 1925, when some products containing lead were briefly banned, that lead from pipes was leaching into the water of homes and businesses across the country. Further installations of lead pipes were banned, but that did not impact existing pipes, most of which are still in place. Plumbers continued to use lead solder in other types of water pipes until the 1980s. Lead faucets and fittings were not outlawed until 1998, so only the newest homes and ice makers are certain to have lead-free pipes.

Potable Water

Water faucets do not have to meet modern lead standards unless they lead to a fixture specifically designed to dispense drinking water. Otherwise, it is legal for them to contain eight percent lead. Children must be taught never to drink the water from the bath, shower, garden hose, utility sink, and laundry tub! Water that has been sitting in water heaters contains the highest concentration of lead, so the EPA says not to drink water from the hot water tap. Turn on the cold water tap and let the water run until the temperature changes before drinking it. That way, water that was sitting in leaded pipes or solder is cleared away. However, letting the water run for a while will not help if the entire municipal water supply is contaminated, which is often the case. This is an especially big problem on the east coast, where some water systems have been in place since the Civil War. Well water in rural areas is not necessarily safe to drink, either. Depending on the type of fertilizer that has been used in nearby fields and pastures, run-off that ends up in wells can contain heavy concentrations of lead and aluminum.

Ensuring Water Safety

To learn about the quality of your local water supply, contact your water department and request a copy of its annual report. The report will list the EPA standards and indicate whether they are being met. Your local department or the EPA's Safe Drinking Water Hotline (☏800-426-4791) can provide information about testing and safety.

Water filters that remove lead and other heavy metals can be purchased from any department store. Be sure to get one that meets ANSI/NSF standards for health effects. Some filters are designed to improve "aesthetics," which means taste and odor are improved but harmful chemicals are not removed. The filters must be changed regularly to be effective, so follow the instructions carefully.

Essential

Water experts say that to revamp big city water systems would require a tax increase of $100 per year per household—less than most families spend on bottled water and a fraction of the cost of a cable television subscription. It is time to make the choices needed to protect our nation's children!

Contaminated Air and Soil

Lead from automobile emissions ends up in the air and settles in the soil, so children living near congested traffic and heavily traveled roads run an especially high risk of lead poisoning. Playing in areas where leaded gasoline, leaded paint, or ceramics were once manufactured, sold, or used in quantity is very dangerous. Long after the gas station has been demolished or the building containing lead has been razed, heavy lead concentrations remain. Also, dust blowing in from contaminated areas causes youngsters living at a distance to be poisoned. The bottom line is that soil in densely populated urban areas and the air near high traffic areas are major offenders.

Taking Action

Every child with ADD/ADHD symptoms should be tested for lead poisoning. Some of the inexpensive do-it-yourself lead poisoning test kits may not register the low levels of lead that the government has now determined are harmful. Blood levels as low as 10 micrograms per deciliter of whole blood produce full-blown ADD/ADHD symptoms. The best way to determine if your youngster has lead poisoning is from a blood test performed by a doctor. Your child may be eligible for free testing through your local Child Health and Disability Program (CHDP). To find out, contact your local public health department. Phone the National Lead Information Center at ✆(800) 424-LEAD for information about how to have your home tested.

 **Fact**

The decline of the Roman Empire has been attributed to lead poisoning, which rendered its emperors insane, sickly, and sterile and its population lethargic, gluttonous, and debauched. Like us, the Romans continued to drink water from lead pipes and to eat lead-contaminated food while knowing of the danger.

Treating Lead Poisoning

The good news is that ADD/ADHD symptoms often disappear once lead is out of a youngster's system. The treatment for lead poisoning is chelation therapy, which involves speeding the excretion of the lead through urination. However, chelation therapy is controversial for children with problems stemming from chronic, low-level lead exposure. The medications that are used can be dangerous, and chelation therapy can actually increase lead absorption. Previously chelation was only used for extremely severe cases of lead poisoning since blood lead levels fall quickly once the environment is cleaned up. However, now that doctors realize the serious effects of even slightly elevated blood lead levels, chelation therapy has become more common. Still, some say that cleaning up the child's environment and letting time work its wonders is best unless the situation is serious.

Public Alerts

In 1997–2000, 6.7 percent of children ages five to seventeen were reported to have been diagnosed with ADD/ADHD, and the figures continue to rise at a rate that is as alarming as it is mysterious. The pharmaceutical industry and many professionals attribute the increased number of cases to increased public awareness, but others are not so sure. An estimated four percent of American children have toxic lead levels. That average includes six percent of toddlers, and increasing numbers of little ones are being medicated for ADD/ADHD. The lead poisoning average also includes eight percent of White non-Hispanic children, and over thirteen percent of White non-Hispanic children were reported to have ADD/ADHD—the highest of any group. The rate for lead poisoning is highest among minority youth in urban areas where lead concentrations are highest.

 *Essential*

Americans traditionally vote according to their pocketbooks and have been unwilling to pay for the clean up of contaminated air and water, and to ban lead. Perhaps it is time to make the financial sacrifices required to protect America's most important resource: its children.

Two to three times more boys than girls are diagnosed with ADHD, and boys' rate of lead poisoning is much higher than for girls. Perhaps boys are more constitutionally susceptible to ADD/ADHD as doctors believe. But given their penchant for vigorous activities, it seems likely that they spend more time outside breathing lead-contaminated air and playing in lead-contaminated soil than their female peers. Do boys also spend more time playing in porcelain bathtubs (many of which contain heavy concentrations of lead) and drink more lead-contaminated water as they splash about? Do they grab more drinks from the garden hose, thus consuming more contaminated water as they sip? These questions do not seem to have been addressed in scientific investigations. More research is needed.

Other Heavy Metals

Other heavy metals can cause ADD/ADHD symptoms. Artists are familiar with paint colors named "cadmium blue" and "cadmium red" (often called "cad blue" and "cad red" for short). They may not realize that cadmium is a highly toxic heavy metal. The mental illness of Van Gogh and many other famous artists is believed to have been caused by cadmium poisoning. Young artists should handle these paints carefully and avoid getting them in their mouths.

 *Question?*

Does aluminum cause ADHD?
Aluminum poisoning does cause the symptoms. However, aluminum pots and pans are reported to be safe. Aluminum apparently does not leach into food unless it is used for acidic foods, such as tomatoes and certain fruit juices.

Certain heavy metals are essential for the human body to function properly, but in excess they cause problems with brain functioning. Heavy metals can disrupt thyroid gland functioning, which helps to regulate activity level. Copper is a brain stimulant and can cause racing thoughts and thinking disturbances. Copper also destroys histamine; low-histamine children are hyperactive. An excess of aluminum has been implicated in learning disabilities and behavior problems. Mercury is a neurotoxin that leaches from dental amalgam fillings. It has been used as a preservative for certain childhood vaccinations which have been associated with autism. It is common for autistic children to also be diagnosed with ADD/ADHD. U.S. companies release forty tons of elementary mercury into the atmosphere each year, and an estimated one in six babies exposed to this poison has developmental delays. The federal government has declined to impose stricter pollution controls, citing the economic hardship such measures would create for the companies.

Overlooked Dangers at Home

After learning about lead poisoning, Kyle's parents insisted that their son be tested for lead, although they really had no reason to believe he had been in contact with it. The psychiatrist seemed as surprised as his parents when the results came back from the lab. Kyle had enough lead in his system to explain his mild anemia, stomachaches, constipation, forgetfulness, attention problems, aggressiveness, and mood swings. Kyle's parents searched for the source of the lead and found several. The water in their house contained lead. The ceramic cup and bowl Kyle had been eating and drinking from contained lead. Kyle's favorite brand of juice was from Mexico, and the cans were sealed with lead solder. Three months after they began using a water filter and got rid of the cup, bowl, and juice, Kyle's lead levels remained unacceptable. His parents were about to have the soil around their house tested. Fortunately, before they went to that expense an EPA official advised them to check the porcelain bathtub for lead. While sitting in the tub, Kyle absorbed lead through his skin, and he had been drinking lead-contaminated water when he played in the bath. After switching to showers, Kyle's lead levels quickly fell. Because the lead poisoning had occurred on the heels of a difficult three-year-old stage and had progressed so gradually, his parents did not realize how much he had changed until he recovered. They were so very glad to have their happy, easy-going son back.

CHAPTER 5

Other Causes and Complications

From low-birth weight to watching a lot of television, an amazing number of factors put children at risk for ADD/ADHD. Moreover, two-thirds of the children diagnosed with it have at least one other psychiatric diagnosis. A closer look at current opinions about the causes of ADD/ADHD and an examination of how psychiatric diagnoses are made raises some disturbing questions. Might ADD/ADHD be just a figment of the medical community's imagination? Lots of people think so, but one undeniable fact remains: many children are hurting.

The Diagnostic Maze

The day Tom started taking Ritalin, his teacher called his father at home to express delight over the amazing transformation. "Tom raised his hand instead of shouting out answers. He did all of his work. He never had to be reminded to stop talking or remain seated. It seems like a miracle!" Through the years Tom's father had only heard an endless litany of complaints from the school. Finally receiving a positive report about his son's behavior meant a lot. That night before bedtime, Tom said he was worried that he might have forgotten to do something for school the next day. His dad told him that it would all work out and to get some sleep, but was secretly delighted. Tom actually cared about doing his work and staying out of trouble! That was another first.

Tom's recitation of his worries about having forgotten to do something for school soon became a long and very trying nightly ritual. Nothing his father said or did reassured him. Tom had a hard time falling asleep because of the troubling thoughts running through his mind. They were always the same: he might have forgotten "something" and would get in trouble with his teacher. At school Tom became so intent on doing perfect work that he could not finish an assignment. He bit his nails and developed a twitch in his eye. His doctor sent him for a battery of psychological tests. The results showed that Tom had a learning disability, anxiety, and might be depressed as well.

 **Fact**

Many youngsters develop obsessions, racing thoughts, compulsions, and tics while taking amphetamines and other stimulant medications. Doctors may then prescribe medication to control the unwanted effects. Or they may diagnose anxiety and prescribe medication to treat it. The more sensible course is to change the original prescription.

Tom's doctor prescribed medication to calm him and referred him to a psychiatrist. When they arrived for the appointment, Tom was groggy, apathetic, and listless from the anti-anxiety medication. Tom's father tried to explain to the doctor that Tom was not usually like this. Still, after interviewing Tom and his father, the psychiatrist diagnosed depression. He pointed to the test report and said that depression and ADD/ADHD had probably been Tom's core problem all along. To treat it, he added a prescription for a regimen of antidepressants. The family medicine chest was starting to resemble a pharmacy. Tom's father decided it was time for a second opinion.

Cause, Effect, or Complication?

Soon after a child is diagnosed with ADD/ADHD, many parents find themselves on a psychiatric merry-go-round as additional diagnoses begin pouring in. About fifty percent of children diagnosed with ADD/ADHD are also diagnosed with a learning disability, reading disabilities being the most common. About twenty-five percent are simultaneously diagnosed with anxiety and/or with conduct disorder. Symptoms of conduct disorder include aggressiveness toward people, animals, or both; serious rule violations such as lying and stealing; and wanton destructiveness toward property. The rate of depression is estimated at about twenty percent, as is manic-depression (now called bipolar disorder).

Alert!

Depression, anxiety, and serious misconduct are often indistinguishable from ADD/ADHD. Determining whether ADD/ADHD symptoms are the cause or result of depression, anxiety, or a conduct disorder is like trying to decide which came first, the chicken or the egg.

If that list of diagnoses seems long, it is really just the tip of the psychiatric iceberg. Hundreds of thousands of abused and neglected children display the kind of impulsive, hyperactive, and inattentive behavior patterns that earns them an ADD/ADHD diagnosis as well as a diagnosis of posttraumatic stress disorder (PTSD). That is the same disorder that afflicts so many soldiers returning from battle, as well as victims of violent crimes and natural disasters. Then there are the children who are simultaneously diagnosed with ADD/ADHD and Tourette's syndrome. The symptoms of Tourette's include tics, twitches, and other uncontrollable movements. Sometimes children make bizarre sounds as well. Children who take Ritalin are at risk for developing this disorder. Autistic children, who have marked impairments in social relationships and communication, are commonly diagnosed with ADD/ADHD as well. So are many youngsters with developmental delays. Large percentages of teens with ADD/ADHD are also diagnosed with substance abuse disorders. In fact, the vast majority of children diagnosed with ADD/ADHD—about two-thirds—have at least one other diagnosis. Many have two, three, four, or even more.

If your youngster is diagnosed with ADD/ADHD, it is undoubtedly distressing to think that several heavy-duty psychiatric diagnoses may eventually be added to his medical chart. However, that does *not* mean that your child is seriously mentally ill. Often diagnoses are added because doctors mistake the side effects of medications prescribed to treat one psychiatric disorder for a completely different disorder. More often, it is because of the way physicians and increasing numbers of therapists conceptualize and go about diagnosing so-called "mental disorders." But to understand that, it helps to first understand the medical community's theory of ADD/ADHD.

Biological Causes

Most doctors trained in Western medicine are predisposed to believe that all psychological, behavioral, mental, and learning difficulties stem from physical processes. They think that anatomy, physiology, neurology, biochemistry, and genetics are the routes to understanding human problems. Ironically, they minimize the role of nutrition or deny it has an effect at all—perhaps because it receives little attention in standard medical school programs. Yet nutritional problems are the leading cause of ADD/ADHD symptoms.

Brain Abnormalities

An electroencephalogram (EEG) can spot various types of brain damage. EEG testing used to be routine for children with ADD/ADHD symptoms, but brain abnormalities were so rarely detected that widespread testing is no longer being done. Certain brain injuries and abnormalities, especially those affecting the frontal lobes, are strongly associated with ADD/ADHD (see Chapter 11, Cutting-Edge

Treatments). Children with certain types of epilepsy are often hyperactive and impulsive, and have difficulties with planning and thinking ahead. Problems caused by a temporal lobe cyst are often mistaken for ADD/ADHD.

Boys under age eight who snore are three times more likely to be hyperactive and to wet the bed at night. Hyperactive boys with attention deficits who wet the bed often have mineral deficiencies or sleep apnea. Both cause ADD/ADHD symptoms.

Although no association between ADD/ADHD and petit mal seizures has been found, parents and teachers often mistake them for signs of inattentiveness. That is because during this type of seizure, children lose consciousness for very brief periods but they do not fall down, twitch, or even close their eyes. They simply do not respond when spoken to and are unaware of what is happening around them. Because they do not remember what went on, it can seem that they were not paying attention. The seizures only last a few seconds or minutes, but can occur hundreds of times each day. They are most common among boys age six to twelve. Many youngsters eventually outgrow the problem.

Prenatal Problems

Despite all of the public service announcements, many people still do not realize that an unborn child's development depends on the mother's health. Problems during pregnancy are associated with an increased likelihood of ADD/ADHD symptoms later in life.

- Maternal ingestion of drugs
- Maternal consumption of alcohol
- Maternal smoking

- Poor maternal nutrition
- Maternal exposure to lead and mercury
- Premature birth
- Low birth weight

Commonly abused drugs such as cocaine and heroin can impair fetal brain development. Babies born with full-blown fetal alcohol syndrome (FAS) from their mother's heavy drinking display many serious abnormalities, including birth defects and mental retardation. FAS babies commonly show behavioral patterns consistent with ADD/ADHD. Some babies born to moderate drinkers show fetal alcohol effects, including mild physical abnormalities and typical ADD/ADHD behavioral problems. Even minor ingestion of nicotine and alcohol during pregnancy is associated with ADD/ADHD symptoms, according to the National Institute of Mental Health. Children with ADHD are twice as likely to have mothers who smoked while pregnant and to have been exposed to alcohol while in the womb. Low-birth weight and premature babies are twice as likely to be diagnosed with ADD/ADHD.

Doctors assume that prenatal toxic exposure and premature birth cause mild brain damage or neurological problems, and that is why the affected children develop ADD/ADHD symptoms later in life, typically in elementary school. However, often emotional factors are involved. Many premature babies are insecurely attached to their mothers, which complicates child-rearing because of their often serious behavior problems. Babies born to mothers with drinking problems are more likely to be reared in chaotic home environments. Children living in families with tense, angry emotional climates are more anxious and angry. Such young people are more likely to develop behavioral and learning problems that involve inattention.

The Genetic Link

The vast majority of physicians consider ADD/ADHD to be an inherited condition caused by the reigning queen of the natural world,

Mother Nature. Most doctors maintain that virtually all emotional, behavioral, and learning problems result from the genetic mix that takes place when egg meets sperm. A number of highly regarded professionals in the field have gone so far as to state that the gene responsible has been tentatively identified. Once its identity is confirmed, many doctors say, geneticists will find a way to inactivate it. Until then, they urge patients to take their medication.

Nature versus Nurture

For all of its appeal, there is nothing to suggest that the "faulty gene" theory is true. In an investigation of one of the genes thought to be responsible for ADD/ADHD, only twenty-five percent of children diagnosed with ADD/ADHD had one of the suspect genes, and ten percent of normal children had it. Geneticists say it is highly unlikely that a lone gene is involved; they guesstimate there will be at least five genes, and perhaps as many as ten. And the idea that genes are fixed in stone at conception was abandoned long ago. A gene for red hair may produce a life-long redhead. But the functioning of most genes depends on the environment. Researchers think that emotional and behavioral symptoms emerge when susceptible children are exposed to certain damaging environmental influences. That is why some children may be able to subsist on junk food without developing behavior problems.

Debunking the "Faulty Gene" Theory

The idea that ADD/ADHD might be inherited started with research on identical twins, who have the same genetic structure. Studies showed that if one twin had a mental or behavioral disorder, the odds were that the other did, too, even though they had been separated at birth and raised in different households. Now it seems that these findings were in error. In *The Gene Illusion: Genetic Research in Psychiatry and Psychology Under the Microscope,* author Jay Joseph describes the many flaws in hereditary studies. The conclusion that genes account for about fifty percent of the variance appears to be vastly inflated. It now appears that genes only account for about fifteen percent. The key issue is not genes; it is how they are triggered by and interact with one another and the environment.

Alert!

The "faulty gene" theory provides the rationale for treating ADD/ADHD as a medical disorder, but environmental effects are key. Parents need to protect their child from known toxic influences: poor diet, lack of exercise, exposure to pollutants, trauma, substandard education, and stress.

False Hope

The idea that a faulty gene is causing a child's behavior problems is definitely appealing. It can relieve parental worries that their child-rearing methods are to blame and reassures them that they do not need to do anything differently. The belief that their youngster has a medical problem overcomes parents' doubts about administering potentially dangerous medications. It also moves parents to be kinder to their children. Many stop punishing them upon learning that they are not misbehaving on purpose.

Although being told that something is wrong with their brain devastates many children, some are relieved. (For suggestions about explaining ADD/ADHD to your child, see Appendix A.) Self-esteem may improve when youngsters are no longer burdened with shame about their lack of self-control, guilt about hurting their parents, and remorse for their continuing misdeeds at school. When the blame stops and medication settles them down, many youngsters reveal how deeply distressed they have felt all along. It is common for them to say things like, "I was good today! Not a devil!" That is when many parents first realize that their child was being hurt by so much nagging. Many youngsters become so alienated, defensive, and secretive from the constant criticism, their parents have no idea what is in their hearts. Teachers are glad to learn that a student's problems are not a reaction to a poor curriculum or ineffective teaching. Doctors dedicate their lives to healing, and they are gratified to be able to quickly and efficiently help their patients by writing prescriptions. Characterizing ADD/ADHD as a genetic condition simultaneously builds an airtight case for an easy medical solution and helps the child and everyone in his life to feel better.

 **Fact**

Doctors buttress their case for the gene theory by pointing out that most children diagnosed with ADD/ADHD have a relative suffering from alcoholism, depression, anxiety, or another major psychiatric disorder. But the same is true for most children who do *not* have ADD/ADHD symptoms. A skeleton seems to lurk in every family's closet.

Avoiding the Diagnostic Trap

Psychiatric symptom lists and diagnoses were actually developed to facilitate research investigations. The current system for diagnosing "mental disorders" that attempts to put people into narrow categories is actually useless for describing the emotional, philosophical, and spiritual problems of children. The widespread practice of diagnosing mental and behavioral disorders was driven by insurance companies. The companies began requiring mental health providers to submit a diagnosis along with their bills so that patients could be reimbursed for their therapy sessions. The goal was to gather actuarial data as a first step toward controlling costs. Many therapists refused to pigeonhole patients into nonsensical categories that did not begin to describe their problems. How to diagnose a child who was too sad, worried, and angry over his parents' divorce to sit still, pay attention, and concentrate on schoolwork? Most therapists agreed that it was ridiculous to use a diagnostic system that had been designed to standardize the way people were chosen for research studies. But since patients needed a diagnosis to receive their health benefits, therapists were moved to accommodate them. Accordingly, a therapist might diagnose a child in crisis over a divorce with depression because he was sad and having a hard time sleeping. Or, because the child was too tense to sit still and too worried about his family to think about much else, the diagnosis could have just as easily been hyperactivity, an anxiety disorder, or an attention deficit. But because the child was angry with his dad for having left home and was taking it out on his mother by being defiant, then oppositional/defiant disorder also applied. And if the distress went on long enough to undermine his academic progress, he could be diagnosed with a learning disability.

Having to affix diagnoses to patients was treated as a waste of time by therapists. Having to record the "date of first illness" and to specify which condition was treated on which date made it obvious that having to use the same health benefit claim forms as physicians was an error. But eventually the diagnoses began to take on a life of their own. Managed care companies wanted case notes documenting that the therapist had in fact stuck to treating the diagnosis listed on the form and had not strayed into other areas.

The practice of diagnosing and treating separate groups of symptoms may be reasonable when a youngster has an ear infection, a broken toe, and a rash, since he might benefit from antibiotics, a toe splint, and some soothing skin cream. Prescribing different medications to alleviate depression, to combat anxiety, to lessen aggression, to boost concentration, to reduce hyperactivity, and to stabilize mood can be dangerous—especially when a child is upset about very real problems. A prime example is the hundreds of thousands of foster children diagnosed with ADD/ADHD. The real problem is their traumatic past and uncertain future. They need stability, love, and therapy. They are more likely to get half a dozen diagnoses and prescriptions to try to alter their mood.

The Brain/Behavior Connection

Tom's father lost faith that medication could help his son and asked his physician whether psychological counseling or psychotherapy might help. The doctor said that sitting in an office and talking about problems might occasionally yield some modest benefits. But he emphasized that medical problems needed medical treatment. He spoke somewhat disparagingly of "talk therapy," which he seemed to classify as so-much voodoo.

Alert!

Research shows that counseling and therapy are powerful and effective treatment methods. Clients reap benefits from solving personal problems and learning new, more effective ways to cope. And the changes run deep. Therapy outcome studies have revealed changes in the structure of the brain following treatment!

Tom's father attended parent counseling, Tom attended play therapy sessions, and sometimes they met jointly with Tom's therapist. It turned out that Tom was still having difficulties coming to terms with the loss of his mother many years before. Tom had gone back and forth between blaming himself and blaming his father—and often his mother, too. Because his father had mourned intensely for about a year, Tom had felt abandoned by both parents and had kept all of his feelings inside. Then he had begun taking out his anger on his female teachers. Every time one of them was absent, he feared she might never come back. Then he felt so sad and guilty that he sometimes cried himself to sleep. Yet he had felt compelled to stir up trouble in the classroom. "I start thinking about my mom when it's too quiet, and I get sad," he said. "Or I think something might have happened to Dad, and I get worried. People say, 'It's so noisy I can't hear myself think.' It's true! When it's loud, I can't hear the bad thoughts." Therapy was a big time commitment, and talking about problems was so painful that Tom did not always want to go. But a year later, he was doing so much better at home and school, they decided he did not need more sessions. Tom's father had not expected to get help for himself, but he was calmer and happier, too.

CHAPTER 6

Little Space Cadets: The ADD Child

Symptoms of attention deficit disorder (ADD) are common among intellectual geniuses, and among all types of artists, poets, musicians, philosophers, sages, seers, and highly creative children. If Socrates, Leonardo da Vinci, Albert Einstein, Benjamin Franklin, Thomas Edison, General George Patton, and Walt Disney were growing up today, they would undoubtedly be diagnosed with ADD. Highly intuitive nonconformists have historically suffered ridicule and rejection because they did not think or act like the majority. Now they are being coerced, even drugged, into conforming to other peoples' ideas of normal. This is a tragedy!

The ADD Child at School

Bernadette's parents were first alerted to their daughter's problems when she was in nursery school. When the teacher read a story aloud and discussed it with the class, Bernadette asked irrelevant questions instead of sticking to the topic. In kindergarten Bernadette was often oblivious to what the group was doing. Right in the middle of a game of Simon Says, she would wander off to the crafts corner or book nook. Instead of playing hopscotch and tag during recess, she played alone in the sandbox. "Her short attention span and poor social skills are signs of immaturity," the teacher said.

Essential

Many students diagnosed with ADD do well in school one year and flounder the next. That should make it obvious that the classroom environment and teaching method are key. It is a mistake to diagnose such students as learning disabled.

Bernadette's first grade teacher had nothing but praise for her, but her second grade teacher said she daydreamed and needed to pay attention. In third grade, the school contacted her parents about "a worrisome incident." While the teacher was explaining double-digit addition, Bernadette stood up and walked to the classroom door. When asked where she was going, Bernadette said, "To play on the playground," as if that were the most normal thing in the world. The other children were startled, and some boys started calling her crazy and induced others to avoid her. Bernadette was unhappy in fourth grade because her messy handwriting, inattentiveness, and failure to follow directions displeased her teacher. An example of the latter was that instead of giving an oral book report, Bernadette staged a puppet show to act out the story. Her parents had thought her puppet show was a creative way to fulfill the assignment. They felt guilty for having encouraged her and angry about the teacher's inflexibility all at the same time.

Fact

Most of the children who are diagnosed with an attention deficit disorder (ADD) are girls. They are usually well-behaved and are not disruptive in the classroom. They are less likely to have problems with delinquency and substance abuse in adolescence than their hyperactive counterparts.

Bernadette's IQ test showed that she was very bright, and her fifth grade teacher recommended an evaluation to find out why her grades were poor. The school psychologist said she had a "classic case" of attention deficit disorder. Her irrelevant comments during conversations and strange answers to questions were caused by a language processing problem. Special education classes and a consultation with a psychiatrist were recommended. Her parents had affectionately called Bernadette "our little space cadet." Now they were being told her spaciness was a sign of deeper problems.

ADD or Creative Genius?

When highly creative adults read about attention deficit disorder (ADD), most recognize that they had all of the symptoms when they were growing up. Some eventually learned to compensate for or even overcome some of the problems that made childhood so challenging for them. However, many still have great difficulty with a number of tasks that come naturally to most people. As adults they feel freer to be themselves, either because they surround themselves with like-minded people or because they have stopped caring about what others think. Still, many successful adults carry the scars from their difficult childhoods.

Educating the ADD Child

Creative children struggle in traditional classrooms and are commonly viewed by their teachers as unintelligent or as underachievers. Many come to think of themselves as not very bright or unmotivated. The real problem is that their minds work differently from most people. They are more holistic in their thinking and are drawn to abstract ideas rather than details. Because they focus on the "wrong" parts of the lessons, they can easily forget, mix up, or simply overlook information that teachers consider important. Many are accused of being lazy because they daydream. Often the real "problem" is that they devote a lot of mental energy to pondering the material being presented rather than simply trying to commit it to memory. They consider its relationship to other things they have learned and contemplate its implications. Creative children are also more intuitive, so when asked what they are thinking about, they may be unable to articulate what is on their mind. If they try, they are often ridiculed by teachers and peers who cannot comprehend the connection between their comments and the subject under discussion. Creative children end up being accused of not listening or of not paying attention—and are diagnosed with ADD.

Essential

Highly sensitive children react strongly to sounds, temperature changes, smells, and tastes that others barely notice. Such acute sensitivity goes hand in hand with artistic, musical, and literary genius. Do not assume your child is exaggerating when he complains about discomforts that to you seem minor.

Peer Problems

Highly creative children are in the minority, and the majority does not understand how they think or why they behave as they do. Peers tend to regard them as strange or odd because of their unusual interests. Especially creative types are often branded as crazy because their heightened sensitivity causes them to have stronger emotional reactions than less sensitive people. Even if creative teens find a social niche in high school, they know that most of their peers regard them as odd. Some creative children are very independent and do not notice or care how others perceive them, but many notice and they care a lot. Feeling lonely, rejected, and being viewed as strange during childhood can cause long-term difficulties with self-esteem. Without their parents' support, many youngsters find themselves without anyone to affirm them as people. Their desperation often propels them toward an antisocial peer group. Others label themselves as crazy and withdraw. Some hold everyone at a distance for fear of having their "insanity" discovered. Some embrace the role and spend years moving through the revolving door of the mental health system. When creative children are not accepted by their peers, affirmation from parents becomes all the more important. Most parents love their children dearly. But too many make creative youngsters feel that something is terribly wrong with them.

Parent Problems

Most people pride themselves on being practical and realistic. They focus on the details of everyday life, accept things at face value, and rarely pause to contemplate abstract matters. They prefer the tried and true to the unknown and uncertain. They devote a lot of energy to trying to arrange the present in order to ensure that the future does not hold too many surprises. They value conformity and are disturbed by independent thinkers who are not careful about adhering to social conventions. Parents may appreciate the artistic, literary, and scientific contributions of creative people and admire their inventiveness and creative problem-solving abilities. But they urge their children to follow the beaten path and make decisions about important issues such as courses of study, careers, and mates based on their heads. Most people consider the heart less trustworthy.

 **Fact**

ADD symptoms can stem from impaired brain functioning due to fetal alcohol syndrome, lead poisoning, allergies, chemical sensitivities, or another brain trauma or injury. However, the ADD symptom list also describes the personality of most highly creative individuals. See Appendix A for a partial list.

Growing up ADD

Good family support is probably more important for creative children because they suffer more peer rejection and find it harder to please their teachers. Youngsters who achieve success in their chosen field often say that their warm family relationships were critical sources of emotional support. Their parents might not have understood what made them tick. But their families encouraged them to develop in their own direction instead of adding to the pressure to conform. Having a supportive parent seems to make for a much happier childhood, but some children received critical emotional support from a teacher, relative, or neighbor who believed in them. That can enable them to maintain feelings of self-worth.

 *Essential*

Please Understand Me by David Keirsey and Marilyn Bates and *Nurture by Nature* by Paul and Barbara Tieger describe the special strengths of different personality types. They should be required reading for parents who are having difficulties understanding their child. Put them on your must-read list!

Struggles to define a personally fulfilling identity typically intensify during adolescence. Feistier teenagers commonly distance themselves from parents who discount their goals, deride their ambitions, and strive to change them. The results are often alienation and family rifts. Compliant teens may let their parents' dictates override their own wishes and pursue college majors and careers their parents consider practical. That can result in poor grades, dropping out of school, or worse: pursuing unfulfilling careers and marrying someone whose main appeal is that their family approves. Too often, such children end up with serious regrets decades later.

Kings of Chaos vs. Absent-Minded Professors

Highly creative children enjoy complex ideas and problems. Routine tasks that do not pose an appealing intellectual challenge try their patience, and repetitive tasks set their teeth on edge. Sorting and putting away clean clothes, doing pages of handwriting practice, or completing dozens of simple arithmetic problems strikes many as too mindless to be of interest. When they finish, they do not feel pride in their accomplishment because it seems meaningless. Praise for a job well done may not motivate them if the job seems mundane. They may prefer to toss all of their socks into a drawer even though they must spend a lot of time rummaging through it each morning to find two that match. This seems nonsensical to people who find organizing easy and enjoy having things in order. Many creative children never learn to write legibly because they cannot bring themselves to do page after page of handwriting practice. Like Einstein, many highly intelligent creative youngsters are very adept at comprehending complex concepts and developing new ones, but they are abysmal at performing simple computations, which require rote memorization. At the same time, tasks that seem to others to involve boring, repetitive practice may strike creative children as fascinating. Young pianists practice scales on the piano for hours because perfecting them poses a challenge.

Alert!

Scientists believe that highly creative people are genetically inclined toward serious psychiatric disorders, especially depression, manic-depression, and substance abuse. However, peer rejection and years of feeling like failures at school and disappointments to their parents predispose children to psychological problems. Be supportive!

Creative children can appear to be hopelessly disorganized, but often there is a method to their seeming madness. They use inventive methods to break the monotony of routine tasks to stave off boredom and remain alert and focused. For instance, they skip around when doing sets of problems for assignments and tests instead of doing them in order. They experiment with different problem-solving strategies instead of finding one that works and sticking to it. In the process, they overlook some problems altogether and make errors that do not seem to follow a pattern. Their uneven performance confuses educators, making such students ripe for a diagnosis of a learning disability.

 **Fact**

Many creative children are mystified by adult reverence for the calendar and clock. Teachers refuse to accept late work, believing that *when* students do their lessons matters more than that they do them. Some children march to a different drummer because they keep time to their internal rhythms.

Life in the Here-and-Now

It is hard to generalize about children who are by nature nonconformists, but many do share certain characteristics. One is that many have great difficulty adhering to schedules. In part, that is because dividing time into slots and assigning activities to each one does not strike them as sensible. If they worry about being late, it may be because they are afraid others will be upset. They do not believe that the passage of time is significant or that the clock should rule people's lives. Many are doers, not planners. The future and past matter less to them than the present. In that, they are in accord with the world's philosophers who teach that the only reality is the here and now. Overly anxious creative youngsters may obsess about the future or ruminate about the past. However, the issue is more likely to be that they do not know how to identify or manage the anxiety they are feeling at the moment.

Seeing the Forest, Not the Trees

Highly creative children typically have a holistic thinking style. Because they focus on how things merge, combine, and connect, they see the big picture. Indeed, the ability of creative children to analyze and synthesize ideas while ignoring details can be mystifying. They do not automatically focus on the elements that define subtle differences, which is required to sort and organize. Teachers commonly see academic failure on the horizon. A matching or true/false test that requires students to recall specific information about Civil War generals and battles is likely to be very challenging. Yet their ability to expound on the strategies used in various military campaigns on an essay test may be very intelligent and incisive. Teachers warn that students cannot succeed academically without getting the details straight. However, if creative youngsters do not give up and drop out altogether, they are likely to find college not only more gratifying but actually easier than elementary and high school. Many do not begin to shine until graduate school where original, creative thought is highly prized.

 **Essential**

Creative youngsters need to learn to organize their possessions and cope with schedules, since these skills are important for school and most job settings. Most children are eager to learn, but staying organized requires an attention to niggling details they do not normally focus on.

Parents often worry about how their child with ADD symptoms will manage a job and a household because she is so haphazard about details. In fact, many creative children go on to be very successful adults. They develop impressive new theories, produce spectacular inventions, and create dazzling works of art, music, and literature that enrich the world and contribute to its betterment.

They may also lose their keys every time they turn around and forget to get their driver's license renewed. Many have to make repeat trips to the grocery store because they keep forgetting things. They do not bother with grocery lists because they know they will lose them. Yet they survive. And those who pursue careers that utilize their special talents thrive. They make fine parents despite being exceptionally messy housekeepers.

Space Cadets vs. Spacious Dreamers

Many parents and teachers very much dislike being interrupted when they are deep in thought or are concentrating on a complicated task because it distracts them. Yet many adults do not recognize that interrupting a child can also create an unwanted distraction. For a youngster to be immersed in her own thoughts is not necessarily bad. In fact, to be able to concentrate intensely and avoid being distracted can be an asset.

 **Fact**

Many great artists honed their skills while relieving classroom boredom. Ask your child's teachers to support your budding artist. Some students listen better while drawing, sculpting, or knitting than sitting with their hands neatly folded on the desk. Many children can do two (or three or four) things at once.

It is of course frustrating to speak to a child and not get a reply—or at least an acknowledgment. But it seems ironic that many parents have such deep respect for their child's body that they consider it a violation to insist that their three-year-old give up diapers and use the potty. Yet those same parents routinely violate their child's mind by insisting that she immediately stop thinking her own thoughts and respond to what is on their minds. Patience is in order!

Recalcitrant Rebels vs. Independent Individualists

Some children are very independent from the time they are tots, and this characteristic is especially common among the intellectually gifted. Individualists often clash with their teachers even though they are not disruptive. Some read books in class instead of doing busy work assignments. Some draw instead of sitting with their hands folded on their desks. Some create complex stories in their imaginations to fend off boredom. They persist because what they are doing interests them very much. Parents' and teachers' negative opinions are less compelling than their desire to learn. The only ways to get them to change may be to use heavy-handed punishments to break their spirits or to drug them.

Alert!

Independent thinkers are often diagnosed with attention deficits because they are so intent on what they are doing, they do not notice what is going on around them. If they do notice, they may not care to join in. Getting them to care may be a losing battle.

Very independent children tend to be outspoken. They are prone to address adults like equals rather than deferring to their authority. If they are generally insensitive to other people's feelings, they may alienate peers and earn a reputation among adults for being ill-mannered. Maintaining good relationships with teachers and classmates can be especially challenging for independent types who love to debate. Some children consider ideas more important than people's feelings.

Help your child understand how his behavior effects others, but let him decide whether he wants to change in order to be liked. It is a mistake to take your youngster's side against teachers, but it is also a mistake to try to change your child into someone he is not. A better approach is to communicate in no uncertain terms that you expect your child to be respectful of others. Discuss ways he can assert himself appropriately. And when he hurts someone's feelings, he of course needs to apologize.

Essential

The social and emotional cost of being different is high, and many parents work hard to get their youngster to act like the other children. During adolescence, the desire to conform and act like peers can lead to trouble. Be careful what you wish for!

Students are expected to participate as members of the class and move with the group even during recess and lunch. If they also attend afterschool programs and extra-curricular activities, they have little time to ponder their own thoughts or pursue their individual interests. Highly intelligent and creative students are not content to soak up bits of information so they can spit them back on a test. Moreover, some are not very adept at memorizing facts and remembering specific details. Nevertheless, they may be masterful when it comes to grasping concepts. But some need to conduct their own investigations and draw their own conclusions. They have a hard time making sense of material that is presented to them orally or in writing. Having an unorthodox method of processing information does not mean they are deficient. It does, however, mean that they are different. And being different is definitely difficult.

Different Strokes for Other Folks

Studies have shown that the brains of children diagnosed with ADD function differently. Doctors view this as a sign that their brains are defective even if there are no signs of organic problems. They could just as easily decide that the brains of organized, detail-oriented people who remain alert to what is happening around them and are attentive even when bored are in need of repair. Such people do not realize how their values, attitudes, and behaviors limit them. Creative people are in the minority, and it is very hard for the majority to comprehend—much less appreciate—values, attitudes, and ways of being in the world so different from their own. Sometimes it helps the majority to understand how their own personality characteristics limit them.

Question?

Shouldn't children be made to follow directions?
Coloring inside the lines results in a tidy picture, but never a great one. For that, children must color outside the lines. Avoid trampling on your youngster's inventiveness by pushing him to do things like everyone else. Creativity needs to be nurtured, too.

Very organized people work hard to keep their ducks lined up in a row, but the world is inherently unpredictable and chaotic. Such people would benefit from learning to tolerate disorder instead of becoming unduly stressed over messiness and distracted by clutter. Many organized parents are too busy straightening and tidying to play with and talk to their children. They need to learn to pay attention to what matters most and not get bogged down in details.

Organized people are good at noticing small differences so they can put things into categories, but they often overlook subtle similarities. That causes them to miss how things merge and connect, which is required for true creativity. Most people are overly preoccupied with schedules and can get very upset when their child is ten minutes late to dinner. Being so aware of time does not mean that they are more productive than children diagnosed with ADD. They might get more done if they were more flexible. Approaching tasks in an organized, methodical manner may improve accuracy, but many people waste time by putting more energy into dotting Is and crossing Ts than is warranted. They need to learn to be less careful.

While most people can readily manage black and white issues, they have a tendency to become immobilized when confronted with many shades of gray. They postpone decisions until they get more details and information, even though it is obvious they will never get enough. They need to become comfortable taking risks. Instead of trying new things, they say, "We have always done it this way," or "Everybody else does it this way." That does not mean that it ever worked well or that the majority is right. Most people need to be more illogical—to listen to their heart as well as their head. Being in an unstructured environment where the rules are unclear makes most people feel so uncomfortable that they cannot function effectively. The categories they create are artificial; their deadlines are arbitrary. Most people would benefit from learning to tolerate disorder, be more flexible, withstand ambiguity, and to cope when events do not unfold according to plan. Diversity is the spice of life, but if more people had ADD symptoms, the world might be a better place.

Alert!

Organized parents benefit from becoming more flexible, tolerant of chaos, less concerned about details and schedules. They also benefit from daydreaming. ADD children can help their parents develop these qualities. Rather than trying to change your child, try to learn from him!

Allergies and ADD

Congestion and swollen tissues caused by allergies are not always confined to the sinuses. The brain may be congested and swollen as well. The result is brain fog that makes it hard for children to remain attentive and to think clearly. Some children with chronic allergy problems are hyperactive and impulsive, but many have problems with motor underactivity. They are sluggish and lethargic. From the list of behaviors that are associated with allergies, it is easy to see why many allergy sufferers are diagnosed with ADD.

- Poor concentration
- Short attention span
- Inattention
- Clumsiness and poor coordination
- Staring into space
- Daydreaming
- Passivity
- Lack of initiative
- Lack of perseverance
- Boredom
- Laziness
- Drowsiness

One of the most common allergies is to mold. Most people think of mold as only being a problem in wet climates, but the moisture in air conditioning systems is enough to activate the spores in homes located in arid regions. There are thousands of different strains of mold, and allergy tests can only identify a few of the more common ones. Children can have a serious mold allergy despite getting negative allergy test results. Mold grows best in the dark, so symptoms of allergy often worsen at night and disrupt children's sleep.

To a Different Drummer

Bernadette did not have allergies or any other identifiable physical problem. After her parents understood the special challenges creative children must confront, they were more accepting of her way of doing things. They realized that telling her to pick up her toys when she was finished did not work because in her mind, she was never quite through. She liked to have many projects going at once so she could move back and forth between them. To hold the chaos in check, her parents simply told her when it was time to put away her projects and stopped adding, "When you are through." Instead of berating her for daydreaming, they trusted that what was on her mind was important. They made it a habit to say her name and get her attention before proceeding to talk to her. When she described her plans to change a school assignment, they pointed out that the teacher might not appreciate her work unless she followed the directions. But they did not discourage her creative approach.

Bernadette's parents explained that if her teachers could not read her handwriting or were offended by messy papers, they might lower her grades. But her parents also said that as she advanced in school, teachers would care more about the quality of her work and her handwriting would not be such a big issue. They helped her focus on details they considered important by saying, "This is important" and asking her to repeat what they told her. The teacher agreed that when Bernadette was daydreaming, she would be given the choice to pay attention or to write a paragraph summarizing the lesson. Often Bernadette chose to write the summary, and her teacher could see that she was learning even if she did not always seem to be paying attention. It would be easier to have a daughter with a personality like the majority. But Bernadette's parents no longer felt ashamed of her differences. In fact, in some ways they wished they were more like her.

CHAPTER 7

Hyperactive Heroes

Most adults slow down and head for bed when they are tired, troubled, stressed, or ill—or at least, they wish that they could. But almost everything that adversely affects your child's physical and mental well-being can cause hyperactivity, inattentiveness, and impulsiveness. In addition, many males and some females have a personality trait known as thrill-seeking. Parents without this trait have a hard time dealing with children who do, but trying to change them is futile. The challenge is to affirm youngsters for who they are instead of trying to stamp out displeasing personality traits.

The Parenting Challenge

Frederick had started taking medication for hyperactivity at age five. At age twelve, his mother was as distressed as ever by his daredevil behavior. He ran into the street without pausing to look for cars and zoomed about on his skateboard as though he had a death wish. The only time he settled down was to play video games, and then he would not let go of the joystick when it was time to go somewhere or do something else. Frederick was finally having a good year in school. His mother thought that was because he had a male teacher who would not put up with his nonsense. Sometimes people complimented her on having such a polite, well-behaved son. "If only you knew him like I did," she would sigh. She wished someone understood what she had to put up with.

Frederick was going to spend the entire summer with his aunt and uncle. They were so strict that they made their kids study an hour every day during the summer. If nothing else, that should convince Frederick how easy he had it at home! When his mother called to check on him, her sister said that she was not giving Frederick his medication, but he was behaving "beautifully." Her brother-in-law echoed her comments. "He's welcome at our house anytime," he said. Frederick's mother could not imagine what their secret might be. After all of the money she had spent on doctors and medication, she could not wait to find out.

Question?

How can I help my son do better in school?
Reading just twenty minutes a day during the summer can give your youngster a big academic boost. Children who do not read during summer vacation are more likely to have academic problems the following year.

Healthy and Active Versus Hyperactive

In generations past, hyperkinesis was the diagnosis for children whose motor activity was so constant and intense, their bodies seemed to vibrate, and their hands shook when they tried to write or play with a small toy. Their activity was markedly unfocused, so they could not complete short, simple projects even when they were highly motivated. Playing meant wildly rummaging through a toy box or drawer as they searched for the toy they wanted, then impulsively dumping the contents onto the floor because they could not instantly find it. No sooner had they spotted what they were looking for than a sound would float in from another room and they impulsively raced off to investigate. Their parents were not exaggerating when they said that their youngsters could not concentrate for ten seconds. Most were suffering from a serious medical problem such as epilepsy, mental retardation, cerebral palsy, or brain damage.

Alert!

Children with a "Sensory-Perceiving" temperament are action-oriented with a fun-loving zest for life. Too often, they are diagnosed ADHD. They have much to teach the more serious, sedate majority about the joy of living in the moment. Read *Please Understand Me* by Keirsey and Bates to learn more.

Now the term "hyperkinesis" has been changed to ADHD and the definition has been expanded. Children are being diagnosed by the millions, including an estimated ten percent of boys! The vast majority would have been viewed as normal in other times, and their behavior is considered typical by parents from other cultures. Some veteran child therapists say they have only seen one youngster who is physically unable to control his activity level in their entire career. Is hyperactivity only in the eyes of the beholder? One research investigation suggests that may be the case. On the standard questionnaire that doctors use to assess ADHD, almost two-thirds of parents rated their hemophiliac child (hemophilia is a rare blood disorder) as inattentive, hyperactive, or both. Almost a third of the youngsters in the study were taking stimulant medication for ADHD. Yet when teachers were asked to rate the same children, they only judged four percent as inattentive and *none* as hyperactive! Why the difference? Even moderately active play is a high-risk activity for children with hemophilia. Because their blood does not clot properly, any small scratch or bump can mean a trip to the emergency room. Even a brief bout of mild rowdiness upsets their parents terribly. A minor lapse of attention is major when bumping into something could prove life threatening. But rowdy behavior is normal and is not dangerous for healthy children. Because it involves vigorous physical movement, it is good for them. Expecting children to behave like somber adults is unrealistic!

Tackling ADHD Symptoms

Symptoms of ADHD are lots of fidgeting and restlessness. Yet, a lot of either or both do not mean that a child is out of control; they mean that she is bored and needs to get some exercise. If your child is restless, do *not* nag or suggest a sedentary activity, such as television or reading. Recommend somersaults, jump rope, hitting a tennis ball against the side of the house, or going for a walk. At least suggest that your child stand up and stretch for a moment.

 **Essential**

The best cure for inattentiveness is to make sure your child is getting enough exercise so he can tolerate sitting still. Switch activities every few minutes to keep boredom at bay. Do not bemoan your child's ability to tune out the rest of the world and concentrate. Be proud!

Lack of exercise is seriously compromising the health of American children. The symptoms include obesity, high cholesterol, high blood pressure, diabetes, and behavior problems. For many students, gym is their only chance to move about, but many schools have cut back so that students only attend a few times a week. Even if they go every day, they average only nine minutes of exercise. The rest of the time is spent watching others or listening to the teacher. A study by U.S. International University and reported in Thomas Armstrong's *The Myth of the A.D.D. Child* found that exercise had positive effects on behavior. Hyperactive, aggressive students participating in jumping or field exercises forty minutes a day, three times a week were less aggressive on the days they ran than on the days they did not! Even as parents bemoan the fact that their children get too little exercise, they chastise them for failing to sit still. Parents should be glad they are moving, even if they are only swinging their legs and wiggling in their chairs!

Being able to shift attention rapidly on the one hand, and being able to concentrate so intensely as to be oblivious to everything else on the other, are considered symptoms of inattention. Parents and teachers find these behaviors frustrating because they want to control what children pay attention to. That is reasonable when the goal is to get them to pay attention during six class periods a day, assuming they have a break between each subject. But expecting youngsters to attend to what others consider important every waking moment is expecting too much.

Most doctors attribute youngsters' difficulties sustaining attention on the one hand and shifting attention "appropriately" on the other to a genetic defect. However, if these behaviors are genetic, they do not necessarily signal a defect! In hunter/gatherer societies, forests were filled with dangerous animals. Survival depended on being aware of and responsive to each small movement and sound that might signal the presence of a dangerous predator. When hunters spotted game, they then needed to be able to hone in on it during lengthy pursuits without becoming distracted by small movements and sounds. Since most hunters were men, this would also explain why the vast majority of children diagnosed with ADHD are male. Times have changed, but being highly alert and responsive to the environment is still an asset in many settings. In fact, being able to respond quickly as situations arise and handle many different problems at once is called multitasking. In hectic job settings, it is highly prized. To do well in chaotic environments, multitaskers must also have extraordinary powers of concentration so that they can at times tune out a dizzying array of distractions. Most women are natural multitaskers. If not, they get lots of practice when they have a baby.

The Boy Factor

ADHD is almost exclusively a young male disorder, with the ratio of boys to girls running at about six to one. The International Narcotics

Control Board estimated that in 1995, ten to twelve percent of all U.S. boys ages six to fourteen were diagnosed with ADD/ADHD and were taking Ritalin. Inattentive girls are more likely to be diagnosed with ADD (see Chapter 6, Little Space Cadets: The ADD Child). When it comes to hyperactivity and impulsiveness, boys still get the lion's share of the labels, the seats in special education classrooms, and the Ritalin prescriptions. Boys also get the majority of the learning disability and conduct disorder diagnoses. The big question is why.

 Essential

Boys need a father to teach them what it means to be a man and how to behave respectfully toward women. Mothers need a man to teach them what boy behavior is normal. Step-fathers and male relatives, neighbors, and mentors can be father figures for boys and consultants to their mothers.

It may be that the physical and psychological absence of men from boys' lives has turned the age old battle of the sexes into a nasty intergenerational war. On childhood playgrounds today as in generations past, young girls look askance at the uncivilized crowd of jostling pig-tail pullers who are too busy arguing about who is "it" to get on with the game. Girls find the insults boys hurl at one another off-putting, their squabbles too aggressive, their practical jokes too mean-spirited, and their classroom antics and interruptions too rowdy and rude. Adolescent girls are surprised to discover that young men have many redeeming qualities and start working to civilize them. Once the boys learn that shoving the fairer sex into lockers, name-calling, and being unspeakably gross do not impress them, they learn to toe the line. Females never do have to confront the typical boy behaviors they find so objectionable—until they become mothers or teachers. And when they do, they are likely to find a lot of typical boy behavior just as objectionable as back on the elementary school playground.

Rethinking Expectations

As compared to girls, young males are more active, aggressive, and independent. Boys are also less compliant and less verbal. Overwhelm them with words, and they will eventually agree to anything. That does not mean they will keep commitments made under duress. Half the time, they do not remember the promises they made when caving in beneath a verbal barrage. Because boys are also less able to identify their emotions, it is harder for them to express their feelings in words. As a consequence, they are more likely to lash out when upset or frustrated. Since many parents discourage crying, many boys learn to keep their tears inside and restrict themselves to displays of anger.

 **Fact**

Boys have a harder time reading other people's emotions. Like their fathers, they find it especially difficult to read and comprehend women. They have a harder time recognizing when their mothers and female teachers are becoming impatient with them.

It is not surprising that growing up in a single-parent household headed by a woman increases a boy's chances for being diagnosed with ADHD. The problem is not just that women find a lot of typical boy behavior objectionable. Boys also are more resistant to doing what women say. Perhaps men's larger size and deeper voices are more intimidating, as many suspect. It is possible that boys are more able to pick up on what men are feeling. Even fathers who never yell, hit, or punish note that their boys are more respectful toward them than toward their mothers. And of course, men of all ages struggle to understand women and to figure out what they want. It is no wonder that little boys fail so abysmally. Women need to communicate clearly.

- Say what you mean and mean what you say. Do not say "Please stop that" when you mean "Stop!"
- Put your feelings into words rather than expecting your son to be able to read your facial expressions. Say, "I am angry. Stop that."
- Be concrete and specific when discussing the meaning of "respect." Say, "Cursing is disrespectful. You are not to curse."
- Spell out your wishes rather than assuming that your son knows what you want and giving hints. Rather than asking, "What are you supposed to do after dinner?" or hinting that the dog wants to go out, say, "It is time for you to walk the dog."

Boys do want to please their mothers. But to succeed, their mothers must tell them how to go about it.

Boys at School
Boys actually do better in all-boy schools, and girls do better in all-girl schools. In co-ed classrooms, boys have more trouble because the rules tend to be designed to appeal to feminine sensibilities. Most lessons emphasize reading, writing, and listening, but most boys learn better through hands-on activities. Most teachers require students to sit still and keep their hands to themselves, but boys like to touch, jostle, push, and shove. Students are supposed to do what they are told; boys prefer to compete than to comply and cooperate. Students are not supposed to argue or fight; boys argue constantly to establish their place in the pecking order and are generally more aggressive. These stereotypes do not apply to every boy, but they do fit for the majority. They also apply to many girls. Children do need to follow the rules, but contact your PTA and school officials and discuss ways to make them more boy-friendly. Too many boys become mental dropouts at an early age.

What Boys Need

Besides needing a male to be an active presence in their lives, boys need a lot of active free play. Rather than enrolling your son in more organized activities, put on his hat and coat and send him out to play. Let him make mud pies on rainy days, snowballs on cold ones, and find safe targets so he can sling and hurl. If he wants to splash in puddles and wallow in snow, he and his clothes are washable. Buy a workbench and tools so he can hammer, pound, pry, and saw; buy a pocketknife so he can whittle. If you cannot find someone to teach and supervise dangerous tools, sign him up for a scout troop or find a Big Brother at *www.bbbsa.org*. Let him light the fire on the grill in summer and in the fireplace in winter. Buy a foam rubber ball and put a small basketball hoop on the door of his room. Teach him to hold down the noise in public and at the dinner table, but set aside time for hearty whooping and hollering. Give him earphones to use when he cranks up the music. Do not deter climbing—guide him to lessen the likelihood of a fall or help him build a tree house. If worst comes to the worst, a broken leg that heals in six weeks is probably healthier than taking amphetamines for years on end to squelch his urge to scale to the top of whatever. Let him play in the creek and fish in the pond. And for the best birthday present in the world, consider a trampoline. Safety nets have eliminated a lot of the danger. Do what you can to keep your child safe, but remember that the quality of life matters, too. Too many repressed boys go wild during adolescence as they unleash the energy their parents successfully contained for years. And too often, the results prove fatal. If you think an activity is too dangerous, consult male friends and relatives. If they approve it, close your eyes and pray. And if you have a hyperactive girl, all of the above can help her as well.

Thrills, Chills, and Spills

Children with a personality trait known as "thrill-seeking" are commonly diagnosed as hyperactive. While most youngsters are content to read adventure stories, thrill-seekers need the excitement of the adventure itself to achieve the same emotional high. They concentrate well when they are immersed in an intensely stimulating activity and have great trouble sustaining attention when nothing much is going on. They are perfect candidates for an ADD/ADHD diagnosis.

Understanding Thrill-Seekers

Thrill-seekers find boredom especially noxious and are happiest when the stereo is blasting, the television is blaring, the strobe lights are flashing, and everything is happening at once. Whether they arrived on earth with their minds pre-programmed by genetics or were re-programmed by television and video games is unclear. For whatever reason, their brains do not register strong reactions to the routine and familiar. Boredom occurs when there is insufficient stimulation and the brain must struggle to keep from falling asleep. It is believed that they are drawn to excitement because they do not derive pleasure from tranquil activities. The fact that they are drawn to danger the way a bookworm is drawn to books puts them at high risk for more than their fair share of injuries.

 *Question?*

Don't daredevils care about hurting themselves?
Thrill-seekers do care, but they have a higher tolerance for pain. Trying to squelch their determination to pursue risk and danger is apt to be a losing battle. They may be terribly accident prone and very athletic at the same time.

Traditional classrooms hold little appeal for them, since opportunities to do things they find even mildly stimulating are so limited. Many cook up trouble to generate some excitement. They may not even consider trips to the principal's office or the many punishments their parents inflict all that unpleasant. Talking does not make much of an impression. Spankings may not have much effect, either.

Parents have to hit so hard to have an impact, those who use physical punishments are at risk for abusing their youngster. Time-outs and being grounded are more motivating, but to avoid defiance and rebellion, keep them short. Although thrill-seekers are not interested in what the rest of the world thinks of them, you can cause much damage by harping on their flaws and failings.

Dosing these youngsters with stimulant medications settles them down but does not alter their personality. Although there is no research on the subject, drugging them seems more likely to postpone serious problems than to prevent them. Many young adolescents refuse to continue taking their medication when they are old enough to just say no, insisting that they want to feel fully alive and do not want their senses dulled with medication. Yet many later gravitate toward stimulants, especially cigarettes, amphetamines, and cocaine.

Protecting Thrill-Seekers

Deterring thrill-seekers from danger is likely to prove impossible. Trying usually fails and alienates them in the process. Parents are better off working to keep them safe while allowing them to be who they are. To that end, you may need to spring for a skateboard and every type of protective pad on the market. Buy a sturdy bike that can withstand a lot of wheelies and leaps, and be prepared to replace it often. Be rigid about requiring your youngster to wear a helmet. Channel rowdiness at the swimming pool by providing diving lessons. To deter fights, try Karate lessons. If the choice is between your teen's hearing and having the entire family go deaf, buy headphones and insist that he use them. Maintaining solid relationships with thrill-seekers and finding enough pro-social activities to keep them busy is critical for getting them through their teenaged years unscathed. And that is no easy task. Their penchant for danger and desire to live on the edge can get them into serious trouble. Their dislike of academics and of being confined puts them at risk for dropping out. Thrill-seekers do not usually aspire to college and do not think in terms of long-term goals. Their aim is to live the present moment to its fullest. Many parents alienate them by trying to get them to forget today and think about tomorrow. Yet indulging in what gives them pleasure often leads to a spectacular outcome. If guitar playing or track turns them on, they may keep playing or running for the sheer joy of it and become accomplished musicians or athletes in the process.

Alert!

If your youngster prefers activities involving physical risk and danger, find some that interest him and sign him up for classes. What he learns about fun during childhood will help to determine whether he spends his adolescence drag racing with the local thugs or white water rafting with fellow scouts.

The allure of exciting peers often proves irresistible, so maintaining a positive relationship is critical. Rather than pressing your teen toward college, look for ways to make his life more fulfilling right now. Since high school courses that teach rock music and racecar driving are not offered, vocational classes in machine shop, automobile repair, and carpentry may satisfy him. If you can get him through high school, he may eventually want to go to college. If not, do not despair. Trade schools and apprenticeship programs are options. If he likes large engine repair or a building trade, both pay well. Brighter, more motivated workers often end up managing or owning businesses. In general, anything that involves action and an element of risk tends to be appealing: police officer, firefighter, war correspondent, security professional, forest ranger, military officer, stuntman, rodeo rider, ski instructor, life guard, animal trainer, nature guide, machinist, heavy equipment operator. If your child can tolerate a lot of advanced academic study—and many do go to college after they have been out of school for a few years—he may want to major in oceanography to work with sharks, geology to study volcanoes, or forensic medicine to piece together crimes. As thrill-seekers mature,

many find satisfaction in mental risks and become entrepreneurs, financial investors, or criminal defense attorneys. Stressful jobs that wear others down may rev their psychic engines.

The Huckleberry Finn Syndrome

When Frederick's mother arrived to see what her sister and brother-in-law were doing that caused her son to behave during his visit, he was playing softball with his cousins out front. Frederick's aunt stepped out to greet her and told the children it would soon be time for dinner. "We're not hungry. Can't we eat later?" one of the children asked. "I don't mind cold food," another called. Frederick said, "Maybe I can do dishes instead of setting the table." His mother was amazed. His aunt explained, "We would rather that the kids exercise. No need to eat if they're not hungry—assuming they don't mind cold food." The adults ate, and when the children arrived they sat together at the table to chat. Frederick's uncle explained. "We think it's important to sit down together as a family, but we don't always eat at the same time."

Alert!

Thrill-seekers are not very good candidates for traditional therapy, but they can benefit by communicating through toys in a therapy playroom, over checkers in a counseling office, or while shooting baskets with their psychologist. To see what great things they can accomplish in life, see Appendix A.

When Frederick tried to argue about why he did not need a bath, his aunt said, "You played outside. You are dirty. You must bathe." Frederick yelled, "I hate baths!" His aunt replied, "Yes, I know" as she walked away. She explained to Frederick's mother, "He does not have to like baths, but he does have to take them." The rules in the house were strict, but the parents never nagged. Frederick's mother learned that neither parent even asked about homework during the school year. They held a quiet hour every night. If a child had no assignments, he could review the day's lessons or work ahead. Since the only thing more boring than studying was doing nothing at all, they studied. The children were not allowed to roughhouse inside and were sent outside to "get their energy out" if they got rowdy. They were not allowed to watch television during the week and did not own any video games. They did own a computer but were only allowed to play educational activities or chat online. "Online chatting involves writing practice," they explained. When it got dark early in winter, the family went to bed very early and took a brisk walk or bike ride before school. They did not have to eat what their mother cooked, but were only offered vegetable slices, fruit, or cereal for snacks—and no sugary cereals were on the menu. Frederick's mother was impressed to see them don protective gear when they went for a dirt bike ride. Still, it made her nervous. "Isn't it dangerous?" she asked. "Yes," her brother-in-law said simply. "It is."

CHAPTER 8

Family Fixes

I t is not surprising that one-third of the average family food budget is spent on junk food—who has time to cook? It is understandable that one-third of children have a television set in their bedroom—who has time to entertain them? And it makes sense that most parents interact with their children by directing, ordering, explaining, teaching, and reprimanding—who has time for a genuine conversation? But growing up in a pressure-cooker environment is not healthy for anyone. To cure what ails your child, you need to find a way to turn down the heat.

The ADD/ADHD Lifestyle

Don's parents both worked long hours, and to say that their days were hectic was putting it mildly. They knew their family was not unique. Everyone else seemed to struggle with the same frenzied schedule. But other people's children did not have ADD/ADHD. It never occurred to them that Don's symptoms had to do with their lifestyle.

The Daily Grind

By the time Don's family got home from work, ate dinner, and Don finished his homework, only about an hour remained until it was time for him to get ready for bed. To free up time, they often ate take-out dinners. Don was a bit overweight, and the rule was no sweets in the evening unless he ate his vegetables at dinner. But other than French fries, he avoided them like the plague. When he begged for a bedtime snack, they usually gave in. Don was a handful, and they had enough conflicts as it was. Nor did they want him going to bed hungry. They figured that if his body was telling him that he needed a certain snack, they should try to go along.

 **Fact**

It is a myth that children naturally gravitate toward the foods they need for optimal health. Humans are genetically programmed to seek high fat, sugary foods so they can survive during famines. But without lean times and proper nutrition, the results are obesity and ADD/ADHD.

Don's parents did not think that spending a lot of time watching television was good for him. But he was unhappy at school, and his parents thought he should have some fun each day. So he watched a couple of shows in the evenings. Besides, while he was watching television, his parents could cook, do dishes, tend to the baby, and perhaps watch a little television themselves. Don's bedtime was supposed to be at 9:30 on school nights, but he employed all sorts of delaying tactics. In truth, he did not seem to need much sleep, so they did not really push the issue. They were lucky to get him in bed by 11:00.

Modern Dilemmas

Stressed. Exhausted. Overwhelmed. That's how most parents feel much of the time. And it is no wonder. Eighty percent manage jobs in addition to raising children. Stay-at-home parents struggle to fill in the gap by volunteering at school and handling endless crises for their neighbors. As the rich get richer and more middle-class families slide toward poverty, having two incomes is often the only way to stay a step ahead of the bill collectors. Only a handful of communities have laws requiring companies to pay full-time employees a "living wage" so they can survive on one paycheck. Many single parents have to work overtime or juggle two jobs. Even the lawmakers who declare their support for "family values" have declined to enact legislation so that parents can properly nurture America's future. Governments in Europe provide family leave so that workers can devote time to infant/parent bonding and tend to their youngsters when they are ill or have an emergency. In the U.S., the economic cost of such programs is generally considered prohibitive. The emotional cost of not having them takes an indeterminate toll.

Alert!

It really only takes one parent to raise a child. It takes an entire village to support a child's parent. Urge your legislators to pass laws that guarantee workers enough money to support a family on a forty-hour work week. Help your single-parent friends and neighbors.

Investing in Family Life

While many parents must paddle frantically to keep from being sucked into a financial sinkhole, many others do not realize that they could in fact work less—and that doing so would be in their child's best interest. Most parents are assailed by unending requests for expensive gadgets and garb that their children see advertised on television and that fill the homes of their friends. It is easy for parents to conclude that youngsters' happiness depends more on having material wants gratified than on having parental time and attention. But youngsters benefit more from playing a game of crazy eights with a parent than from playing an expensive video game by themselves. The best possible start in life does not come from the best school money can buy, but from the most loving relationship you can manage. Time to play outside does more to round out children's lives than a schedule packed with lessons and organized activities.

Re-evaluating Priorities

Surveys show the truth of the old saying that money does not buy happiness. Life satisfaction has continued to drop as prosperity has increased. Although growing up in poverty increases family stress, sacrificing time with your children as you quest for more dollars to buy luxuries increases family stress, too. It is common for children to refuse to wear many of the clothes their parents worked to buy for them. Children do not play with many of the toys they asked for. They do not eat most of what is put on the table because they have been consuming snacks that have little or no nutritional value. They are excited at the prospect of taking lessons or signing up for a sport but drag their feet when it is time to go, refuse to practice, lose their equipment, fail to bring home the schedule, and do most everything else they can think of in order to avoid going.

Fact

When youngsters share what is in their hearts in family therapy sessions, their number one wish is *not* for a new video game or family car. Rather, they wish that their parents had more time for them and were not so often in a bad mood.

Responses on surveys administered to high school students reveal that the wish for more time with the family is widespread. A minority says that they have as much time with their parents as they would like; the majority say they want to be able to see and talk to their parents more. But time is not the only issue; quality matters, too. On those same surveys, teens also say that they wish that their parents would listen and try to understand them.

Young Materialists

When a youngster voices a wish for more family time, his parents typically defend themselves by saying that they work long hours for their child's benefit. They point out that they would not be able to afford that new bicycle or special pair of shoes their child has been wanting, and he would have to sacrifice trips to restaurants and special activities. When such issues are discussed in family counseling sessions, most children immediately agree to give up the fringe benefits of their parents' paychecks so their parents can work less. They spontaneously start listing ways they could help save money. Parents may choose to dedicate long hours to their jobs because the work is fulfilling and they want to enjoy more of life's material pleasures. But they should not assume that working long hours is also best for their children. Youngsters need their parents more than they need trinkets and toys. Many of the songs you sing together in the car will linger in you child's memory for a lifetime. The piles of expensive CD's cluttering the console will soon be forgotten.

The Decline of the Family

Parents used to be their children's heroes, but that has changed. Even members of the tween crowd are more likely to choose a celebrity or popular peer than Mom or Dad for the subject of their "Who I Most Admire" essay. Given how most youngsters spend their time, it is understandable that media stars and peers are esteemed more than parents. Half a century ago, the average U.S. child spent over three hours a day interacting with parents or extended family members. Today, the average is a mere fifteen minutes. Meanwhile, the average time of watching television each day is four hours. The quality of the time with parents has deteriorated, too, according to parenting author Josh McDowell. He reports that on average, parents spend twelve of their fifteen minutes criticizing, correcting, or teaching their children. That leaves just three minutes a day for conversing and enjoying one another as people.

If your child cares more about what television commercials and peers say about what to buy and wear, it may be important to put more time and energy into strengthening your relationship. If asking about school draws non-answers (e.g., "OK," "Fine"), try talking about *your* day. Your youngster cannot feel close to you if he does not know you! Children tend to feel closer to single parents because they share more about what is happening in their lives. This helps to make up for having less time together.

Alert!

If your child only wants to go on family outings when a friend can come along, watch how you communicate when no guests are present. Be courteous and respectful when dealing with behavior problems. Concentrate on getting to know your child and on having fun.

Quality Time

Many parents struggle to find extra-curricular activities that children with ADD/ADHD symptoms can enjoy and use as a steppingstone to making friends. Suggestions for spicing up your youngster's social life are presented in Chapter 18, Building Social Savvy. But between daycare, school, and afterschool programs, most youngsters have more than enough time with peers. What they really need is more time with their families. That does not mean that they need their parents to spend more time teaching, directing, controlling, and instructing them, however. They need more opportunities to enjoy one another's company. To do that, families need to look for ways to pull themselves out of the daily do-your-homework-and-clean-up-your-room rut that makes everyone tense and edgy.

To free up time, you may need to forego activities like working out at the spa, if the only real contact is on the trip there and back. Turn off the radio in the car so you can converse while chauffeuring your youngster about town. Being on the soccer field while you chat with other parents in the stands does not count as spending time together. For most families, the biggest time sink is the television.

Television and ADD/ADHD

American teachers have long insisted that watching a lot of television adversely affects students' academic performance and behavior. Educators claim that watching televised stories and movies instead of reading, conversing, and engaging in creative play left students with little imagination. When asked to write a story, many could only relate an episode from a show they had seen.

Children need lots of vigorous exercise, and teachers maintained that sitting in front of the television all evening made students more restless and hyperactive in class. Most veteran teachers expressed the conviction that viewing so much televised sex and violence was contributing to the steady deterioration in behavior and moral values they saw over the years. Others declared that viewing so many commercials was warping children's values. The consensus was that so much stimulation from rapid-fire images had reduced the attention span of the average student to that of a flea. They pointed out that children grew restless at predictable intervals, as if their systems were geared to the rhythm of the once-every-eleven-minutes commercial break. Research investigations examining the impact of television viewing on children's development concluded that the teachers were correct. Children who watch a lot of television are less imaginative and have shorter concentration spans than those who watch none or only an hour per week. Heavy viewers are more easily distracted, more impulsive, more hyperactive, more aggressive, and have more learning problems.

 *Question?*

Will turning off the television help ADD/ADHD?
Common sense dictates that families should outlaw television and video games, at least on school nights, to allow time for homework, exercise, and free play. It is harder for children to sit still in school if they sit all evening, too.

In 2004, research findings on the effects of television made headlines across the country. It was reported that watching a lot of television between birth and age two increased the probability of subsequently being diagnosed with ADD/ADHD by twenty percent! The American Pediatric Association urged parents to protect their babies under age two by not allowing them to watch any television whatsoever. Parents were also advised to limit how much older children watch. Physicians conjecture that intense, prolonged visual stimulation of the brain during such a vulnerable stage of life interferes with the development of the central nervous system. If that is true, older children may be adversely affected as well, since their brains are still developing, too. And video games are probably equally dangerous. Be that as it may, it is clear that putting a baby in front of a television program can have serious repercussions. For older children, eliminating television altogether on school days makes good sense. Eliminating it altogether makes even better sense.

Dietary Delights

Children clearly need to watch less television, to have wholesome entertainment, to learn how to manage a household, and consume a well-balanced diet. Youngsters also need more quality time with their parents—and for children, there cannot be quality without a large quantity. Parents need help with housework, to tighten the family budget, and to spend more enjoyable time with their children. The one solution for all of these problems is to stop eating out and turn cooking into a family hobby. To make meal preparation fun, you may need to change the way you operate in the kitchen. When children get involved, their usual role is as the servant. They are told to set the table, pour the beverages, or wash the dishes. Many resent being ordered about and being given the worst jobs. Meanwhile, parents are saddled with all of the responsibility for figuring out what to cook, for shopping, for doing almost all of the cooking, then battling to get their youngsters to come to the table and eat what they prepared.

A happier arrangement for everyone is to turn the job of preparing meals into a partnership. The first step is to include your youngster in the cooking. Even toddlers can shred lettuce for salad, wash radishes, scrub potatoes, butter toast, stir batter, spread peanut butter on celery sticks, and arrange rolls on a plate. Let your child make some of the menu decisions—not just by deciding whether he would prefer spaghetti or pizza, but by pulling out a cookbook and seeing what he would like to learn how to make and serve. Rotate responsibility for the meals. When it is his turn, you will have to help your child, but try to keep him in charge.

- Let your child create menus. Going through the cookbook provides practice in reading and learning to think ahead.
- Let your child create the grocery lists. It provides great practice for spelling, handwriting, organizing, and learning to think ahead.
- Let your child shop for the needed groceries. Checking the ingredients on labels is a great way to practice reading; comparison shopping provides practice using a calculator; learning to stay within a budget is a good way to practice math and decision-making. All of the above are great cures for grocery store misbehavior born of boredom.
- Let your child be in charge of cooking. Letting him direct who does what teaches leadership skills. You can keep the chain of command and provide prompts as to what needs to be done by asking, "Do you want me to put the noodles on to boil?"

Alert!

Young chefs are more likely to eat foods they cooked themselves, including the foods they usually disdain. And young farmers who normally gag on vegetables think the ones they have grown themselves are absolutely wonderful. Present your child with seeds and designate a patch of ground for a garden.

To make the time in the kitchen more enjoyable, it is important to talk as well as to listen. Share what is going on in your life and your opinions about happenings in the news. Make it your goal to get to know your child—but remember that for him to open up, he has to know who he is talking to. And if he never does say much about himself, that is fine, too. Many children are doers, not talkers. Spending pleasant time with a parent literally means more to them than words.

Essential

Children diagnosed with ADD/ADHD have to get enough sleep at night. They just do. That alone may be enough to clear up thinking, improve memory, and lessen crankiness. See Chapter 20, Ending Bedtime Battles, to learn how to help a night owl get proper rest.

Wonderful Weekends

Finding activities to do together as a family is not hard. Many bicycle stores sponsor Saturday morning family bike rides. Bait and tackle stores hold fishing meets that are open to all ages. Family outings with the Sierra Club for hikes and with other nature groups for bird-watching expeditions are fun and provide great exercise. Mountain Man clubs are for women, too, and participants whittle, cook meals over open fires, tan leather, and engage in lots of other old-time activities that fascinate children.

Help connect your youngster to the community by donating time to neighborhood cleanups or another worthy cause, such as Habitat for Humanity and local homeless shelters. Seeing the realities of poverty up close does more to convince children about the need for education and a career than a thousand lectures. Make it a habit to read the weekend guide of your local paper, and set a goal to attend at least one activity each month until you find a hobby or activity the whole family can enjoy. After a trip to a garden show, you may decide to get serious about growing tulips. A visit to a cat show may convince you that raising fabulous felines or volunteering at the local animal shelter is a project that everyone can get behind. Some families spend years building a boat in the garage. The boat may never see water, but the shared dreams and the hours spent tinkering bring parents and children closer.

Alert!

Churches, synagogues, mosques, and temples offer a wealth of family activities. If you are not religious, try attending a different one each week. That way your child can experience them all while learning about the many fascinating customs. Afterwards, you will have lots of fodder for interesting conversations.

Revamping Your Lifestyle

After realizing the impact of their family's lifestyle on Don's ADD/ADHD symptoms, his parents decided to make some dramatic changes. They were all cranky the first week after they got rid of the television, because they did not know another way to relax. Don considered the loss of the television a form of child abuse. They started cooking dinner together and taking walks afterwards. It was cold and rainy, so they bundled up and carried umbrellas. Don's parents belted out renditions of "Singing in the Rain," while Don glowered and acted as though he might die of embarrassment. In addition to a bedtime story, they started reading a book aloud that they could all enjoy. Don sat on the floor and played with Legos, yawning noisily at regular intervals to indicate his disdain for the story.

Don's parents were determined to keep the project of cooking dinner together relaxed and enjoyable. However, his mother began to cave in under their son's unrelenting ill humor. As she was at the sink spraying the lettuce one evening, Don started carrying on that she could fix him a salad but could not make him eat it. She just lost it. She grabbed a handful of lettuce and hurled it onto the floor in anger. "OK! There's your salad! You do not have to eat it!" she snapped. Everyone froze in horror, and she was appalled at what she had done. "I guess I need to cool it, huh?" she asked meekly, turning the sprayer on herself. "What in the world . . . ?" her husband demanded. "You need to cool it, too," she said, turning the sprayer on him. One thing led to another, and they ended up in a riotous food fight that took days to clean up and that still made Don chuckle when he told the story to his own children decades later. It was an unorthodox way to get the family onto a happier footing. But the magic of shared laughter turned Don around. Not only did Don start eating salads, but the next time his parents belted out "Singing in the Rain" as they walked down the block, he joined in.

Essential

A family outing to a farmer's market is an important educational experience for city kids, and visiting can improve your child's attitude toward vegetables. Let her make some of the selections and handle all of the financial transactions.

CHAPTER 9

Medication Maze

The drug companies provide physicians with information about their products, so it is understandable that so many doctors believe ADD/ADHD medications to be safe. However, the side effects range from troubling to tragic. Stimulant medications dramatically reduce ADD/ADHD symptoms for many children but are not meant to be taken long term. Many parents have trouble getting their children to take medication. They resist taking pills at school for fear of being stigmatized. By teaching your child to respond assertively to teasing, she can acquire a valuable interpersonal skill she can use long after the prescriptions stop.

A Potpourri of Problems

Amy was initially delighted over her son's response to Ritalin. Unfortunately, when the pill started wearing off after about four hours, withdrawal set in. Then Jake was so cranky, he was harder than ever to deal with. He struggled with nausea the first few weeks, and even after it went away he lost weight, because he did not have much of an appetite. His pulse increased by twenty-five beats per minute. That was to be expected, but his mother worried that an extra million beats per month would put an undo strain on his heart. She saw cardiac problems listed as side effects on the Ritalin insert and called the doctor. He reassured her that since Jake was healthy, she should not worry. But she did.

Question?

Are there non-stimulant medications to treat ADD/ADHD?
Strattera (Atomoxetine) was recently approved by the U.S. Food and Drug Administration (FDA). The effects typically last for five hours but may last all day for slow metabolizers. It is one of the newer ADD/ADHD medications and was only tested on about 200 children for longer than a year before receiving FDA approval.

Jake resisted taking medication at school after being teased by some classmates. Over the next few months, the doctor tried him on several different types of time-release and long-acting tablets so he would not have to join the line outside the nurse's office. None of them worked very well and they returned to the rollercoaster of tablets that only lasted four to six hours. Although his mother was delighted with the improvement in Jake's behavior, she was not entirely comfortable with the change in his personality. He had lost his sparkle and seemed somewhat dazed, as if he were not fully awake.

Medication Evaluations

Children should undergo a thorough psychological or psychiatric evaluation before taking mood-altering medication. Psychiatrists are the experts in this highly specialized field, so it is advisable to see one before you fill a prescription. If more than one medication is being prescribed, it is essential for the doctor to be an expert in psychopharmacology.

Unfortunately, it is common for family physicians and pediatricians to diagnose ADD/ADHD and to prescribe medication during a single thirty-minute appointment. In that case, the traditional second step of the ADD/ADHD evaluation process is a follow-up appointment to see whether there is a need to adjust the dosage, add another medication to control problematic side effects, or switch the youngster to a different medication altogether. Once the optimal dosage is achieved, brief medication checks are usually scheduled every three months for a time, then scheduled at six-month intervals. Yet the medications are only for short-term use. Some require constant monitoring for specific complications, such as reduced liver functioning. Problems with prescriptions abound. Ritalin has not been approved for children under age six. Nevertheless, in one year doctors wrote 3,000 prescriptions for babies under twelve months of age.

Essential

Most pharmacies store patient records in computers that are programmed to issue alerts when a patient is taking a combination of drugs that might interact. That is a compelling reason to fill all of your child's prescriptions at the same store.

Prescribing medication without first conducting a thorough psychological work up can have tragic results. Some family doctors and pediatricians are trained to treat patients with serious mental health problems and are well-informed about psychotropic medications. But this is not true for most. A thorough psychological evaluation is imperative, because the most commonly prescribed ADD/ADHD medications can make some psychiatric problems worse and are believed to trigger more serious mental disorders in susceptible children. For instance, Tourette's syndrome, tic disorder, psychosis, and bipolar disorder should be ruled out before stimulant medication can be safely taken.

Since amphetamines stimulate the nervous system and make normal people "speed," it seemed obvious that such drugs would cause hyperactive children to start bouncing off the walls and make it even harder for those with attention deficits to concentrate. Instead, it was discovered that amphetamines had the opposite effect: hyperactive children settled down and children with attention deficits became more focused. In the past, it was common practice for doctors to confirm a questionable ADD/ADHD diagnosis by prescribing medications containing amphetamine, methamphetamine, or methylphenidate to young patients. If they settled down and their concentration improved, that was viewed as proof that they in fact had ADD/ADHD. It was later realized that although amphetamines and their chemical cousins make some people feel jittery and nervous, they boost almost everyone's concentration enough so that they can sit still and remain focused for long periods. That is why "speed" has long been the drug of choice on college campuses among students who are cramming for exams. All physicians should have long since abandoned the practice of administering trial doses of stimulants to diagnose ADD/ADHD, especially now that it is understood that some children have such serious reactions to even a single dose. Nevertheless, some doctors have continued the practice.

What Your Doctor May Not Know

Professionals who favor medication for treating ADD/ADHD say that when children are out of control, drastic measures are needed. Most never see the research showing that diet, exercise, and sleep are as effective as Ritalin. The research they do see has a strong pro-medication bias. They do not consider that without concurrent child, parent, or family counseling, children do not learn to control their behavior and must continue to rely on pills.

The Pharmaceutical Industry

Physicians receive most of their information about ADD/ADHD from pharmaceutical company sales representatives. They supply doctors with reports and brochures about their companies' products, provide free samples to distribute to their patients, and offer all-expense paid trips to medical conferences so doctors can hear about recent research. It is not surprising that myths about ADD/ADHD and stimulant medication abound. Physicians are reassured that they can accurately diagnose ADD/ADHD by conducting a parent interview and having a teacher complete a behavior checklist. Most say that ADD/ADHD is genetic in almost every case, that diet does not make a difference, that sugar does not affect thinking or hyperactivity, and that problematic side effects of amphetamines are rare. Many warn that children diagnosed with ADD/ADHD run a greater risk of adolescent substance abuse if they do not take medication. A careful review of the research does not support any of these contentions.

Alert!

Even if research findings that reflect poorly on medication are submitted for publication, they are less likely to end up in print. This is even true for America's most prestigious medical publication, the *Journal of the American Medical Association*, according to a 2004 FDA advisory committee report.

Biased Research

When research studies are funded by private industry, doctors and the general public may not get to see the results. Companies obviously do not want their unfavorable findings published. They release required reports to the FDA, which often fails to distribute troubling results, according to the 2004 FDA advisory committee report. The U.S. government used to fund most of the university research on medication safety and effectiveness. In the last two decades, pharmaceutical and biotech companies have increased funding of university research from under thirty million to two billion dollars. An investigation found that even at America's most prestigious universities, whoever pays the piper is apparently calling the tune. Drug research is more likely to show positive results if it was funded by a drug company than by the government. And research that appears to be paid for by government grants sometimes has invisible strings attached to the drug companies. A National Public Radio report revealed that top employees at the National Institute of Mental Health have been receiving huge sums from pharmaceutical and biotech companies. Some research scientists and officials in charge of awarding government research grants were being paid up to two million dollars for their "consulting services."

Facts about Stimulant Medications

While taking psychostimulants, disruptive behaviors decrease dramatically and attentiveness improves for most children. The effectiveness of stimulant medication tends to decrease over time, and studies of long-term use have generally been disappointing. Initial improvements in behavior and grades are not followed by significant long-term improvements on achievement tests. Psychostimulants appear to be more beneficial when combined with educational interventions, psychological treatment (especially cognitive-behavioral therapy), and parent counseling. In 2002, children received eleven million prescriptions for psychostimulants, including:

- Ritalin, Metadate, and Concerta (Methylphenidate)
- Dexedrine (Dextroamphetamine)
- Adderall (Dextroamphetamine and Amphetamine)
- Cylert (Pemoline)

Methylphenidate is more powerful than amphetamine. For most children, Ritalin is the most effective ADD/ADHD medication and has the fewest side-effects. Cylert does not contain amphetamine. The mechanism of its action is unknown. Because Cylert can cause liver damage and failure, the FDA says it should only be prescribed after other medication options have been tried. Liver functioning should be tested every two weeks while taking it, according to the *Physician's Desk Reference*. A new, non-stimulant medication, Strattera, has not been tested on children under age six. It can take up to a month to take effect. Side effects include upset stomach, decreased appetite, nausea and vomiting, tiredness, and mood swings—to name a few. A Web site called rxlist.com has extensive information on ADD/ADHD medications.

Alert!

Keep track of your child's stimulant medication! Many middle school and high school students boost their allowances by selling off their pills. Thirteen percent of high school students and four percent of middle school students admitted to illicit use of Ritalin in a Massachusetts Department of Public Health survey.

Drawbacks of Stimulant Medication

The FDA classifies methylphenidate (Ritalin) and amphetamine as Schedule II substances because of the extremely high potential for abuse and dependency. Other Schedule II substances include cocaine, morphine, and opium. Diet pills containing amphetamine were widely prescribed until the FDA cracked down because they are so addictive. Amphetamines remain the drug of choice among many "speed freaks." Doctors deny there is a risk of addiction when taken as prescribed. However, a 1999 study reported in the *International Journal of Disability, Development, and Education* followed children from first to fifth grade. It found that Ritalin dosage levels tended to be increased over time (the dose depends on the rate of metabolism, not body size). About one in three children cannot tolerate the side effects of stimulants or their behavior does not improve. There are some predictable side effects:

- Reduction of spontaneous behavior
- Rapid pulse
- Loss of appetite
- Growth suppression
- Insomnia

The list of other common side effects is very long. While Ritalin elevates mood and creates feelings of well-being or even euphoria in adults, this is uncommon for children. Instead, increased irritability and crying, along with a general sense of feeling unwell and/or unhappy are more typical. Obsessive-compulsive and perseverative behaviors may appear. The latter involves doing something repeatedly, past the point of being productive. A big problem with stimulant medications is that they cause nervousness. After taking them for a time, many children are diagnosed with generalized anxiety disorder, obsessive-compulsive disorder, tic disorder, Tourette's syndrome, mania, etc. Ritalin patient information sheets warn that even when taken at the recommended dosages, psychosis can occur. By some estimates, the incidence of psychosis and paranoia runs at nine percent—almost one in ten! Psychotic children are severely disoriented, have bizarre and illogical thoughts, and may hallucinate. The symptoms usually disappear when the medication is stopped. Some doctors believe that only a very disturbed youngster would react so dramatically. Instead of immediately discontinuing the medication, they diagnose a more serious mental disorder and prescribe more medications to treat it.

Alert!

Some doctors put an inordinate amount of faith in stimulant medications. If ADD/ADHD symptoms worsen or do not improve, they conclude that the problem is more serious. A poor response to a medication does *not* mean something else is wrong!

In the "crash" as the drugs wear off, it is common for children to become more aggressive than they were to begin with. (This has led to the stereotype of the violent adult "speed freak" that is in the throes of withdrawal.) Some children become more depressed than aggressive when they "crash." In either case, the "rebound effect" as stimulant drugs wear off is so problematic that most doctors now recommend children stay on them all of the time rather than only taking them at school. Periods of abstinence have been considered essential for trying to combat some of the harmful long-term side effects, especially on growth. On days that Ritalin is not taken and when the prescription is stopped altogether, the production of growth hormone increases, as if the body is trying to make up for lost time. But now most experts say that children may not outgrow ADD/ADHD. If they do not find another solution for their symptoms, they could need medication for life.

Essential

Lessen problems with appetite by administering stimulant medication after meals rather than before. To lessen insomnia, do not administer it in the evening. It should not be administered to a chronically anxious child. Check with your doctor about how to discontinue a prescription. Do not terminate abruptly unless advised.

It is hard to tell whether children who take Ritalin for several years eventually reach their growth potential or not—who can tell how tall they would have become if they had not taken Ritalin? One study found that youngsters who had a lot of problems with nausea and vomiting during their first year on Ritalin ended up a bit shorter in height even though they had drug holidays. Their adult height was compared to children who never took Ritalin, as well as to children who took it but did not have a lot of digestive side effects. Disturbingly, some professionals have warned that it is wrong to assume that only height is adversely affected. Peter Breggin, psychiatrist and the author of *Talking Back to Ritalin*, suggests that long-term adverse effects on the brain may be significant as well. Many doctors assume that once the most prominent effects of stimulant medication have worn off, which happens in a matter of hours, the child returns to normal.

In truth, even after stimulant medication can no longer be detected in the system, a youngster may not return to normal for quite some time, according to Breggin. He cites studies suggesting that changes in the brain can linger for months, even though only a few doses were taken. After longer periods of regular use, brain scans have shown shrinkage in certain areas of the brain. It is possible that this occurs because Ritalin decreases blood flow to the brain.

Ritalin and Later Drug Abuse

Clinical reports have long suggested that children taking Ritalin and other stimulant medications are at risk for amphetamine addiction later on. Then an article entitled "Pharmacotherapy of Attention-Deficit/Hyperactivity Disorder Reduces Risk for Substance Use Disorder" by Joseph Biederman, Timothy Wilens, Eric Mick, Thomas Spencer, and Stephen Fanaone published in *Pediatrics* in 1999 made headlines. But the study on which the headlines were based did not warrant that title! Nineteen participants that had not taken medication for their ADD/ADHD had the deck stacked against them and were at higher risk for abusing drugs. Unlike the fifty-six teens who had taken Ritalin (sixty-six percent of whom were receiving psychiatric treatment), the non-Ritalin group members were significantly older (average age of nineteen), few were receiving psychiatric treatment, most came from poor families, and eighty-four percent had a parent with a history of drug abuse! Nevertheless, based on that study, doctors have been telling parents that *not* taking Ritalin puts children at risk for abusing drugs when they get to be teenagers.

 **Fact**

A major review of all of the Ritalin research concluded that it sensitizes children to stimulants. Taking it *increases* the likelihood of using amphetamines, cocaine, cigarettes, and coffee later in life.

Antidepressants

There are three main types of antidepressants. MOAs (monooxidase inhibitors) are so dangerous they are rarely prescribed. Tricyclic anti-depressants have been approved for treating ADD/ADHD. It is easy to see from the list of common side effects why the tricyclics often exacerbate problems with hyperactivity.

- Anxiety
- Hypertension
- Insomnia
- Nightmares
- Mania
- Tics
- Tremor
- Psychosis

 *Question?*

Is Prozac safe for children?
The American Pediatric Association has issued increasingly urgent alerts about the dangers of some commonly prescribed antidepressant medications such as Prozac, and has strengthened warnings about adverse reactions.

The so-called third generation antidepressants or SSRIs, which include famous names such as Prozac, Paxil, and Zoloft, are widely prescribed to children to treat depression and anxiety. However, they have not been approved for use by minors and have not been shown to be better than placebo in controlled studies. Doctors continue to prescribe them because many adults and some children do get positive results. The FDA has issued increasingly severe warnings about administering SSRIs to children and adolescents, because these medications often worsen suicidal behavior. Their use for children with hyperactivity is questionable. In one study, almost half of the children taking SSRIs experienced increased motor restlessness. A further complication is getting off of them. Withdrawal, which is now being referred to as "SSRI Discontinuation Syndrome," involves a range of difficult physical and emotional symptoms. Children discontinuing any type of antidepressant need medical supervision.

Social Stigmas

Lots of students refuse to take medication at school and are horrified by the prospect of having their peers discover that they are taking it. At home being told they are acting "hyper" is a criticism, and being similarly criticized by peers seems too humiliating. But peers do not necessarily use the term "hyper" derogatorily. It depends on the context and tone of voice. Many students say, "I'm hyper," or "He's hyper," as straightforwardly as if they were saying, "I'm in fifth grade," or "He's a hockey player."

 **Essential**

A sensitive or defensive youngster may overreact to comments about taking medication. Help your child understand that the intent may not be to upset him. If that is in fact the goal, he needs to find out what an attacker is mad about and not get sidetracked by name-calling.

There is a big difference between teasing and harassment. Students aren't usually harassed because they have been seen standing in line at the nurse's office. They are more likely to be targeted due to their disruptive classroom behavior and inappropriate interactions on the playground. Some youngsters are able to improve their standing in the social pecking order once their symptoms are under control and they are less disruptive. Popular children with good self-esteem use humor to diffuse tension, or they respond assertively to let others know that insulting, demeaning treatment is unacceptable. Aggressive responses tend to alienate others and make matters worse. You can help your child devise ways to turn enemies into friends—or at least, to stop harassment—by role-playing at home.

Provocation: "I think you need another pill. You're acting hyper."

Aggressive Responses

Technique:	**Trade insults**
Response:	"Look who's talking, four-eyes."
Typical Reaction:	Hostilities escalate
Technique:	**Challenge**
Response:	"Oh yeah? So what are you going to do about it?"
Typical Reaction:	Fight
Technique:	**Bully**
Response:	"Maybe you wouldn't say that if you were missing a few teeth."
Typical Reaction:	Fight; or back down and retaliate later.
Technique:	**Retaliation**
Response:	(Pushes antagonist later in the day while passing in the hall)
Typical Reaction:	Alienates his antagonist as well as peers who witness the provocation and do not know the background
Technique:	**Tattling**
Response:	"I'm telling on you."
Typical Reaction:	Teased about being a tattle-tale; however, reports to the principal may get results.

Assertive Responses

Technique:	**Humor**
Response:	"You want to see hyper? (twirls in circles like a whirling dervish)
Typical Reaction:	Laughter; tension diffused
Technique:	**Sarcasm**
Response:	"I am shocked to hear such rudeness from a fine lad. Get up on the wrong side of the bed? Try the other side. It can work wonders."
Typical Reaction:	Embarrassed smile
Technique:	**Self-disclosure**
Response:	"You wouldn't want someone teasing you about being overweight. Let's drop the insults, OK? I'd rather play."
Typical Reaction:	Backs down
Technique:	**Find allies and stand together**
Response:	"Last week you picked on Wesley, now me. We don't like it and want it stopped. You're welcome to play with us if you can behave."
Typical Reaction:	Bullies eventually learn to keep a distance.
Technique:	**Identify the problem as a first step toward solving it**
Response:	"If you can't say what you're mad about straight out, maybe we need a mediator."
Typical Reaction:	"What's a mediator?" Tensions may subside during the ensuing conversation.

Even if children never use the humorous comebacks they invent while role-playing, laughter can help them gain a better perspective.

Children often reject parental suggestions for handling peer conflicts because they sound too "dumb" or "dorky." Usually that means the comments sound too adult. Try to help your youngster understand that although some bullies rule by brute force, most leaders rise to power because they are more mature than their peers—or at least more verbal. Saying, "Maybe we need a mediator" to a bully may draw derisive hoots on the playground, but onlookers are likely to be a bit impressed as well. That can translate into heightened respect.

When discussing ways to resolve peer conflicts, emphasize the importance of not backing an opponent into a corner. Otherwise, he may feel compelled to fight to save face even if he would rather forget the whole problem. A back door should be left open so an antagonist can save face while retreating. At the same time, the front door should be left open to create the possibility of future friendship. To that end, a child can say, "You're welcome to play with me if . . . " or "Why don't we just play and talk about this some other time?" Comments like, "OK. So I'm sorry already. What are you going to do about it?" stir the proverbial pot. "OK. So I'm sorry, already. Can we please just get on with the game?" can move a relationship forward.

A Success Story

Jake had come to feel all right about taking medication at school and had adjusted to the side effects when his mother decided to take him off of it. She was just too uncomfortable with the whole idea that her son's growth might be adversely affected, and she was concerned about his rapid heartbeat. Since the long-term benefits of stimulant medication had not been established, she realized it should not be used as a permanent solution. She signed up for parenting classes to learn new ways to help him at home. After the first class, she realized that she was going to have to make a lot of changes, and none of them would be easy. She would need to improve Jake's diet and ensure that he got more exercise and sleep. She would need to look for ways to reduce stress. She would have to talk to the school counselor to see if she had suggestions about ways his teacher could manage his classroom behavior. Jake's mother did not believe that her son was actually suffering from an illness, but he was definitely a high-maintenance child. The trade off for having such an active, inattentive child was his sparkle and zest for life. And she just did not want to squelch those special qualities.

CHAPTER 10

Over-the-Counter Remedies

Certain herbs and Chinese medicinals can reduce ADD/ADHD symptoms as effectively as Ritalin. So can caffeine. Properly used, many over-the-counter treatments produce fewer debilitating side effects than prescription medications. But remember that you are still sending the same wrong-headed, very dangerous message to your child: pills cure problems. Every child (and every adult!) becomes restless and inattentive when bored. It is normal to be upset over problems and to rail at being confined and controlled. The best non-prescription treatments are parenting classes and family counseling. So sign up!

Treatment Dilemmas

When Seamus was in seventh grade, he flatly refused to keep taking the medication the doctor had prescribed for his hyperactivity. His parents understood his refusal to go to the nurse's office each day to get it. They tried the long-acting formulas, but they bothered his stomach. His parents could see the differences in him when he was not taking his medication and were worried, but Seamus complained about how the drugs affected him, too. "I want to feel like myself," he maintained. His parents could not understand. "Who would want to feel moody and hyper?" they wondered aloud. "I would!" Seamus snapped. And so it seemed that whether or not his parents liked his decision, it had been made.

Alert!

Underage drinking is illegal; the mixture of an inattentive teen driver, alcohol, and cars is lethal. One drink is one too many, so get your child into AA. Do not debate whether or not your teen has a drinking problem. If you have questions, attend an Al-Anon meeting and discuss them there.

Reports of problems at school began to flow in a week later. Seamus's math teacher sent home a note saying that he had not turned in any homework all week and was disrupting the class. They got a call from the principal saying that he had sworn at his English teacher and stamped out of her classroom in a rage. As was his custom, Seamus blamed everyone else. His parents tried to be tactful when suggesting that he might want to start back on his medication, but he swore at them and stamped out of the room. His father followed him to his bedroom. "You have two choices," his father said. "Take your medication and go to the special education class to get resource help twice a week. Or see a naturopath, take whatever herbs are prescribed, go to counseling every week, and attend tutoring. You have until tomorrow to decide." Seamus had attended counseling in the past and had quit going because he said it did not help. His parents were sure he would choose medication and special education. They were wrong.

Buyer, Beware!

It is a dangerous myth that herbs are "natural" and therefore safe. Belladonna is an herb and can be fatal if taken in large quantities. Mint is from plants, but it is not produced by the body, so it is hardly "natural." Since many children have serious allergic reactions to it, it makes no sense to declare that mint is "safe." Herbs can be as potent and unsafe as any manufactured medication. And like a prescription product, an herb is ineffective if the dose is too small and taking too much can be dangerous. Herbs like St. John's wort do not take effect immediately. Adequate doses must be taken regularly for several weeks in order to build up in the system. The change in mood is subtle, just like for prescription antidepressants.

Combining herbs and prescription medications can be like doubling the dose of either one. St. John's wort and manufactured antidepressants boost serotonin levels. Children must stop taking the prescribed medication for one to two weeks before they start taking St. John's wort and vice versa. Also, some herbs interact with one another, with over-the-counter products, and with prescription drugs. Gingko biloba dilates the blood vessels and should not be taken with blood thinners. Gingko and a number of other common herbs (garlic, ginger, bilberry, dong quai, feverfew, ginseng, turmeric, chamomile, motherwort, horse chestnut, fenugreek—to name a few) interact with aspirin and acetaminophen to increase the risk of bleeding. Some herbs interfere with the action of prescription and over-the-counter medications, rendering them *less* effective.

 Essential

Many parents are accustomed to picking up over-the-counter medications on the advice of an advertisement or friend. Store clerks in herbal and health food stores may consider themselves experts, but that does not mean they are! Get a referral from the American Herbalists Guild at *www.americanherbalistsguild.com.*

Cashiers and employees charged with stocking and straightening the shelves are not experts! Yet customers keep approaching them with questions and employees blithely declare, "It's safe. People buy this all the time." Clerks commonly look at the label and report that "It's all natural—it can't hurt you." But herbs either affect the system or they do not. If they do, caution is in order. If they do not, there is no point in buying them. The FDA will take products off the market if it receives enough reports of serious adverse reactions, but otherwise consumers are on their own. Unless you are a trained herbalist, you owe it to your child to get professional advice! Unfortunately, that is easier said than done.

Finding an Herbalist

The lack of funding for herbal research and the fact that herbal products do not need FDA approval make it hard for consumers to know what to use and to determine the proper doses. Over half of parents give herbal remedies to their children to treat ADD/ADHD symptoms, but one study found that only eleven percent discussed the matter with their child's doctor. Their reluctance is understandable, since the medical community is largely uninformed about research on herbs. Many professionals discount their value, and some refuse to treat patients who admit to using them. Still, for your child's safety, it is important to confess and then find another doctor if necessary. Graduates of naturopathic and acupuncture medical programs have taken courses in botanical sciences, so they are the most trustworthy sources for advice. The Institute for Traditional Medicine has an online practitioner reference guide as well as information about Chinese medicine at ✍*www.itmonline.org*. Great Britain has standards for certifying practitioners, but the U.S. does not. Many naturopathic physicians and alternative medical practitioners are very knowledgeable about botanicals. Personnel at herb stores can often provide referrals.

Herbs for ADD/ADHD Symptoms

In Europe, St. John's wort is more widely prescribed as an antidepressant than Prozac. The herb is commonly used to treat ADD/ADHD symptoms of anxiety and irritability, which commonly manifest as hyperactivity and inattention. It is also used to treat bedwetting. Other names for St. John's wort are *hypercium*, goatweed, klamath weed, binbirdelikotu, *chin su tsao*, tipton weed, and amber. Studies show that St. John's wort is as effective and has fewer side effects than tricyclic and so-called third generation antidepressants (SSRIs) such as Prozac. Unfortunately, the advertisements on some boxes of tea extolling St. John's wort as a mood enhancer are highly misleading; drinking an occasional cup will not work. Doses must be taken regularly for several weeks to build up in the system.

Gingko biloba is often prescribed by naturopaths as a memory enhancer. It works by increasing circulation to the brain. *Centella asiatica* promotes mental clarity, enhances memory and brain function, and alleviates anxiety. Studies suggest that it also improves cerebral blood flow. In general, herbs that increase blood flow to the brain seem to improve memory. Improved cerebral blood flow is also the goal of HEG neurotherapy, which is an effective ADD/ADHD treatment (see Chapter 11, Cutting-Edge Treatments). Amphetamines significantly decrease blood flow to the brain, which may explain why long-term use results in significant shrinkage of the frontal lobes. Gotu kola, an herb from India, also aids memory by helping to convert amino acids into neurotransmitters. Rosemary is purported to boost memory and is an energizer. It contains chemicals that prevent the breakdown of acetylcholine, which is involved in memory functioning. Acetylcholine deficiency has been linked to memory impairment. Passion flower extracts are helpful for relieving tension, restlessness, and irritability.

Alert!

Kava Kava has been widely appreciated for its anti-anxiety properties, but the FDA warns that it might contribute to the development of liver problems. The American Herbalists Guild protested. Meanwhile, many ADD/ADHD medications pose a known threat to the liver.

Panax ginseng has been used in Chinese medicine for more than 5,000 years to reduce stress, increase energy and motivation, strengthen the immune system, and decrease fatigue. Studies have shown that Panax ginseng enhances physical performance in athletes by normalizing body functions, reducing stress, and preventing disease. Studies in Japan and India have demonstrated that rats fed with Panax ginseng were able to learn tasks quicker, perform at a faster rate, and make fewer mistakes than those in the control group. It may be useful for memory problems. Panax ginseng is different from Siberian and American ginseng. Yizhi syrup stimulates the production of neurotransmitters and has been shown in studies to be effective for lessening behavioral problems and improving grades. Ma Huang is a powerful sedative and should be used with caution. Like prescription sedatives, it depresses the central nervous system. Like some prescription antidepressants, it may aggravate anxiety and suicidal tendencies. Fish oil and flaxseed oil are commonly prescribed in Europe to treat depression and manic-depression. A massive review of 102 studies on SAMe (S-adenosyl-L-methionine) conducted in 2002 found that it was more effective than placebo for relieving depression. A copy of the report can be obtained by calling ✆(800) 358-9295.

Some Herbal Combinations

Naturopathic Doctors (NDs) and Doctors of Oriental Medicine (DOMs) often use herbal combinations to treat ADD/ADHD symptoms.

- **Liquid Serenity** is a formula to combat depression. Other ingredients are St. John's wort, oats (*Avena sativa* or "green oat extracts"), Siberian ginseng, skullcap, chamomile, schisandra, plus lavender and orange essential oils.
- **Focus Formula** contains oats (*Avena sativa*), lemon balm, hawthorne, ginkgo, and skullcap.
- **Compounded Melissa** contains lemon balm, chamomile flowers, passion flower, skullcap, fresh wild oat seed, gotu kola (*Centella asiatica*), and mineral salts from seaweeds.

- **Tiaoshen Liquor** is a Chinese herbal formula that has been used to treat hyperactivity. In one large study, attention and grades improved for ninety-four percent of the children who took it! In animal studies, Tiaoshen Liquor has been found to improve memory for newly-learned material.

When treatment with Ritalin was compared to treatment with a special combination of Chinese medicines (*Bupleurum chinense, Scutellaria baicalensis, Astragalus membranaceus, Codonopsis pilosula, Ligustrum lucidum, Lophatherum gracile*, and thread of ivory), it was as effective as Ritalin. IQ scores and behavior problems improved and EEGs normalized for children in both groups. However, there were fewer side effects with the Chinese medicine. Calm Dragon Formula is commonly used by master herbalists. It is only available through licensed practitioners. A combination of Crataegos, Biloba, Pasiflora, and Valeriana, which are mild sedatives, were combined with Cola and Paullinia, which are mild stimulants. They were administered to children diagnosed with mild anxiety in a controlled research study. The herbs were found to be more effective than placebo for reducing anxiety.

The Caffeine Cure

Caffeine is a stimulant, and its effects are similar to amphetamines. Although it makes some people nervous, jittery, and hyperactive, many feel energized and their concentration improves. A number of studies have been conducted to see whether caffeine can relieve ADD/ADHD symptoms. The results have been mixed. Some found that caffeine did not help. Others found dramatic reductions in impulsiveness and aggressiveness, and improvements in attention span and performance on visual-motor tasks. The latter usually suggests improved concentration and hand-to-eye coordination. Parent and teacher ratings of behavior have at times been as impressive as for Ritalin. Some studies have found that combining Ritalin and caffeine produces the best results of all.

Caffeine Considerations

More research is needed, but at this point it appears that different children respond differently to caffeine: drinking a caffeinated beverage with breakfast, lunch, and perhaps dinner helps some youngsters, does nothing for others, and makes others nervous and jittery. When researchers examine the effects on groups of children diagnosed with ADD/ADHD by assessing their concentration and hyperactivity, they average the scores. That makes the overall results look as though the effects of caffeine are minimal or nonexistent. Hence, many doctors dismiss caffeine as an ADD/ADHD treatment. In fact, the behavior of some youngsters in caffeine studies improved dramatically, others not at all, and some worsened.

Question?

Is caffeine safe for children?
Like Ritalin, caffeine increases the heart rate and can cause tachycardia (rapid heart beat) and arrhythmias. It is a vasoconstrictor, causes insomnia, and is highly addictive. Check with your health care provider before dosing your child with it—or with anything else!

Not surprisingly, how much caffeine children consume makes a difference in how it affects them, and more is not better! A study reported in the *Canada Journal of Psychiatry* ("Responses to Methylphenidate and Varied Doses of Caffeine in Children with Attention Deficit Disorder" by BD Garfinkel, CD Webster, L Sloman, 1981) found that low doses of caffeine (158 mg) were better than no drugs, better than large doses of caffeine, and about the same as taking 10 mg of methylphenidate (Ritalin). Combining low doses of caffeine with 10 mg of Ritalin yielded even better results than either caffeine or Ritalin alone. However, when high doses of caffeine (308 mg) were combined with 10 mg of methylphenidate, the children's behavior deteriorated.

Caffeine Dosages

A strong cup of coffee, tea, or cocoa contains a lot more caffeine than weak, but how much caffeine is present also depends on the variety of the plant and how it is processed. For a comprehensive list of products and the amount of caffeine they contain, see the National Soft Drink Association Web page at *www.nsda.org*. Guarana, a dietary supplement made from the *Poullinia cupana var sorbilis* plant, also contains caffeine.

Caffeine Dosages		
Product	**Milligrams of Caffeine**	**Serving Size**
Guarana	40	1 dose
No Doz	100	1 tablet
Decaffeinated coffee	2–4	8 ounces
Espresso	30–50	8 ounces
Cocoa	3–32	8 ounces
Chocolate milk	5	8 ounces
Instant tea	10–30	8 ounces
Brewed tea	20–35	8 ounces
Coca-Cola Classic	23	8 ounces
Diet Coke	31	8 ounces
Pepsi-Cola	24	8 ounces
AMP Energy Drink	75	8 ounces
Planet Java's Tremble	129	9.5 ounces
Milk chocolate	1–15	1 ounce
Semi-sweet chocolate	5–35	1 ounce
Baker's chocolate	26	1 ounce
Chocolate syrup	4	1 ounce

Like traditional stimulant medications, caffeine causes insomnia. Supposedly no link has been found between heart disease and caffeine, but check with your doctor before giving it to your child. It is actually quite a heavy-duty drug, and the long-term effects on children are unknown.

Parenting Classes

Parenting classes teach parents to communicate with and discipline their children. All teachers cover both subjects in detail but some emphasize one more than the other. Parent Effectiveness Training focuses on compassionate, nonjudgmental listening and learning to talk without blaming, nagging, or criticizing. This is the hardest parenting approach for many parents to learn but is especially effective for improving relationships with alienated youth. Tough Love parenting programs emphasize limits and discipline. They are especially helpful for parents with a very manipulative, disobedient, out-of-control child. Participants learn to hold firm and follow through with discipline. Love and Logic parenting classes strike a good balance between loving communication and learning to set limits and enforce consequences.

 **Question?**

Where can I find a parenting class?
Check with your child's school counselor about classes in the community, or contact a child guidance clinic or juvenile probation office. If none are available, urge your PTA to sponsor one! It would be hard to find a worthier cause.

Although busy families are reluctant to add parenting classes to their hectic schedules, it is hard to find anyone who is less than enthusiastic once they have attended. Afterwards, participants typically say that parenting classes should be mandatory before having children. Support groups for parents of children with ADD/ADHD are also valuable, as long as the members provide one another with feedback. Having a chance to commiserate with other suffering parents can bring some much needed relief, but the benefits of simply sharing war stories are limited. For on-going support, parents usually find it more helpful to take the same parenting class again and again—and many do just that! Learning the material takes eight to twelve hours. Learning to apply it takes a lifetime.

Psychological Counseling

Child guidance clinics, public mental health agencies, and private practitioners provide individual and family counseling. Child guidance professionals also teach parenting classes privately and in the community.

Choosing a Therapist

In addition to psychologists, licensed clinical counselors, and social workers, some psychiatrists provide therapy. However, many psychiatrists restrict their practices to prescribing medication because medical school programs do not emphasize counseling and therapy. School counselors provide group counseling and classroom guidance. Most are too busy to work with individual students. Physicians are not trained to treat mental health problems, and since they typically schedule fifteen minute appointments, they do not have time. Those who try to counsel parents soon learn that dispensing tidbits of advice usually backfires. Parents respond by defensively blaming their child for being restless and inattentive, and end up angry with the doctor. Pediatricians commonly complain that parents lack the motivation to do what is needed: to change their child's diet, school placement, and their disciplinary methods. Broaching parenting problems and mental health issues with your child's pediatrician to ask for medication is fine. But for help with behavior problems, you need a professional with psychological training and experience— and the time to use them.

Although there has been a push in the mental health field for professionals to use empirically proven therapy techniques, there are really too many variables to conduct meaningful studies and draw sensible conclusions about specific approaches. The results show that therapy is effective and is not just a "feel good" proposition. Regardless of which theory therapists subscribe to, research suggests that experienced clinicians are more alike than different in how they actually work with clients. The most important factors in successful treatment are the therapists' warmth, non-judgmental acceptance, congruence, and unconditional positive regard. Thus, the person matters more than the degree. Ask for recommendations from friends, attend a session, and see whether you are comfortable with the therapist.

 **Fact**

Brain imaging studies have demonstrated that therapy alters the structure of the brain. This is not surprising since the brain is altered by all kinds of life experiences. For instance, from examining brain scans, scientists can tell which hand a violinist uses to pluck the strings and which hand she uses to draw the bow!

Assessing Progress in Therapy

Admitting to and facing problems is not easy, and some children raise a ruckus about having to attend counseling. "You can make me go but I won't talk!" is a common threat. Parents can expect to hear other statements designed to convince them that the sessions are worthless or are doing more harm than good.

- "All we do is play."
- "It's a waste of time; it's not helping me."
- "That counselor is weird."
- "My therapist said you shouldn't ground me anymore."
- "My counselor said my problems are your fault."

Children use similar excuses to get out of going to school. They complain that they are not learning anything and that their teacher is "weird." They undermine parents' trust to convince them to take their side against the teacher. Often a joint session with the child, the parents, and the counselor to discuss the situation is in order.

Essential

Boys tend to reap more benefits from seeing male therapists. Girls who are separated from their fathers due to divorce may also benefit more from seeing a man. But ask your child's opinion. Like adults, some youngsters are very adamant about who they do and do not want to talk to.

Even if therapy sessions are inexpensive because of insurance, sliding scale fees, and government funding at public clinics, the investment of time and energy is substantial. It can be hard for parents to know what to do if their child insists that the sessions are not helping. Note whether your youngster is calmer and more able to handle challenging situations after having attended for a month or two. He may be upset before sessions because he does not want to face difficult problems or would rather play. He may be moodier after a particularly intense session. It is common for children who have kept their angry feelings inside to become more irritable at home, and those who are very defiant to cry more easily. A typical progression is for youngsters to feel worse before they feel better, and then stabilize and show signs of improvement. If you have doubts or concerns, discuss them with the counselor. Some therapists do not know how to work with involuntary clients. They can handle oppositional children until the children are oppositional toward them! If in doubt, get a second opinion. However, do not make a hasty decision to terminate your youngster's sessions. Therapy relationships are very intense, and losing a therapist can precipitate a grief reaction. One or two sessions for proper closure is needed to avoid a setback.

Family Therapy

Soon after Seamus stopped taking his medication, his parents found a counselor for him. Seamus tried to renege on his promise to attend therapy. "I'm not the one who needs help. You do!" he said when it was time for his appointment. When they announced that they would sign up for parenting classes, Seamus was still not appeased. But he emerged from his first therapy session smiling and had a better week. When he said, "Aw, do I have to?" before his second session, his parents were tempted to call the whole thing off. Knowing that Seamus was confiding in a stranger had been uncomfortable for them. They had imagined him making up all kinds of stories to convince the counselor that they were the cause of all his troubles. Worse, they imagined him revealing some of the things they had done and said that they were not proud of. His parents said they would attend the session with Seamus to see whether his counselor thought the sessions would be likely to do any good.

They ended up having a family session, and it turned out to be very helpful. Seamus talked about why he had yelled at his English teacher, and they discussed what he could have said to make his point respectfully. Then they role-played what he could say to repair their relationship. His parents said that Seamus's cursing was a problem at home. It upset them so, the point he was trying to make was often lost as they argued about his language. The counselor drew up a contract wherein Seamus promised not to swear, and Seamus signed it. The agreement specified that if he broke his promise, he would have to meet with their pastor to learn the church's position on swearing. When the session ended they had only tackled two problems, and there were many, many more to go. But the counselor reassured them that once their communication improved, they could hold family meetings and work out problems at home. And in a few months, they were doing just that.

CHAPTER 11

Cutting-Edge Treatments

Some old cures are by far the best. If your youngster still has problems after improving his diet, sleep, and exercise consider homeopathic medicine. No one understands how or why remedies formulated in the 1700s work, but controlled studies demonstrate that they do. And the low cost makes them worth a try. Acupuncture is very pricy, but this ancient treatment benefits ninety percent of those who stay the three-month course and most maintain their gains. Biofeedback, which was popular in the 1970s, is now popular for teaching youngsters to control their brain waves. The long-term success rates are astounding!

Desperate Cases

Hal had always been very insistent about getting his own way, and when he wanted something he would not take "no" for an answer. He had many violent temper tantrums when crossed. When his parents and teachers were careful to keep after him and be consistent with consequences for misbehavior, he became sneakier and more artful about blaming others. In fourth grade, Hal pulled the fire alarm at school and was caught vandalizing the bathroom of the neighborhood youth center. While visiting his grandmother, he kicked her television because he was angry that it did not work. When he was sent outside to play, he proceeded to pelt the dog with stones. By the time he was ten, his parents were helpless to control him.

He laughed in their faces when they imposed a punishment and said he would turn them in for child abuse if they spanked him. He was accused of having stolen money from the teacher's desk, and when confronted, his only comment was, "So, arrest me." Between the defiance, sneakiness, lying, stealing, and destructiveness, his parents feared they were in fact raising a criminal.

Essential

If parents invested a fraction of what they spend on medication for troubled children and on lawyers for troubled teens in private schools and treatment with long-term benefits, they would save dollars and heartache. The usual problem is not a lack of dollars but of sense.

Hal was diagnosed with ADD/ADHD and attended neurofeedback sessions during the summer. After thirty sessions, the change in him was dramatic. When school started in the fall, Hal had his first good day at school. As his parents tucked him into bed that night, he said proudly, "I wasn't bad once! I just hope I can be good again tomorrow." That brought tears to his mother's eyes. Neither parent had thought he cared about behaving. How they had misjudged him!

The Frontal Lobe Factor

Many areas of the brain play various roles in behavior, but the frontal lobes are particularly important. They are considered the brain's emotional control center because of their key role in motor functioning, problem-solving, memory, attention, judgment, impulse control, aggression, and social behavior. The left frontal lobe specializes in language and the right in non-verbal abilities, although both are involved in almost all aspects of behavior. Still, damage to one side or the other has been associated with specific learning disabilities. And because the frontal lobes are located in the forehead, they are very susceptible to injury. Follow-up studies have shown that after receiving a mild blow to the head, learning problems commonly develop even for youngsters who were pronounced healthy afterwards.

Alert!

For surgical lobotomy, portions of the frontal lobes were destroyed to improve behavior. The result was loss of spontaneous behavior. Ritalin has been called a "chemical lobotomy" because the results are similar. Fifty percent of children taking Ritalin long-term have been found to have frontal lobe atrophy.

Besides injuries, poisoning from exposure to lead and other heavy metals, carbon monoxide, and air pollution, the frontal lobes can be damaged in a number of ways, including:

- Lack of oxygen (from drowning, smothering, choking)
- Head injury (including mild closed-head injuries)
- Shaken baby syndrome (shaking a baby, usually in anger, bruises the brain)
- Fever
- Infection (especially meningitis and encephalitis)
- Seizures (especially absence seizures)
- Insulin-dependent diabetes
- Brain tumor
- Chemotherapy for cancer
- Renal disease
- Thyroid disorder

Impaired frontal lobe functioning causes children to have difficulty making sense of cues about how to respond appropriately. They do not properly interpret feedback and cannot use it effectively to guide their behavior. Accordingly, youngsters may not recognize the signs that someone is becoming upset with them. Or, they may take untoward risks because they do not properly size up situations and evaluate dangers. Add to that their difficulties with memory for new learning, and even after receiving the painful feedback that a dog bites, they may turn right around and try to pet the snarling animal again.

 **Fact**

Besides medical tests such as MRIs, PET scans, EEGs, and QEEGs, frontal lobe problems can be picked up with the Wisconsin Card Sorting test, the Finger Tapping Test, the Token Test, the Test of Variables of Attention (TOVA), and the Stroop Test.

Neurotherapy

When using QEEGs (quantitative electroencephalographs, which are a type of EEG) to study the brain waves of children diagnosed with ADD/ADHD, scientists found some unusual patterns. Their frontal lobes produced fewer beta waves than their peers. Beta waves predominate during focused, analytical thinking. Instead, children with ADD/ADHD symptoms produce more alpha and/or theta waves. Those waves predominate when people are in a dreamy, unfocused mental state. Scientists reasoned that if children's brain waves could be normalized, they might achieve greater mental clarity. Biofeedback had long been used to teach patients to control their blood pressure, pulse, muscle tension, skin temperature, and other automatic physical processes. Investigations were conducted to see if patients could be taught to control their brain waves using similar techniques. It turned out that they could! The techniques have become very precise as the equipment required for brain wave training has improved. Unfortunately, many physicians do not refer patients for training, saying that the benefits have not been established through research. But the physicians who say this are wrong!

EEG Biofeedback

One type of neurotherapy is variously called neurofeedback training and EEG biofeedback. It is as effective as stimulant medication for treating inattention and hyperactivity. In one study, two-thirds of the children diagnosed with ADD/ADHD were able to decrease or stop taking Ritalin after twenty neurofeedback training sessions. One ten-year follow-up study showed that many children maintained their gains for a decade! This type of therapy has also been used to control seizures, overcome learning disabilities, improve autistic children's ability to function, and enhance creativity.

Essential

EEG biofeedback may not be appropriate for extremely disturbed children, e.g., those with bipolar or manic-depressive disorder. Because most families with a special-needs child have a variety of problems, including unrealistic parental expectations, poor communication, and unsatisfactory relationships, family counseling is usually required as well as EEG training.

A study of prison inmates demonstrated that EEG biofeedback can significantly reduce aggression. In fact, the drop in recidivism rates among convicts who learned to control their brainwaves was about the best anyone has seen to date: seventy percent for those treated with neurotherapy versus fifteen percent for the untreated control group. "Clinical reports indicate that neurofeedback training is effective for seventy-five to eighty percent of children with ADD/ADHD," according to Dr. Brotman. His company trains EEG clinicians and sells equipment to professionals as well as to the public. Parents can provide neurofeedback training under an experienced clinician's supervision. For information, call ✆800-735-9171 or see *✐www.biof.com.*

EEG Biofeedback in Action

Neurotherapy involves hooking up young patients to an EEG and assigning them a task that requires them to remain alert and focused. The children are rewarded whenever their EEG reading shows that they are producing the type of brain waves needed to think clearly. The reward might be the sound of a pleasant tone. New breakthroughs in technology have eliminated the need to attach electrodes to the scalp with messy gels. Children wear a cap that contains an amplifier and a wireless transmitter. This has significantly improved the accuracy of EEG readings. The transmitter feeds data to a computer. Children usually need twenty-five to forty sessions, but they may need an occasional booster session after several months to maintain their gains.

Alert!

"The big question about neurofeedback is no longer whether it works," writes Jim Robbins in *A Symphony in the Brain*, the best introductory book on the subject of neurotherapy. "The questions are why it is as effective as it is." Another question is why so few people use it.

Learning Self-Control

Most children enjoy their neurotherapy sessions. They sit comfortably in front of a computer monitor wearing a special electronic cap. Then they are instructed to watch a DVD or play a specially designed video game, such as Pac Man, while their brain waves are monitored. The Pac Man game looks like a regular video game, but there is no joystick. The game is programmed so that whenever the child emits the proper type of brain wave, Pac Man responds by zipping through the maze, gobbling dots on the screen, and artfully avoiding attackers. When the child's mind wanders or he gets too excited so that he produces the wrong type of brain wave, Pac Man takes a wrong turn, stalls, and may get gobbled up. Children begin with a trial and error approach to try to get Pac Man to move. They try relaxing and concentrating until they chance upon the mental state that produces the proper brain waves. They are rewarded by seeing Pac Man move. When they lose focus Pac Man stalls again, and when they resume producing the correct type of brain waves, Pac Man prevails. In time they are able to remain alert and focused. Children do have to be motivated to change—or at least, they must be willing to play a lot of Pac Man.

HEG Biofeedback

HEG stands for hemoencephalography. This new type of neurofeedback is showing great promise for ADD/ADHD sufferers. The concept is the same as for EEG biofeedback, expect that instead of learning to control their brainwaves, children learn to increase the blood flow to their frontal lobes. The training time for HEG in one study was less than ten minutes, as opposed to five to seven hours for EEG biofeedback. HEG biofeedback training reportedly helps many of the youngsters who have not responded to EEG training. In general, the expectation is that children will start with EEG biofeedback and finish up with HEG training.

During HEG biofeedback, children wear a headband that shines light into their brain. Like holding a flashlight against the hand at night, the skin and bones are translucent. Oxygen-rich and oxygen-starved blood are different colors, and the sensors in the headband can detect colors. A tone or other signal lets the child know whenever the oxygen level in the frontal lobes increases. Some children can raise it dramatically in a matter of moments simply by imagining that their foreheads feel warm.

Obtaining Neurotherapy

Neurologists are familiar with this procedure and should be able to provide good referrals. Specially trained psychologists are usually the ones who offer neurofeedback training sessions. However, little training is actually required—most neurofeedback therapists are trained in a week's worth of classes and then see clients under the supervision of an experienced neurotherapist for several months. However, one study examining the effectiveness of HEG biofeedback found significant differences based on the experience level of the therapist. The children treated by more experienced clinicians made much better gains. It is possible for parents to purchase the equipment and software needed to do neurotherapy biofeedback for under $2,000. They can train their youngster on their home computer and feed the data to an experienced clinician at a remote location via a modem. Clinician fees cost extra, but neurotherapy is often covered by insurance. The clinician analyzes the data and instructs the parent as to how to proceed. Alternatively, the equipment can be leased. However, this does not necessarily save money, since some children need an occasional "booster" training session.

Acupuncture

Controlled research studies have demonstrated that acupuncture is as effective as Ritalin for treating ADD/ADHD. A 1999 investigation reported in *Chinese Medical Psychiatry* by Bob Flaws and James Lake, MD, Blue Poppy Press; (2000) compared 155 children ages five to fifteen who were treated five days a week for three months with acupuncture using *Jiu San Zhen Liao Fa* (Jiu's three needles treatment method). Fifty-five members of the control group received Ritalin. Eighty-three percent of the children receiving acupuncture and eighty-nine percent of the children on Ritalin were completely cured or their symptoms improved. The difference was not significant. However, the behavior of most of the children who took Ritalin was back where they started a month after treatment ended. All of the children on acupuncture maintained their gains. The three viscera of the heart, liver, and kidneys are believed to be involved in ADD/ADHD. But it is interesting to note that the needles (they are painless!) are placed in the scalp, so it may be that the frontal lobes were being stimulated. Be that as it may, the researchers noted that a few children received some symptom relief from acupuncture in the first two weeks. However, most youngsters require the full course of treatment.

Alert!

Over two thousand MDs and DOs across the country are using medical acupuncture to help the body heal itself. Insurance often covers their services. To find a practitioner near you, call ☎800-521-2262 or visit the Web site for the American Academy of Medical Acupuncture (AAMA) at ✎*www.medicalacupuncture.org.*

Another study compared acupuncture alone to acupuncture and Chinese medicine for children age three and older for three months. *Jingo Ling Kou Fu Jin* (Stilling, Magically Orally Administered Fluid) was administered orally. It contains *Shun Did, Shan Yak, Shan Zhu Yu, Noshed Zip, Wu Weir Zip, Fu Ling, Fu Sheen, Yuan Zhan, Long Go, Mud Li,* and *Zen Xiao.* Ninety-five percent of the group receiving the Chinese herbs and acupuncture, and eighty-five percent of those receiving acupuncture alone showed substantial improvement. Three months later, only three percent of the children who had received both treatments had deteriorated. Thirteen percent of the acupuncture only group did not maintain their gains. While the combination of acupuncture and Chinese herbs was more effective, the vast majority in both groups remained cured or much improved.

Homeopathic Medicine

Founded in Germany in the 1700s, the first U.S. college of homeopathy opened in the mid-1800s. Still, this type of medicine remains as mystifying to the scientifically-minded as acupuncture. And like its oriental cousin, double-blind research investigations and a large body of clinical evidence demonstrate that it is a powerful and effective form of treatment. The FDA has approved many homeopathic over-the-counter medications, but this type of medicine never really caught on in the U.S. However, homeopathy is very popular in other parts of the world, especially in Europe. In Britain, family physicians routinely refer patients to homeopaths. In France, homeopathic treatment is reimbursed through the national health-care system, and over a third of the population has received it.

Unexplained Benefits

Exactly how homeopathy works is unclear. The remedies consist of tiny amounts of various substances that somehow stimulate the body to heal. The substances are chosen based on the principal of similarities, not unlike the principal behind vaccinations. When given a small dose of certain foreign substances, the body begins producing antibodies to defend against it. Once the antibodies are in place, they can tackle an infection in the event of a serious exposure. The difference is that for homeopathic treatments, the original substance has been diluted hundreds or even thousands of times, to the point that the original molecules can no longer be detected in the solution. How can a substance help if there is too little of it to detect? The exact mechanisms remain shrouded in mystery. However, that should not serve as a deterrent to using them. Treating an overly active child with stimulants follows the principal of similarities. Amphetamines were prescribed for decades before scientists began unraveling how they worked. The same goes for acupuncture, which has been used for thousands of years and continues to elude Western medicine's attempts to understand it.

Alert!

Qualified homeopaths can be hard to find. Judyth Reichenberg-Ullman, ND, DHANP, LCSW and Robert Ullman, ND, DHANP, authors of *Ritalin Free Kids: Safe and Effective Homeopathic Medicine for ADHD and Other Behavioral and Learning Problems*, treat patients by telephone as well as in person. See ✍*www.ritalinfreekids.com* for information.

Homeopathic Procedures

Rather than viewing ADD/ADHD as a single problem and prescribing the same treatment for everyone, homeopaths view particular symptoms as stemming from a lack of systemic balance. They consider a range of physical attributes, sensitivities, behaviors, and personality variables when determining which remedies to prescribe. The child with problems centering on aggression who likes sour foods and is sensitive to cold will need a different remedy than one who is hyperactive, inattentive, upset by loud noises, and likes very salty dishes.

Question?

What is the least expensive treatment for ADD/ADHD?
Dollar for dollar, homeopathy is usually the least expensive treatment. Homeopaths' fees are high, but only a few appointments are usually required. The medications may seem expensive, but they only have to be taken for a few weeks, perhaps followed by a booster dose.

Homeopathic kits and individual remedies are sold at herb stores. Parents can administer them to treat common ailments like colds, flu, and infections on their own, but cannot treat more serious problems like ADD/ADHD. Moreover, over-the-counter products are not as strong as those available through homeopaths. And an accurate determination as to which remedy or remedies are needed depends on having someone with considerable expertise conduct a detailed diagnostic interview. Afterwards, the child's reactions to the prescriptions need to be monitored. Some of the most common homeopathic remedies for ADHD are *Hyoscyamus*, *Tarentula*, and *Stramonium*, but an individual child may need one of over two thousand remedies, depending on the individual symptoms. Although the initial homeopathic consultation can be as expensive as an office visit with a regular physician, homeopathic remedies are considerably less expensive than standard ADD/ADHD medications and only have to be taken for a short time.

Finding a Homeopath

To select a homeopath, the first step is to understand the credentialing process. Some physicians and doctors of osteopathic medicine study homeopathy as a postgraduate specialty and receive board certification as Diplomates in Homeotherapeutics (DHt). Naturopathic physicians (ND) study homeopathy as part of their naturopathic school training and may become board certified as Diplomates of the Homeopathic Academy of Naturopathic Physicians (DHANP). Other practitioners hold a Certificate in Classical Homeopathy (CCH). Before selecting a homeopath, The national center recommends asking a number of specific questions.

- Has the practitioner treated children for ADD/ADHD symptoms?
- Does the practitioner specialize in homeopathy?
- Does the practitioner use classical homeopathy?
- Where was the practitioner trained?
- How long has the practitioner actively been using homeopathy?
- Is the practitioner board-certified in homeopathy?

Information from the National Center for Homeopathy notes that the competence of individual practitioners varies widely. It advises consumers to seek referrals from friends or consider joining a study group. A listing of groups is posted at *www.homeopathic.org*.

Success Stories

Hal was much calmer and less quick to anger after he learned to control his brain waves in the neurofeedback training sessions he attended at the psychologist's office. He still had the usual disagreements with his parents over bedtimes, not wanting to do homework, and having to be reminded everyday to carry his coat or sweater, book bag, and anything else he happened to have with him to his room instead of dropping them "wherever" when he arrived home. The latter might have seemed insignificant, but since it happened 365 days a year, it really drove his father up the wall. They discussed some of their family problems with the psychologist, and they ended up agreeing that Hal would put his things in the hall closet just inside the front door. His parents did not believe for a minute that would actually solve anything—they fully expected him to drop his things on the floor as was his custom. But after the first reminder of their agreement, Hal picked up his possessions from the floor, put them inside the closet, and they never had to remind him again. Years later they learned that he had not wanted things in his room that reminded him of school, because thinking about school made him unhappy. Had Hal been able to tell them, it would have avoided years of daily struggles. But at least they had solved the problem in fourth grade with a therapist's help, even though it took them ten more years to find out why.

CHAPTER 12

Behavior Management

Trying to get children diagnosed with ADD/ADHD to behave at home and school is the biggest challenge parents confront. They explain, lecture, admonish, nag, criticize, bribe, take away privileges, assign time-outs, and even spank. Too often their child's behavior does not improve or worsens. Aggressive youngsters become increasingly alienated, defiant, and antisocial with each passing year. Compliant children become more upset, depressed, and self-destructive. Parents simply must end the negativity that creates so much upset and frustration. A behavior modification program may provide the solution your family needs.

Teaching Tactics

Six-year-old David was a very bright boy, but his hyperactivity and short attention span kept getting him in trouble at home and school. He could not sit still or keep his hands to himself. Every little thing distracted him. Because he could not concentrate for more than a few minutes at a time, he didn't get much schoolwork done. Soon after he was given an assignment he would notice that his pencil was dull and get up to sharpen it, or he would decide that he was thirsty. En route to the pencil sharpener or water fountain he would strike up a conversation with a classmate, and his teacher would have to tell him to sit down and get to work. After writing his name on his paper he might see that his shoelace was untied. After retying it several times to get it just right, he forgot about his assignment and began carving designs in his pencil with his fingernails or drawing a picture. After just a few months, David's teacher was at her wit's end and David was behind in all subjects. She contacted his parents and said it was critical for the adults to work together to get his behavior on track.

Alert!

When therapists ask children how their parents can get them to do their chores without an argument, youngsters commonly say, "Mom and Dad should ask me nicely instead of yelling at me." If your child misbehaves, ask her what you can do differently and try following her suggestions.

David's teacher and parents developed a behavior improvement plan and carefully explained it to him. The teacher would put a check mark on the board each time he misbehaved. If he got three checks, he would have to stay inside during recess. If he got four checks, the workers at David's afterschool program would keep him inside during the free play period and have him do his unfinished schoolwork. If David got five checks during the school day, he would not be allowed to watch television or play video games at home that evening.

David's behavior improved for a few days, but then it got even worse than before. He dragged his heels when it was time for school in the morning, was more hyperactive and distracted in school, and was more argumentative and oppositional at home. Things came to a head two weeks into the program when David's parents announced that he would not be able to watch a video with the rest of the family because he had received so many check marks at school that day. The video starred a talking hamster that David had wanted to see. He began yelling that everyone was against him. His parents firmly reprimanded him and said that if he didn't go to his room immediately, he would be grounded for the weekend. David kept yelling, they grounded him, and suddenly David's anger turned into a flood of tears. "I never do anything right," he sobbed. "I'm so bad, I wish I wasn't even born! I wish I would just get hit by a car and die."

David's parents were horrified. They called his teacher and told her what had happened. "The program isn't working," they said. "It needs to stop." The teacher pointed out that David was obviously capable of much better behavior since he had improved for a time. "Don't let him manipulate you!" she urged. "You've got to let him know you mean business." What she said sounded completely reasonable but felt terribly wrong. If they went along with her against their better judgment, were they allowing *her* to manipulate them?

Alert!

The secret to a successful behavior modification program is to define small, readily obtainable goals and systematically reward each small accomplishment until new habits are formed. Children must be set up to succeed. Failure results when the tasks are too difficult or the rewards insufficiently motivating.

The Miracle Cure

By systematically rewarding selected behaviors in a consistent, highly organized fashion and ignoring undesirable behaviors, trainers teach animals to perform amazing feats. They teach dolphins and lions to jump through hoops. Pigeons learn to carry messages to distant locations. Seeing Eye dogs master the art of guiding the blind about town without becoming distracted by passing cars, animals, and crowds. In short, animals learn to respond in ways most people never would have thought possible. Psychologists have long recognized that the same straightforward principles and simple procedures work well for animals of all kinds, from human beings to fruit flies. Behavior modification programs are effective for helping children and adults alike eliminate troublesome behaviors, break destructive habits, develop better self-control, and respond in healthier ways. At least, impressive results are commonplace when trained professionals conduct behavior modification programs in controlled environments. When scientists methodically follow carefully designed protocols in laboratories and special education teachers work with students in self-contained classrooms, they typically get excellent results. When ordinary parents and teachers try to carry out behavioral programs at home and school, the results often prove very disappointing.

Question?

Isn't it wrong to train children as if they were circus animals?
Using rewards to control behavior is coercive, though arguably less so than medication. A major benefit is that parents must acknowledge and respond to their child's good behavior. Hence, behavior modification reverses negative communication patterns and strengthens the parent/child relationship.

Many parents are sure that behavior modification won't work for their child, because their past attempts to solve behavior problems by doling out rewards and imposing punishments followed a predictable pattern: most everything they tried worked for a time, but nothing worked for long. Although parents typically conclude that failures mean that their youngster is especially difficult, strong-willed, defiant, or resistant, the real problem usually lies elsewhere. *The success of a behavior modification program depends on the adult, not on the child.*

Defining Problem Behaviors

The first step in developing a behavior modification program is to create a list of the behaviors you want to eliminate or to increase.

Examples of behaviors to eliminate are interrupting when someone else is speaking or arguing when told to do homework. Examples of behaviors to increase include being in bed by 9:00 p.m. and remaining seated during dinner. Behaviors that are general, vague, or subject to interpretation such as "don't be rude" must be rewritten so that they reflect specific, concrete, observable actions, such as "do not curse," "do not walk out of the room while I am talking to you," and "do not slam the door." Similarly, internal states of mind and attitudes such as "don't be so argumentative" must be rewritten as specific behaviors, such as "do homework when instructed without arguing."

 Essential

Ask your child which behaviors she would like to work on, and add them to the list. You may be surprised to hear her express a desire to learn to control her temper or remember to do her chores. Most children are more motivated to improve than parents think!

Defining behaviors precisely is a must. Saying that you expect your child to be polite when relatives are visiting really does not tell your youngster what to do. Is she to preface her answers with "Yes, Sir," "No, Ma'am," and "I'm not sure," instead of mumbling, "Yeah," "Naw," and "I Dunno?" Should she say, "Please" when she wants a piggyback ride, "Thank you" when given a present, and "Excuse me" before interrupting a conversation? Or would you just be happy if she would refrain from punching her little cousin, using the sofa as a trampoline, and asking the company to go home so she can watch television? Parents often think that their child knows how to behave properly and is simply being stubborn, lazy, or defiant. Time and again it turns out that the youngster truly does not understand that when mother says, "Do the dishes," she also means "put away the food, wipe the table and counters, and carry out the trash."

After creating a list of target behaviors to modify, try to eliminate the negatives and replace them with positives by changing the "don'ts" to "do's." Saying that your daughter is not to hit her little brother does not explain what she should do when he takes her toys or taunts her. Telling her to ignore a tormentor may not be realistic and doesn't teach her how to set limits and defend herself.

Rewarding Good Behavior

Children tend to repeat behaviors that are consistently followed by positive consequences. Behavior modification programs use rewards to reinforce desirable behaviors. There are two types of rewards: material rewards and social rewards. Material rewards include toys, treats, outings, privileges, and permissions. Social rewards include hugs, smiles, congratulations, compliments, and kudos. Negative reinforcement, which entails withholding a reward to discourage misbehavior, can also be used but is generally less effective.

Material Rewards

For a behavior modification program to succeed, you must reward your child for a few simple behaviors she can readily accomplish. Then you must reward her every single time until she has thoroughly mastered them before presenting her with more challenging tasks. Since you will be providing many rewards each day, material rewards must necessarily be inexpensive. Items such as stickers, marbles, or trading cards appeal to some children. Many parents give a piece of sugarless gum or candy, although it is not a good idea to give artificial sweeteners or sugar to youngsters—especially youngsters diagnosed with ADD/ADHD. Outings such as a trip to the mall, city park, or library are popular. Privileges might be getting to play a video game for ten minutes, being allowed to choose the restaurant when the family eats out, or deciding which video the family rents. Some children appreciate permission to do something special, such as being allowed to watch television on a school night and being exempted from a chore.

Since rewards must be given immediately after a desired behavior occurs, it may be easier to give tokens that can be traded for a bigger prize. However, as everyone who has tried to diet knows, it is hard to remain motivated to work toward a far-off goal. Reward systems only work when children *feel* rewarded. If you discover that your child is not motivated by certain rewards, change them. If she cannot readily earn rewards, make them easier to obtain.

Essential

Solicit your child's input before deciding how many stickers she needs to accumulate in order to earn a trip to the skating rink or to get a new toy. She must view the rewards as worthwhile and believe she can earn them for a behavior modification program to work.

Children should be involved in all phases of a behavior modification program, and their help determining what rewards they can earn and what they must do to get them is important. Explain that you are going to begin rewarding her for good behavior and help her brainstorm a long list of the toys, treats, outings, privileges, and permissions that she would like. Record all of her wishes. You may not be willing to fulfill her heart's desire for a horse by moving Black Beauty into your backyard. But learning that horses mean that much to her may provide clues as to highly motivating rewards. You might consider providing stickers with pictures of horses for her to affix to a chart, renting *The Black Stallion* video, driving to the country so she can pet a horse, letting her take a riding lesson at a stable, going to see a rodeo or horse show, transferring a picture of a horse onto her T-shirt, riding a pony at an amusement park, and helping her arrange to work at a stable.

Social Rewards

Social rewards are interactions that your child enjoys and that are affirming. They can be smiles, hugs, pats on the back, the thumbs up sign, praise, expressions of appreciation, positive acknowledgments, overhearing glowing comments, and spending pleasant time with a parent. Pleasant time can include wrestling, making brownies, planting a garden, turning off the car radio and singing "Row, Row, Row Your Boat," reading a bedtime story together, etc. When asked, children usually choose material rewards over social rewards, but social rewards are powerful and important. They are more meaningful to most children in the long run.

Make it a habit to administer verbal or physical pats on the back whenever you give your youngster a material reward. Some children are indifferent to praise, smiles, and kudos because every other sentence their parent utters is "Good job!" until it sounds like a verbal tic. Youngsters come to regard such glowing comments for what they are: meaningless and empty. Tell your child you love her often, be affectionate, but only praise specific achievements. And when you do, provide a detailed description of the behavior you like: "I'm impressed that you remembered to ask your brother to pass the salt instead of reaching across the table."

Combining material and social rewards is especially powerful. Trainers provide material rewards such as scraps of meat to puppies at the outset of training. By combining praise and pats with the food, dogs soon learn to associate the two. Once they make the association, praise alone serves as a reward and keeps their behavior on track. Similarly, children eventually associate the positive feelings about material rewards with their parent's smiles and expressions of pleasure. In time, approval is enough to keep them going.

Shaping Desirable Behaviors

Because a youngster sometimes manages to control his temper or clean his room doesn't mean that he can do either easily. If your child quickly loses interest in earning rewards, you are asking too much of him. Behavior modification programs work because they set children up to succeed. To do that, you must break each target behavior into a series of small tasks that your child can easily manage. Each small success builds confidence and creates the can-do attitude that motivates children to tackle new challenges.

Defining Tasks

Perhaps you want your youngster to clean his room without an argument, but his usual response when told to turn off the television and get started is to ignore you. If you turn off the television and firmly tell him to clean his room, he has a fit and promises to clean it later, but later never comes. Or, he goes to his room but does not work. To solve this problem with a behavior modification program, the first step is to get him to respond when you speak to him, whether he is busy doing something else or is purposely ignoring you. Inform him of this goal, write it on his behavior chart, and specify the reward or the number of tokens he can earn each time he achieves it. Then, when you want to speak with him, go to the room where he is playing, say his name in a normal tone of voice or gently touch his shoulder, and then reward him when he looks up, even if he only glances your way by chance. As you hand him a token, sticker, or another predetermined reward, say, "I appreciate your stopping what you're doing when I need to talk with you. Thanks." After he has been reinforced a number of times in this way, he'll be better at noticing that you are speaking to him. After he is consistently responding, compliment him on his accomplishment and announce that he is ready for the next challenge, which might be to accompany you to his bedroom without protest when it is time to clean his room. Describe the rewards he will earn for each success. Then, if he willingly accompanies you to the bedroom, reward him even if he doesn't proceed to clean up his room. Help him pick it up or pick it up for him, and reassure him that he will be able to handle that task in time. Don't advance to the next step until he can consistently walk with you to the bedroom and refrain from arguing. When you are sure he has mastered that challenge, describe the next goal: he will pick up his clothes from the floor and put them in the laundry.

If it takes an entire month for your child to pick up his dirty clothes each evening without an argument, don't get discouraged!

Many parents of children diagnosed with ADD/ADHD have to yell to get their attention for years on end. Many adults are too undisciplined to put their dirty clothes in the laundry each day, and the result is arguments with roommates and marital strife. Do not underestimate the importance of small accomplishments!

Negative Reinforcement

Negative reinforcement entails withholding something that a child finds rewarding, such as watching television or playing video games. Ask your child's opinion before deciding what the penalty should be for a particular type of misbehavior, and then watch carefully to see if losing privileges really deters misbehavior and motivates your child to behave correctly. Many children are motivated by negative reinforcement, but others decide they would rather forego television or be grounded than clean their rooms or do homework.

Alert!

You have probably told your youngster a million times, "If a classmate is bothering you, just ignore her and she'll stop!" Try taking your own advice. If your youngster's behavior is bothering you, ignoring it is often the most effective way to get your child to stop!

In general, negative reinforcement is not as effective as positive reinforcement. The exception is withholding attention for misbehavior. Many youngsters misbehave in order to get a reaction from their parents. Even negative attention is better than no attention, so being scolded can actually be more rewarding than being ignored. Many children simply do not know how to get positive attention. Their parents ignore them when they are playing quietly, refuse invitations to play board games, and decline requests to go outside to toss a football. They are chronically stressed and exhausted and only find the wherewithal to respond when a behavior problem compels them to get involved.

Behavior modification programs often succeed simply because parents are forced to notice and respond to their child's good behavior.

Strategies for Success

There are some limits on what can be taught using behavior modification. Chickens can learn to play the piano but cannot master the art of conversation, or even be induced to utter a single word. You must be realistic when targeting behaviors to change. It is doubtful that you can turn your shy, artistic bookworm into a football star. At the same time, do not underestimate how much your child can ultimately achieve. Through a process called shaping, scientists teach a chicken to play "Twinkle, Twinkle Little Star" on the piano by rewarding it when it accidentally pecks the first note, and by continuing to reward it until the chicken hits the correct note one hundred percent of the time. Then rewards are withheld until the chicken plays the first note and accidentally pecks the second note of the song so that they are played in the correct sequence. The chicken is rewarded until it correctly plays the first two notes every time; then it must play the first three notes to earn a reward. Progress is excruciatingly slow at first but then speeds up dramatically. Chickens learn to play the entire song in short order.

 Essential

The strain of behaving in new ways is very taxing. Mental exhaustion leads to mistakes. To evaluate whether a behavior modification program is working, consider trends over a period of several weeks. Do not assess progress based on a few exceptionally good or bad days.

Learners usually understand what they are to do and should be able to earn rewards in short order. Being able to sustain their new behaviors over time is more challenging. Most people can diet or stop smoking for a day or two, but continuing to abstain from fat and cigarettes gets harder rather than easier as time passes. That's because the strain of behaving in unfamiliar ways wears them down. Similarly, although a hyperactive youngster may be capable of sitting still for five minutes at a stretch, doing so requires a tremendous effort. Until your child finds a way to calm his mind, he may well feel as if his nerves are on edge, screaming for him to move about—just as dieters feel that every cell in their body is crying out for food. Your child is likely to require bigger rewards to stay motivated. Until new habits are established, the urge to revert to familiar patterns can be very strong. New behaviors have to be enacted consistently for about three weeks to become habits.

Alert!

Stress from another problem or difficulty that happens to arise while a behavior modification program is in progress can readily cause a setback. Reverting to old behavior patterns does not mean that no progress has been made. Until new habits develop, lapses are to be expected.

Do not hold back from giving a reward because your child is playing quietly or is busily doing homework for fear your interruption will create a distraction and end your precious moments of peace. Otherwise, you will quickly revert to the same destructive patterns of nagging your youngster when she does something wrong instead of rewarding her for good behavior, and progress will stall. Until rewarding your youngster for every positive behavior becomes a habit, remaining consistent is not easy. Be patient with yourself, and reward yourself for your successes at carrying out the program. What you must do to succeed is to modify some of your behaviors—perhaps the very same behavior you are trying to get your child to embrace. You must plan ahead to be sure you have enough rewards on hand.

You must keep your promise and apply yourself so that you reward your child each and every time he earns one. You must avoid slacking off when you feel stressed, tired, or unmotivated. Behavior modification programs really are a lot of work. But you and your child will reap the rewards for years to come.

Behavior Modification in Action

After David's parents learned how behavior modification programs were supposed to be run, they understood why the program his teacher had developed was not working. The teacher's negative approach (punishment and negative reinforcement), poorly defined expectations ("behave"), and overly challenging requirements ("sit still and do your work") had set David up for failure. He had learned that his behavior was bad but not how to behave correctly. His parents proposed a new program, and after the teacher agreed to give it a try, they explained it to David. When given an in-class assignment, he was to remain seated and do three problems. Then he was to take his paper to his teacher. If his answers were correct, she would draw a star on his paper. If he made it to her desk and back to his seat without pausing to chat with a classmate, he would get an extra star the next time he approached her with three more completed problems. That way, he wouldn't have to remain seated for very long. He was encouraged to do his work and was discouraged from disturbing other students. He would take his papers home to show his parents. Five stars were worth a Pokemon card and ten stars were good for an extra bedtime story. Or he could save them up, and when he got 100 stars, he could use his allowance to buy a hamster.

Within two days, David was doing all of his schoolwork; a week later he felt ready to tackle the challenge of completing five problems before showing his paper to his teacher. Best of all, he was enjoying school and was happier at home. His dream of owning a hamster was still a way off, but his mother had begun checking the want ads for used cages. At the rate David was going, she suspected a fuzzy critter would soon be moving in.

CHAPTER 13
Tempering Temper

Large percentages of children diagnosed with ADD/ADHD are very challenging because of their tantrums, fighting, incessant arguing, defiance, and refusal to comply with rules. These youngsters often progress from getting into trouble at school and home during childhood to delinquency during adolescence. Children are not born knowing how to manage anger appropriately; they must be taught. Reacting by becoming angry yourself and throwing a tantrum of your own does not help either of you. As you teach your child to manage anger, you may find that you benefit, too.

The Mask of Anger

For the three years that the social worker had known Henry, he had acted as though everybody was out to get him and he was ready to throw the first punch. Henry got in trouble for fighting with peers and for defying his various foster parents and teachers. He loved his younger brother but was sometimes very vicious toward him. It took two hands to count all of Henry's psychiatric diagnoses, and he attended a special education class for emotionally disturbed students. Henry's current foster parents suspected that when he threatened and bullied people, he was repeating things that had been done and said to him by his abusive biological parents.

Henry's social worker, psychiatrist, and therapist said that his foster parents must take a firm stand and not let him get away with being such a bully, especially toward his younger brother. He needed to learn to follow rules and obey. But his foster parents knew it would require brute force to get Henry to do anything against his will, and more abuse was the last thing he needed. They loved the boys, but Henry kept the household in an uproar. After some terrible confrontations, his foster parents decided to stop trying to control him and focus on trying to control themselves instead.

 Essential

> Very angry, defiant youngsters can turn adults with the patience of saints into raging maniacs in short order. Despite their tough appearance, many children are wounded and frightened. What they need most is to feel safe so they can heal. For that, the best treatment is kindness.

The Angry Child

Some children are so hypersensitive, anything and everything sets them off. Other chronically angry youngsters are reacting to how they are treated. Many parents who see themselves as strict disciplinarians come across as harsh and rejecting. The modern style is to be over-indulgent and to tolerate a good deal of misbehavior, then frazzled parents explode when they reach the end of their rope. Other youngsters are irritable because they do not feel well physically. They do not realize that anything is wrong because they always feel about the same. They suffer from chronic sleep deprivation, lack of exercise, stress, lead poisoning, toxic overload from pollutants, food allergies, and/or poor nutrition.

Food allergies are a more widespread cause of crankiness and irritability than most parents realize. Several studies on prison inmates found that previously undiagnosed nutritional allergies are rampant among this chronically angry, very aggressive, and sometimes violent population. The increase in food allergies in the general population has been astronomical. Peanut allergies alone doubled between 1997 and 2002 to affect 600,000 children, and even parents who try to protect their allergic child's diet usually find they cannot. Food manufacturers have thwarted labeling laws by listing the names of common allergens in Latin or as "natural flavoring." A bill is currently before Congress to require readable lists of ingredients, at least for the most common foods that produce allergic reactions.

 **Fact**

One researcher suggested that chronic sleep deprivation may explain why children taking Ritalin or amphetamines do not improve academically despite their better classroom behavior and attentiveness. Stimulant medication settles them down but produces insomnia. They can concentrate better but remain unable to think clearly.

Understanding Anger

Sometimes anger is a mask for fear, as when an abused child's fight-or-flight response is stuck on "fight" from having been repeatedly terrorized. Some children seem to be addicted to anger and appear to search for things to be mad about. But for most children most of the time, anger is an important, useful, and normal, emotion, even if it is unpleasant for their parents. Anger is not necessarily destructive, as some parents and professionals maintain. People who grew up in violent households often equate anger with rage, but these two emotions are not the same. The goal of anger management is not to make your youngster's anger disappear, but to teach him to use it so that it works for him rather than against him.

Anger 101

The emotion of anger varies in intensity from mild disapproval to blind rage. In between those extremes are dissatisfaction, displeasure, crankiness, irritation, resentment, aggravation, frustration, indignation, exasperation, enmity, animosity, ire, hate, wrath, and fury. Angry feelings are the internal signals that let people know that some sort of change is needed. Accordingly, they have important survival value. By screaming to get their parents' attention, hungry infants are more likely to be fed than if they passively wait for someone to offer up some sustenance. During the days of the cave dwellers, mobilizing aggression to fend off marauding tribes and animals increased the chances that a clan could hold onto its family members and food supply. Lots of angry children would have made great warriors!

Alert!

Beneath the tough exteriors of many defiant children are youngsters in pain. Criticism causes them to retreat further into their shells. Focusing on what they do right can help build trust that you are on their side. Start commenting on small accomplishments!

Anger provides the impetus for children and adults alike to protect themselves, to confront obstacles, to right wrongs, and to make the world a better place for themselves and others. Whether angry feelings are triggered by real or imaginary events is actually irrelevant; the feelings are the same in either case. In many ways, anger is like pain. It may be very unpleasant, but it is not in and of itself good or bad, right or wrong. It is the signal that lets people know that something is wrong. It makes as little sense to say, "You have no right to be angry" as it makes to say, "You have no right to be in pain." How people express their feelings is another matter altogether.

Anger in Action

Angry feelings can be expressed through body language (from rolling the eyes to raising a fist), verbally (from whining to making threats), and through action (from pulling a classmate's pigtail to committing murder and mayhem). It is possible to feel angry and not express it. Some children express anger in such convoluted ways that their parents do not know that anger is an issue. An example is the child who cries over homework, not because he is sad or worried, but because he is angry that his parents are making him do it. Constant pleas for help can then ensure that if he must suffer, his parents must suffer along with him. Some children internalize their angry feelings and turn them back onto themselves or their possessions. They destroy their toys or harangue themselves for being worthless. Often the torrent of self-directed rage is triggered by something that someone else said or did that angered them. Being angry at oneself can feel safer than being angry with someone else.

Alert!

If your child purposely destroys a toy, ask what he is angry about. He may not answer, because he may not know. But the question will prompt him to consider the matter. When he can identify and say what he is angry about, you may be able to help him find solutions to whatever is upsetting him.

Keeping too much anger inside can be dangerous. It is like turning up the heat on a pressure cooker and failing to open the vent to let the steam out. Sooner or later there is an explosion. Many children keep a tight lid on their anger at school during the day and explode at siblings when they get home. Others contain their anger at home and release it at school. Some children keep their anger inside for years and it seems to eat away at them. Digestive ailments and other psychosomatic disorders were once thought to result from keeping anger inside, though it turns out that stress in general rather than anger in particular may be responsible. School shootings and teen suicides are tragic examples of the consequences of storing too much anger.

Essential

Nagging and criticizing are parental expressions of anger that rarely bring about change. Pick a problem, discuss it with your child when you are both calm, define some clear rules, and work out straightforward consequences.

Teaching Temper Control

The best way to avoid losing one's temper is to prevent too much anger from building up in the first place. For that, dealing with issues as they arise takes the blue ribbon. But there is no guarantee. Coping with traffic jams, a jammed photocopier, and a surly boss, then learning on arriving home that one child needs cupcakes for school tomorrow while the other is whining for dinner can create an instant angry adrenaline rush for a parent. Not getting enough sleep, having to rush to get ready for school in the morning, being teased on the playground, making a poor grade on a test, and being told to set the table can undo children. For those situations, the best solution is to follow the advice that parents have been handing down to their children for generations: take a deep breath and count to ten. Deep breathing is relaxing, and the distraction of counting provides a momentary respite so people can collect themselves.

By making a point of taking some deep breaths and counting aloud when you are upset, you teach by example. You may need to provide a verbal nudge to remind your child to use the breathe-and-count technique. If you are still frazzled when you finish, tell your child that you are going to go to time-out until you are ready to continue the conversation. Tell your child to do the same when he is starting to escalate, and instruct him to return as soon as he is calm enough to discuss whatever he is angry about.

Reducing Aggression

Physical outlets are effective for reducing aggression. Any sort of physical exercise, such as jogging, going for a fast walk, or swimming, are proven ways to relieve stress. That includes relieving the tension born of anger. Some youngsters find it more helpful to engage in a more aggressive activity, such as:

- Pummeling a pillow
- Shredding a phone book
- Working over a tree stump with a baseball bat
- Throwing rocks at a chain link fence
- Drawing ugly or silly pictures of someone
- Punching a large inflatable Bobo clown
- Wrestling with a bean bag chair
- Kicking soda cans
- Beating a carpet with a broom
- Banging metal pots and lids together

Repeatedly hitting a tennis ball into a brick wall, shooting baskets, or going for a bike ride helps some youngsters. However, these activities require some self-control, so they are usually more helpful when anger is mild or moderate. Riding a bicycle when furious can be dangerous. Provide a few ideas of physical outlets that other youngsters use to discharge anger, and ask your child what he thinks would be a good way for him. Some children get more relief from hammering a wooden block than pounding a pillow with their fist because of the noise; others find noise an irritation. Some prefer kicking to punching or vice versa. Installing a punching bag in your teenager's room can deter him from putting a fist through a wall or door when angry, thus protecting the house as well as his hand.

Once your child chooses a physical outlet for his anger, offer to direct him to it when you think he might benefit. Enraged youngsters cannot think clearly, so it never crosses their mind to go to the basement to kick cans or to go outside to throw rocks at a designated tree. They automatically hurl or kick whatever is handy, and they hurt people or objects in the process. Be sure that the selected outlet for physical aggression is safe. Clear the area, and look for potential hazards. If the plan is to beat a tree stump with a baseball bat, check to be sure that wild swings won't accidentally hit someone or damage property.

Teaching Anger Management

Psychologists used to believe that airing grievances via no-holds-barred verbal confrontations was a good way to clear the air. They now know that such an approach is destructive. It undermined relationships, worsened hostilities, and caused people to say vicious things they did not mean and could not later take back. Therapists began providing assertiveness training to teach family members how to broach disagreements in a considerate, respectful, and controlled manner.

 **Fact**

Besides being more aggressive than girls, boys act out more because it is harder for them to identify and express their feelings with words. Before admonishing your son not to cry or be scared, consider the alternative! Too many boys express sadness and fear as anger.

You may feel that your child explodes and has tantrums out of the blue, is resentful or destructive for no reason, and is vindictive and spiteful without cause. Before you can help your youngster manage anger appropriately, you must accept that there is in fact a reason for his anger. Detecting the reason can be difficult. Because infants can only howl when they want something, they end up doing a lot of angry crying. They do not actually know what they want—they only know that they are uncomfortable. Their parents must try to figure out what is wrong. They may be hungry and need to be fed, lonely and need to be held, wet and need a diaper change, or have a tummy ache and need to be burped. After having their needs met time and again, infants begin to associate certain physical discomforts with what helps them to feel better.

To be able to manage anger appropriately, children must be able to do three things:

1. Identify their wants and desires
2. Communicate their wants and desires
3. Cope when their wishes are not gratified

Many parents overlook the first two steps and skip to the third. That means they are trying to get their youngster to settle down and contain himself when they do not even know what is wrong. Many do not even consider that their child needs or wants something, and automatically conclude that he is angry for "no reason." If a four-year-old is screaming for another cookie when he has not yet eaten the one he is holding in his hand, the reason may be that he is sleep deprived, stressed, or actually upset about something else altogether. But trust that there is a reason!

Identifying Feelings

By the time they are toddlers, children should have learned to identify many of their needs and wants. They can often point or use words to signal their desire to be fed, changed, played with, or handed a toy, and parents spend less time having to guess what is upsetting them. Some children are more adept at identifying feelings than others. Girls usually find it easier than boys. Still, learning is a lifelong task. Parents need to help by saying, "You look tired," "You sound happy," "You must be thirsty," "You seem excited." Reading body language is an inexact science at best; only your child can know for sure what she is feeling. The point of commenting is to get your child to consider her feelings so she can learn to identify them. Be sure to ask what is wrong whenever your youngster is upset. Your youngster may not know the answer, but asking will encourage her to engage in a bit of introspection so she can eventually become better at deciphering her feelings.

Communicating Feelings

To teach a toddler who is about to deck another child how to express anger appropriately, take the flying fists in your hands and teach him how to put his feelings into words, saying, "You must not hit her! Tell her you want your toy back. Can you say 'my toy'?" Many older children do not put their angry feelings into words, and they benefit from the same sort of lessons by being given the proper words to use.

When children do not believe that they have been heard or properly understood, they repeat themselves, whine, raise their voices, and become increasingly frustrated. Make it a habit to summarize what you think your child is attempting to communicate whenever she is upset. "You are mad about having to carry a lunch to school because you want to buy it in the cafeteria." "You are upset because you want to go out and play and do your homework later." It is easy for parents to assume they know what the problem is; too often they jump to the wrong conclusion. And just knowing that their parent understands often keeps children from having to create a major scene to get their point across. For children with certain personality types, being heard and understood is often enough to soothe them. When they are upset over a run-in with a teacher, friend, or sibling, they do not need someone to fix their problem. They merely need to be understood, although they may also appreciate compassion. A simple hug or statement such as, "I'm sorry that happened to you" is enough to restore their good humor.

Learning to Tolerate Frustration

Often youngsters need more than a sympathetic ear; they need some concrete help to solve whatever problem is making them angry.

After they identify and communicate what is upsetting them, the next step is to teach them to cope when they cannot have what they want when they want it. Learning to delay gratification and tolerate frustration tends to improve as children mature, so they recover from disappointments with less upset. But not every youngster figures out how to do that without help. When your child is angry, respond by offering comfort, perhaps by saying, "I know you are disappointed about not being able to have candy. If you are hungry, I'll fix you something when we get home." Depending on your tone of voice, you can communicate empathy, compassion, and a willingness to meet your child's needs. After hearing many similar comments, your youngster will learn to talk himself through similar situations. Then instead of grabbing for the candy bar when he is in college, he may be able to wait to eat until he gets back to his apartment and can fix himself a decent meal.

Alert!

How can I stop my daughter from whining about minor discomforts? Many children with ADD/ADHD are especially sensitive to thirst, hunger, temperature changes, pain, etc. Have water, a snack, a sweater, comfortable shoes, etc, in the car. She needs to learn to anticipate her needs.

Responding to continuing howls by starting a conversation on another subject can be a way to communicate what people must do when they are angry about something they cannot change: they need to move on. Thinking about other things can help. Howling can be a way for children to discharge some of their anger, which helps them to calm down. When they finally do, it is understandable that a parent is reluctant to say, "I'm glad you're feeling better" for fear the youngster will remember his previous distress and start howling again. But at some point it is essential to point out, "You were really upset when you could not have the candy you wanted, but you calmed down." Children need to know they can cope and recover—that their feelings change and their anger passes. When they can count on being heard and comforted or learn to turn their thoughts to something else, they acquire the ability to soothe and distract themselves. That will not stop them from getting angry, but it will ensure they have some essential skills for coping with life's frustrations and disappointments.

Teaching Problem-Solving

When children are angry, it is often because they have a problem that needs attention. If an issue comes up repeatedly, it needs to be confronted directly and solved. Extend the olive branch by saying you recognize that the issue obviously needs to be addressed so something can be worked out. Schedule an appointment so both of you have time to calm down and prepare. When you meet, begin by identifying the problem as you see it, for instance, "You don't want to take a bath every other day, and the rule is that you need to take a bath every other day." Inserting subtle digs ("because you do not care how you smell and never cooperate") is an invitation to argue, not to solve the problem. Be sure to summarize in a straightforward manner, and do not proceed until you and your child agree as to what the problem is.

The next step is to determine what the underlying concerns are for each of you. Assuming you have already explained yours (e.g., regular bathing is required for hygiene and to eliminate odor), find out what is on your child's mind. Understanding his concerns often helps with the next step, which is to brainstorm solutions. Make a list of every solution that comes to mind without judging them. Silly solutions can often relieve tension, so never bathing again could certainly be added to the list. If the problem is that baths are boring, possible solutions might be to listen to music while in the tub, figure out some new bath toys, or take a shower instead. If the problem is that baths interrupt play time, perhaps bathing before school would work better.

The next step in the problem-solving process is to try out some solutions, then to meet to see how well they worked and to determine what else might be tried. Alternatively, if you cannot reach an agreement, you may both decide to give the matter some more thought. Most parents are surprised that even many intractable problems can be solved in short order once their children's underlying concerns are addressed.

Essential

Even if the first few attempts at problem-solving fail, it is important to keep trying. The model does work. Once children learn it, they can apply it to solving conflicts with peers, teachers, siblings, and someday with colleagues and employers.

Anger Management in Action

Henry's foster parents realized that his rages were driven by fear. Given that they could not make him do anything he did not want to, they said that the only rule was that he must not hit his brother. Henry agreed to let them handle him. The foster parents continued to tell Henry when it was time to clean his room, do his homework, or get ready for bed. But then they went on about their business and let the matter drop. Henry's brother said it was not fair that he got in trouble for disobeying while Henry did as he pleased. "Henry is learning to feel safe at our house," his foster father explained. "You are learning to follow rules. You each need to learn different things. It would be unfair to one of you if we acted as though you both had the same needs."

Although Henry's foster parents did not enforce any rules, there were still plenty of conflicts when they would not buy him a toy or do what he wanted. His typical response was to fly into a rage. They knew better than to try to reason with someone in such a state. When

Henry calmed down they praised him for being able to recover. After a month, there were signs that he was softening. One night when they announced that it was bedtime, Henry said he thought he would turn in, as if it had been his idea. A few days later when they told him it was time to do his homework, he said he knew perfectly well what time it was. But then he actually studied for a few minutes. As Henry came to trust them, he became less hostile and hyperactive. When he got angry and started yelling, he would follow their suggestion to take some deep breaths and count to ten and wait until he calmed down to talk about upsetting issues. They then worked on teaching Henry to be assertive instead of so aggressive, and he began asking for things instead of impulsively grabbing whatever he wanted. That helped his relationships at school. They never did get around to enforcing consequences. Henry was able to behave without them.

CHAPTER 14

Chaos Control

C hildren diagnosed with ADD/ADHD have serious difficulties organizing objects, projects, and time. As a result, they constantly lose and misplace things; employ a scattered, haphazard approach to homework; misjudge how long it will take them to complete tasks; and are chronically late. Whether organizational difficulties stem from neurological problems, personality traits, or both, youngsters do need to learn how to create, maintain, and cope with structure. Teaching this is a job that falls to parents. Get ready to teach!

The Disorganized Child

Mary's parents did not know how concerned they should be about their daughter's messiness, forgetfulness, and chronic tardiness. Mary's mother was somewhat scattered and disorganized herself. She procrastinated and often had to scramble to meet a deadline or get to an appointment on time. Mary's father had heard other parents complain that their children lost and misplaced things, kept their rooms in a mess, put off doing homework and studying for tests until the last minute, and had to be nagged to get ready for school on time. Mary's parents vacillated between worrying that she would never be able to handle living on her own and thinking that they were simply over-reacting. All they knew for certain was that her disorganization was driving them crazy.

Alert!

Families can easily get caught up in the chaos of an ADD/ADHD child. Criticism will not teach youngsters to keep track of his possessions or be on time. A consistent schedule, simple rules, to-do lists, a school planner, a digital watch, and careful instruction can make a difference.

Mary's parents argued about how to help their daughter. Her father advocated taking a firmer approach. "If Mary forgets her homework or can't find her soccer shoes, let her get a bad grade or sit out the game," he said. "If she suffers the consequences, she'll learn fast enough." Her mother thought that sounded hardhearted. "Mary gets upset when she forgets an assignment because she wants to get good grades. Her teammates are counting on her to be at the soccer games, and she takes her responsibilities seriously. We should be glad she cares and should do what we can for her. She can't help the way she is."

Essential

Withholding praise until a child succeeds at a big task, such as remaining seated through dinner, sets him up to fail. You must work with him on being able to sit still for two minutes and help him focus on this accomplishment before expecting more.

Despite their differences, both of Mary's parents responded to her many crises in much the same way. When her father was in charge, he would criticize her for being so irresponsible. Nevertheless, he helped her finish the schoolwork she had put off and rushed forgotten assignments and lunch money to school when she called him at work. Although Mary's mother usually stepped in to solve the crisis of the moment, she was often impatient and berated her daughter for being careless and forgetful. Mary felt guilty, but that did not help her improve.

The Parent Factor

Many parents worry that their own poor example is responsible for their youngsters' organizational problems. While setting a good example is always a worthy goal, it is important to remember that plenty of very organized parents have extremely disorganized children. Some messy housekeepers feel that it is unreasonable to expect their children to straighten their rooms when the rest of the house is brimming with clutter. They think that it is unfair to make an issue of messy school notebooks when stacks of unpaid bills and unopened mail are lying about. Yet adults may function well in chaotic environments while their children flounder. There is nothing wrong with holding children to a different standard. Most youngsters diagnosed with ADD/ADHD could make better grades in school and get along better at home if they learned to organize.

Alert!

If you think you are doing your youngster a favor by cleaning up after him, think again. That is like doing your child's homework for him. The real favor is teaching and monitoring until your youngster learns to clean up after himself and develops self-discipline.

Even the most scattered adult is likely to be more adept at organizing than a child, so parents can feel confident about their ability to teach their youngster. In fact, because disorganized parents have consciously struggled with organizational problems and know it is a complicated business, they can make excellent teachers. They realize that there are many different ways to organize and that the system that works for one person may not work for another. Very organized parents, on the other hand, often have more difficulty teaching. They tend to underestimate the level of skill involved and think their way of arranging things is best. They try to get their youngster to organize his things the way they would, which means the child must memorize where everything goes rather than learning to use categories to solve organizational problems. Many such parents embrace the myth that getting organized is simply a matter of motivation. Too often, they attribute problems with messy rooms, lost homework, and tardiness to their child's poor attitude rather than to their own poor teaching. In truth, learning to organize is like learning to play the piano. Inborn talent and motivation speed learning, but they are not enough. Good lessons and lots of practice are required.

Teaching Organizational Skills

Most parents have an intuitive understanding of why organizational skills are important. They have lots of experience organizing everything from meals and linen closets to car pools and birthday parties. In order to teach their child to organize, they also need to grasp the concrete benefits so they can explain them and boost their youngster's motivation to learn. They need to know the precise steps involved so they can walk their youngster through the steps.

A New Beginning

To set the stage for a new beginning, tell your child that perhaps cleaning up his bedroom and keeping track of his school papers and possessions have been hard because you did not sit down and teach him how to organize them. An apology for not having provided enough help can be a good way to extend an olive branch and convince a defiant youngster that you are on his side. Explain the benefits of learning to organize a bedroom and notebook and keep them in order: It will be easier for him to find his things. He can use the same skills to organize his school desk, locker, backpack, toys, collections, and computer files. There will be fewer frustrations and upsets over misplaced and lost possessions.

Alert!

Someday your child will need to keep an entire house and an office, desk, or work area in order. The best way to prepare is by teaching him how to manage his bedroom and school papers—and helping him develop the discipline to actually keep them organized.

Organizing 101

Organizing objects of any kind entails putting related items into a group and storing them together in a specific location, such as clothes in a closet, toys in a cabinet, school supplies in a drawer, soiled clothes in a laundry hamper, school papers in a notebook, etc. It is obvious to parents that it is easier to find a particular worksheet if papers are kept in a notebook than if they are randomly tucked into various pockets, books, and folders, and it is easier to find a pair of clean socks if all of them are kept in the same drawer. This is not necessarily obvious to children, however. Parents need to explain that although organizing takes some time and effort up front, it saves lots of time and many headaches in the long run.

With a good organizational system, your child should be able to locate any item in about two seconds. If much more time is needed, that usually means the group is too large. In that case, the usual procedure is to divide the group by creating some new categories. For instance, most students put their school papers into different sections of a notebook or keep them in separate folders so they can find individual papers more easily. Different students use different systems, but the usual approach is to group papers by subject. If it is still hard to locate a particular item, some of the sections may need to be subdivided. The papers for social studies, arithmetic, spelling, etc., could be divided so that homework assignments, tests, and notes are stored separately. Another possibility is to put the items within a section in some sort of order. For instance, all of the social studies papers could be filed in chronological order. It may be necessary to add a new category from time to time. When the teacher assigns a major report, it might help to keep all of the associated papers in a separate section. It usually takes a lot of experimentation to come up with a system a student likes. In the process of trying different ways of arranging papers he gets lots of practice organizing. To recap, there are several simple steps for organizing objects.

1. Putting related items into a group
2. Deciding where to store them
3. Dividing large groups into sections and/or ordering the items

These steps apply to any task that involves organizing objects. A child might organize her video collection by putting the comedies and dramas in different areas of the cabinet. If it is still hard to find one that she wants to see, she could create a separate category for cartoons or could alphabetize them by title.

 **Fact**

Many parents decide where their youngster should store her toys, books, and clothing. However, the arrangement that seems sensible to them may not be convenient or make sense to their child. That makes it hard for her to find things and to know where to put them when tidying up.

Bedroom Management

Accompany your child to the bedroom and tell him that you will help him figure out how to organize all of his things in a way that works for him. Explain that a group of related objects can be organized in many different ways. Books can be lined up on a shelf by height, color, subject, or alphabetically by title or author. They can be arranged so that reference books are grouped together on one side of the bookcase and the rest of the books are in no particular order. People usually put things they rarely use in the back of a closet, in the middle of a notebook, or on a high shelf and store frequently used items in more accessible locations. However, special collections and objects with sentimental value are often placed within easy reach on desks and dresser tops even though they are rarely used.

The point of organizing is to make it easier for your child to find and put away his things, so he really needs to be in charge of the decisions about where his possessions are kept. Determining the arrangement also deepens children's sense of connection to their personal space, which can heighten their desire to keep it clean and in order. It is fine to explain why *you* keep your jeans and pajamas in separate drawers, but try to honor your child's wishes even if you do not agree with them. As you go through his things together, ask where he would like to keep everything from his socks to his toys. Help him sort and arrange, but have him make the decisions. If he chooses unusual places to put things, so be it. Just be sure to repeat the key question often: When he wants to find or put away his baseball mitt, will he be able to remember that it is with the school supplies that he has chosen to store in a box under his bed?

 *Essential*

When the missing salt turns up in the refrigerator, don't just say, "It doesn't belong there! It goes in the cabinet!" Explain that moisture causes salt to clump, and since it is a seasoning, you keep it with the other spices. For your child to organize, he must learn the categories.

Coming up with the perfect bedroom arrangement the first time through is not necessarily desirable; your child will learn more by experimenting to see what works best. Offer to help him rearrange his things if he wants to try a different organizational system in the future.

Organizing School Papers

Organizing school papers simply involves designating different sections of a notebook or different folders for particular subjects. Each section or folder should be organized so that homework, projects, class notes, quizzes, and tests are in some sort of logical order. One possibility is to organize the papers by date, with the most recent papers on top so they are readily accessible.

Your teenager may insist that her messy room is her own affair. But being able to care for a bedroom is an important skill. It prepares teens to take care of a home. Your child will benefit from the time you spend teaching and monitoring.

A student may feel overwhelmed if it is late in the semester, her papers are in total disarray, and her notebook needs a complete overhaul. By sitting at her side to help her figure out where to put each paper, you can start teaching her how to organize, provide some solid hands-on practice, and help her straighten out her notebook all at the same time. Whether the job is finished in a single sitting or after several sessions, the secret is to communicate the goal clearly: to create a system so that any paper can be located and filed quickly. Sit down every school evening and help her file the miscellaneous papers until she can handle her papers by herself. At the start of each school year, help her organize a new notebook.

Organizing Projects

Projects that seem simple to an adult can seem overwhelming to a child. Many youngsters are accused of procrastinating when the real problem is that they are frozen due to confusion or fear. They feel lost because they do not know how to get started. Or they do not think they can finish because of a problem they expect to encounter or have already run up against. Since children are often unable to identify or describe the problem, their parents and teachers may assume their lack of progress is due to laziness.

The method for organizing projects such as getting ready for school in the morning and doing a book report is the same as for organizing a neighborhood club, wedding, or a multinational company. It is important for youngsters to understand that once they learn to organize small projects, they will be able to organize big ones with equal ease. Organizing a project involves dividing it into a series of simple, straightforward tasks.

1. List the tasks.
2. List the materials and special resources needed for each task.
3. Put the tasks in order.
4. Review the list of tasks and mark those that seem difficult.
5. Divide difficult tasks into a series of steps.
6. Review the list of steps and mark those that seem difficult.
7. Divide difficult steps into a series of smaller steps.
8. Review the list of smaller steps and mark those that seem difficult.
9. Brainstorm ways to get help with difficult steps.

After each task is finished, it should be checked off. The trick is to make sure that the child considers each task on the list to be simple and straightforward. If one of the tasks seems too hard, the solution is usually to subdivide it into a series of small steps. If one of the steps seems too difficult, it should be subdivided into a series of still smaller steps. If a step cannot be made any smaller and it still seems too hard, that usually signals a need for outside help. But after having subdivided the steps several times, the child should be able to identify the sticking point and be able to identify exactly what kind of help he needs.

For many children diagnosed with ADD/ADHD, having to do a lot of homework can seem like a huge, complicated project. Some avoid it like the plague; others run to parents and teachers every two minutes with desperate appeals for help. When parents try to find out what the problem is, their youngster may only be able to say, "I don't know what to do." If children start by listing the tasks they need to do for each subject, chances are that the project will look pretty straightforward to them. However, it may turn out that some of the assignments seem hard. The solution is to list all of the steps involved, review them, and subdivide any that still look difficult. You will probably need to provide lots of help breaking tasks into steps and mini-steps until your child learns how.

If an assignment to do twenty math problems seems overly intimidating, they might be subdivided into two steps consisting of ten problems each. If that still seems too hard, they could be subdivided into four sets of five problems or ten sets of two. If the first step that consists of two problems still seems hard, it might be subdivided into steps that include reviewing the appropriate section of the textbook, reading the directions, working the examples, contacting a classmate for help, and doing two problems. Project plans can be long, which can make them seem even more overwhelming than a brief note to "do the problems on page 64." Urge your child to concentrate on one step at a time and not to worry about the rest.

 Essential

Sit down with your child each evening and show him how to record assignments, tasks, and steps in a homework planner until he can handle the job himself. Help him divide up long projects that span several evenings and enter the steps into the planner on the appropriate dates.

Tuesday's Homework

Task 1: Math Homework
    Step 1 Do problems 1 and 2
        Ministep 1 Review the textbook
        Ministep 2 Read the directions
        Ministep 3 Work the examples
        Ministep 4 Do problems 1 and 2
        Ministep 5 Have Dad check to see that I'm doing them right
    Step 2 Do Problems 3–10
    Step 3 Problems 10–20
    Step 4 Have Dad check my work

Task 2: Spelling
    Step 1 Homework—do the worksheet
    Step 2 Study for test on Friday
        Ministep 1 Learn to spell 4 words

Teaching Time Management

Prioritizing is a basic time management skill. A good time to help your child learn is when helping him decide on the order for doing homework assignments. Some students prefer to do the easiest ones first, because it boosts their confidence. Others prefer to tackle the harder items first because they are fresher, and they can relax once those are finished. Help your child list the tasks and put them in order before he sets out to do any project that has given him difficulty in the past. Consider making and posting lists in convenient locations to guide him through washing the dishes, straightening his room, and packing his book bag. Children with poor memories for such details should use as many aids as possible. After referring to their lists and checking off each completed task and step over a period of weeks, months, or years, they will undoubtedly memorize the procedure.

Children diagnosed with ADD/ADHD tend to be remarkably unaware of the passage of time. As a consequence, they commonly misjudge how much time is required to complete routine tasks. A common pattern is to underestimate how long it will take them to get ready to go somewhere or do a chore, and to exaggerate the amount of time they spend on activities they dislike. Poor students commonly report that they do an hour of homework every evening, when they actually average only about fifteen or twenty minutes.

Fact

Knowing how much time is actually required to complete chores can make them easier to face, and working on them for shorter periods of time at a stretch sometimes makes them a lot less arduous.

To learn to cope with deadlines, youngsters need to be able to judge how much time various projects will take and set up schedules matched to their capabilities and, whenever possible, their desires. The first step is to collect lots of data about how long it takes them to do all kinds of routine tasks: taking a bath, completing a set of math problems, gathering their things together for baseball practice, walking home from a friend's house, etc. That information will eventually enable them to make realistic estimates about how much time they need to allow themselves for various tasks. Fortunately, most children get a kick out of timing themselves and enjoy searching for ways to do disliked projects more efficiently so they can finish them faster. Becoming a time management expert can be a lot of fun.

Getting Ready on Time

To get ready for school on time in the morning, children can follow the same procedures as for managing other projects. They list all of the tasks, and then review the list to pinpoint difficult ones. They divide the hard tasks into a series of simpler steps and identify the areas where they need help. They put all of the tasks in order and note the special materials and help they need for each step. Then they need to create a schedule. The first step is to determine how much time they need for each task so that they can get ready on time. Most children enjoy timing themselves to see how long it takes them to get out of bed after they are called, get dressed, eat breakfast, wash their hands, brush their teeth, collect their belongings, etc. That information can be used to figure out when to get up in the morning so they can move at a comfortable pace and be ready to leave the house on time. After working out a schedule, many youngsters enjoy setting an alarm on a watch to notify them when it is time to proceed to the next activity.

Alert!

Your child may need to eat breakfast at a particular time, but let her control her morning schedule as much as possible. Lingering in bed for a few minutes after being awakened and being able to dawdle after breakfast may get her day off to a happier start.

To free up time in the morning, many children decide to do some of their morning chores the night before. They decide what to wear, lay out clothes, make lunch, and pack their book bag. When a child is allowed to work out his own schedule, his parents are often amazed to hear him decide on an earlier bedtime so he can get up earlier and not be so rushed in the morning. Nagging during a madcap race to get out the door day after day is as miserable for children as for their parents. Once youngsters have the time management skills to avoid such unpleasantness, most are happy to use them.

Staying Organized

Teaching children to organize is simple enough. Helping them develop the self-discipline required to remain organized is more challenging. Until new habits are firmly established, youngsters need to be carefully supervised and monitored. Otherwise, they tend to revert to their usual chaotic approach. Until tossing soiled clothes into the laundry hamper becomes such an entrenched habit that they can do it without pausing to think, they may persist in dropping them onto the floor. To remember hundreds or even thousands of details so they can keep their room in order or get ready for school on time requires them to remain focused. The moment they are distracted, they slip up. Ritalin and amphetamines reduce spontaneity and increase obsessiveness, so children's organizational skills typically improve while taking these medications. However, the improvements disappear as soon as the drugs wear off. Medication cannot replace teaching.

Steps Toward Independence

Teaching Mary to organize her room, notebooks, homework projects, and before-school activities was easy. However, her enthusiasm wore off after a few weeks, and her parents were dismayed to see how quickly the chaos reasserted itself. When they stopped issuing reminders, she stopped doing what was required to keep her room in order, get needed items back and forth to school, and get ready on time when they were going somewhere. Teaching her to stay organized obviously entailed considerable time and consistency on their part and more patience than they could muster. Soon they reverted to their old habit of doing their daughter's thinking for her to head off problems and rushing in to solve her crises.

While trying to organize the project of helping Mary to stay organized, her parents realized that what wore them down was having to issue constant reminders. They hated having to tell her to pick up after herself, not to forget things, and to hurry when they were trying to get somewhere. They could not follow her around the house to make sure she put everything back where it belonged so she could find it again. After dividing their tasks into steps, they identified the main problem: having to do Mary's thinking for her. They decided her lists and digital watch could remind her about what to do when.

Alert!

Special watches for children with ADD/ADHD can be programmed to remind them to do particular chores. A vibrating alarm can be set to go off at regular intervals to remind them to pay attention in class or when studying. For instance, see ✍*www.watchminder.com.*

Mary added "room check" to her before-school and bedtime chore lists. She was to call a parent to help her collect her possessions from around the house and straighten her room. Instead of issuing a hundred other reminders each day, they simply had Mary add items to her lists or start a new one. She even had a bath list to remind her to rinse the tub and hang up her wet towels. Instead of nagging her, they reminded her to check her list or set the alarm on her watch. If she could learn to make and check project lists and get into the habit of setting her watch alarm, she would eventually develop the basic organizational skills needed for independence. In the meantime, Mary would have fewer upsets and their lives would be much less chaotic.

CHAPTER 15

Calming Young Worry Warts

W hen adults are anxious, they typically become agitated, cannot sit still, and are so restless that they may pace. They have trouble sleeping and are cranky, irritable, and distracted. They have difficulty concentrating, make poor decisions, and act impulsively. Anxious children are the same, except that instead of pacing, they engage in a lot of disorganized activity. What they need most is to learn to relax. A number of treatments are available to help them learn to control their thoughts and calm down.

Posttraumatic Stress Disorder

The Lopez family was in a serious car accident. Although the car was totaled and the accident was traumatic for everyone, no one was seriously injured. Soon after the bruises and cuts were healed and a new car was purchased, life returned to normal—for everyone, that is, except eight-year-old Jillian. Jillian became hysterical when it was time to get into the car, and the intensity of her upset was unnerving. Still, her parents insisted, believing she needed to face her fears so she could overcome them. At first she trembled in the back seat and gasped every time a car went by. Before a week had passed she was doing so well, she had to be reminded to buckle her seatbelt. Her parents thought she was out of the woods. But then a number of other problems emerged.

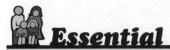

Essential

Abuse and exposure to domestic violence are the most common types of childhood traumas. Anxiety, hypersensitivity, and difficulties concentrating commonly manifest as agitation, impulsiveness, and inattentiveness. Medication can provide symptom relief. What they need is to come to terms with the trauma and learn new ways to cope.

Posttrauma Symptoms

Although Jillian overcame her terror of the car, other worries began to surface. She was fearful that something would happen to her parents while she was at school, and on many mornings she became hysterical about having to leave them. She had always been nervous about sleeping in the dark; now a light and an open bedroom door were not enough; she insisted on sleeping in her parents' room. She had always been very anxious to please, but she now required constant reassurance that people were not upset with her. She complained of headaches and said she was too sick to go to school, but the doctor could find nothing wrong. Her grades dropped because she was so distracted in class.

Question?

Will my traumatized son recover from our burglary?
Estimates for posttraumatic stress for children range from one to fourteen percent. Over half of the victims of natural disasters and violent crimes develop PTSD. Children with ADD/ADHD tend to be more sensitive and have more trouble recovering. Take him for counseling.

Jillian's teacher started to lose patience with her constant worrying and need for reassurance. Her parents wondered if she was trying to manipulate them to avoid her responsibilities. She did not want to leave her parents to go to school, but she had no problem going to the movies or to play at a friend's house. She was too distracted to concentrate on her schoolwork but she could pay attention to games and television shows. When Jillian's doctor diagnosed ADD/ADHD, her parents were not surprised. She certainly had all of the symptoms.

Posttrauma Patterns

Traumas are events that provoke intense "fear, hopelessness, or horror" according to the latest edition of the *Diagnostic and Statistical Manual of Mental Disorders*. It is common for children to react by becoming agitated and disorganized. Trauma can result from having been directly injured or threatened or indirectly from witnessing someone else being killed, injured, or threatened. The former is common among childhood abuse and neglect victims, and the latter among witnesses to domestic violence. Everything from violent movies to divorce can traumatize young children. Brain functioning is altered, so that afterwards youngsters startle easily and have intense reactions to mildly stressful events that they would not have reacted to previously. Instead of becoming a bit out of sorts when excited, they may become markedly hyperactive and disorganized.

Children react differently to trauma. Some have a short-lived, intense reaction but bounce back quickly. Others develop enduring or chronic emotional problems. Some children seem unaffected at the time but develop symptoms months or even years later. This is common after the death or loss of someone dear to them. There is a tendency to deny children's grief and not allow them to attend funerals and other ceremonies designed to help people heal. During and after a divorce, both parents are often so upset that their children work overtime to keep their feelings inside for fear of adding to their parents' problems. These youngsters do not show signs of distress until their parents recover a year later. There are a number of common signs of posttraumatic stress.

- **Intrusive thoughts about the trauma.** Young children often ask the same question again and again at strange moments, such as repeatedly asking, "Where's Daddy?" after a traumatic separation.
- **Nightmares.** Children often are at a loss to recall the content of their dreams or say why seemingly innocuous dreams were so terrifying.
- **Re-enacting the trauma.** It is common for children to repeatedly act out traumatic events through play.
- **Massive upset on receiving actual or symbolic reminders of the trauma.** A child who was abused by a woman wearing a large hat may become hysterical on seeing any strange woman in a large hat.
- **Physical symptoms.** An exaggerated startle response, being hyperalert for signs of danger, and intense reactions to mildly stressful events are common, as are psychosomatic illnesses ranging from asthma attacks and outbreaks of hives to stomachaches.

 *Fact*

Childhood is considered to be a happy time of life, and children have a reputation for being extremely resilient. Yet exposure to domestic violence creates long-term problems for most. A sensitive youngster can be traumatized by parental arguments.

Despite constantly re-enacting and talking about whatever traumatized them, many children simultaneously strive to avoid thoughts about it, refusing to answer questions or discuss the subject even after they bring it up. Children who were more sensitive or troubled to begin with are at greater risk for being traumatized. Enduring a very intense trauma or being repeatedly traumatized alters brain functioning by sensitizing a structure called the amygdala.

Afterwards, a small upset or minor stress can activate a full-blown fight-or-flight response. "You're over-reacting," adults say when youngsters become hysterical over some minor disappointment or difficulty. They are over-reacting, but that does not mean they can help themselves.

Treating Posttraumatic Stress Disorder

Because the effects of PTSD are so difficult to combat, it is important to seek treatment sooner rather than later if your child does not recover quickly from a trauma. Parents often hope that their youngster will simply forget what happened, and they fear that focusing on the upsetting events in therapy sessions will serve as a constant reminder. Although many children do suffer amnesia for much or all of what happened or seem to have forgotten the incident, they may nevertheless develop symptoms of posttraumatic stress. Many sexually abused children do not have problems until adolescence. A competent play therapist will not push a young client to discuss what happened but will be alert to traumatic events being enacted through toys and games.

Internalizing Behaviors

Besides posttraumatic stress disorder, a number of other anxiety disorders are commonly diagnosed as ADD/ADHD, including:

- **Generalized anxiety disorder**—general feelings of tension and anxiety
- **Obsessive/compulsive disorder**—repetitive thoughts and the enactment of rituals
- **Panic disorder**—panic attacks
- **School phobia**—intense distress or even hysteria about having to go to school
- **Separation anxiety**—fears of a parent being killed or injured
- **Tic disorder**—muscle twitches
- **Tourette's syndrome**—involuntary movements and/or sounds

Parents of children with ADD/ADHD symptoms commonly engage in a lengthy quest for the correct diagnosis, believing that when it is found, the correct treatment can be started. They become increasingly confused and overwhelmed when every doctor they consult comes up with a different diagnosis. Many conclude that "head doctors" are incompetent and have nothing to offer. In truth, psychology remains in its infancy. The day may come when knowing the exact diagnosis will dictate the precise form of treatment, but psychology remains more art than science. It is more helpful for parents to direct their attention to two main types of difficulties: internalizing and externalizing behaviors.

Children who act out their feelings are said to be engaging in externalizing behaviors. They are aggressive, oppositional, and defiant. Externalizers are overwhelmingly male. Because they are so disruptive, many are diagnosed with ADHD. The problems of children who "act in" or internalize their distress center on anxiety, exaggerated fears, and depression. They are often diagnosed with ADD. On the outside, they show signs of nervous tension by biting their nails, twirling or pulling their hair, engaging in rituals, or through psychosomatic illnesses. On the inside, their racing minds are filled with worries, commonly about grades and tests, a parent dying or being injured, or burglars invading their house at night.

The percentages of children with externalizing and internalizing behaviors are estimated to be about the same. But because internalizers are usually anxious to please adults and to follow rules, they tend not to be as disruptive. That can make them easy to overlook, and such youngsters are less likely to receive special psychological or educational assistance than those who act out. Some children engage in both externalizing and internalizing behaviors. They are aggressive and defiant, and also have significant problems with anxiety, fear, and depression. They are often diagnosed with the combined type of ADD/ADHD. This difficult mix is common among children with attachment problems. Attachment therapy, an experimental but controversial treatment, may help them. See ✑*www. instituteforattachment.org.*

Internalizing behaviors tend to be fairly stable throughout childhood. Overly anxious, fearful seven-year-olds are likely to have similar emotional difficulties at age fourteen, with depression often intensifying during adolescence. Since children do not usually outgrow their tendency to be fearful, nervous, and depressed, it is important to teach them how to control their thoughts and manage their emotions.

"Chemical" Treatments

Ritalin and amphetamines are not usually effective for children with internalizing behaviors. Psychostimulants tend to increase muscle tension, obsessiveness (preoccupation with a highly disturbing thought), and tachycardia (heart rate), which are symptoms of anxiety. Depression and anxiety often go together, and Ritalin can increase feelings of unhappiness, malaise, and irritability. Hence, stimulants often make internalizing behavior problems worse. The trend in recent years has been to try to treat internalizing behaviors with antidepressant medications. Unfortunately, most have not been approved for use by children and their track records tend to be poor.

 Essential

Youngsters who internalize their distress are good candidates for psychological treatment. Much heartache and suffering could be avoided if parents would work with their children at home and take them for counseling or therapy.

Exercise has been proven time and again to be the best antidote for stress and anxiety, and it is useful for relieving depression as well. After just a few minutes of vigorous aerobic exercise, the body begins to produces endorphins, a chemical with properties similar to morphine. Take your child for a bike ride or outside to play in the snow. Or suggest she jog in place or do jumping jacks indoors.

Reassuring Worriers

Talking can be a good way for children to relieve worries, and you may be able to find simple solutions to problems that have kept your youngster tossing and turning at night and biting her fingernails during the day. Some little perfectionists are convinced that having lost a library book is the ultimate crime, and that they will never be forgiven. Reassurance that "accidents happen" may not be enough to put their minds at ease. Offer to help look for the book and explain that if it cannot be found, paying the replacement fee will satisfy the librarian. To err is human; knowing how to correct errors afterward is divine. For many youngsters, the big challenge is teaching them to reach out for help when they have a problem.

Alert!

When people are anxious, the muscles in the chest tighten, which prevents them from getting enough oxygen. Encourage your youngster to take some deep breaths when he is upset and to concentrate on the rise and fall of his abdomen to block worrisome thoughts.

Sometimes the things children worry about reflect deeper issues, and identifying them requires some detective work. Starting a new school year sends many youngsters into a tizzy. They worry that the work will be too hard, the teacher too mean, or they will not be able to find their classroom. Reassurance does not get very far, because the real issue is their fear of the unknown. Scheduling an appointment to meet the teacher before the school starts can do a lot to restore their calm. Similarly, turning on the light in a youngster's bedroom to prove that no monsters are hiding in the closet or under the bed rarely helps for more than a moment or two. As soon as the light is turned off and the parent departs, the child's uneasiness about being alone in a darkened room returns. What these youngsters need is to have their underlying feelings of helplessness and vulnerability addressed. Providing a magic flashlight to stave off monsters may be enough to restore their sense of being powerful and in control. Similarly, rubbing a magic stone or amulet to activate its protective powers whenever a child senses that a parent might be in danger can relieve separation anxiety.

Learning to stop thinking about problems that cannot be solved at the moment is an important skill. Help your child learn to distract himself by telling him to think happy thoughts, and help him do it by telling a funny story or having a tickle session. Save his favorite jokes, cartoons, and funny e-mails to re-read when he needs to lighten up. Meditating for ten minutes is an effective quick fix for stress and worry, and daily practice can bring about lasting changes.

Confronting Worries Head-on

If your little worry wart cannot stop thinking that lightning might strike the house, terrorists are going to attack the country, or some natural or manmade disaster is going to lead to your demise, provide some simple reassurance. Let your child know that the disasters she fears will not come to pass, or that if something bad does happen it will be dealt with. If that is not enough, it may help to play out a terrible possibility your child is fixated on to its grisly conclusion. If lightning were to strike and the house burned down, what then? All of the family pictures and mementos would be lost. The family would have to find a new house, but at least you would all be together. If terrorists attacked the country, lots of people might be killed. There would be lots of heartache and suffering. But the army would protect the survivors and life would go on. If you were to die in a car crash, keel over with a heart attack, or be whisked away by kidnappers, acknowledge that your child would of course be terribly sad. Tell her who would finish raising her. Let her know that you would want her to treasure the happy memories and go on to have a happy life. Then, try to lighten her mood with a little humor—perhaps by telling her that you want your ashes placed in a gift box covered with Snoopy wrapping paper and placed on her desk. That way you can keep tabs on what she is up to, and if she does not make her bed in the morning or leaves her clothes on the floor, you will haunt her from the Great Beyond.

Alert!

Praying can relieve your child's anxiety, and your prayers for her may well be answered! Cardiac patients recovered more quickly when their names were disseminated to prayer groups across the country, even though the patients did not know that people were praying for them.

Relaxation Exercises

People cannot be physically relaxed and emotionally upset at the same time, so an effective way to relax the mind is to relax the body. Psychologists have developed some relaxation "exercises" for that purpose. Do the exercises yourself while guiding your youngster through the steps to get a better feel for how they work and to avoid moving too fast or too slow. Have your child sit in a comfortable chair. Speak slowly in a soothing voice. Children tend to be nervous the first time through, and some respond by acting silly. It is usually better to ignore disruptions and continue. Getting angry will not help your child relax! Youngsters are usually more cooperative after they have been through the entire exercise once and understand how it goes.

Deep muscle relaxation involves tensing and then relaxing the major muscle groups to heighten awareness of the physical sensations. With practice, children can learn to relax on cue. Have your child close his eyes and take some long, deep breaths, inhaling as you count to five and then exhaling slowly. Next, tell him that when you say "go," he is to tense the muscles in his legs, making them as tight as he possibly can. He should curl his toes, stiffen his ankles, feel his calves go into a knot, and tense his thighs until his feet come off the floor and his legs begin to tremble. Count to five, telling him to try to make the muscles even tighter as you count. Then tell him to relax all at once and to notice the sensations of heaviness and warmth as the tension is released from his muscles.

 **Fact**

> After doing deep muscle relaxation for ten minutes a day for a few weeks, your child should be able to relax all of his muscles instantly. Tell him to use this technique to calm himself whenever he is feeling tense, worried, angry, or "hyper."

After having tensed and relaxed his legs, tell your child to raise his arms to shoulder level. He should tense all of the muscles by making fists, locking his elbows, and tightening his lower and upper arms. He should continue to tighten his muscles as you count to five, until his arms are trembling from the exertion. Then tell him to relax the muscles and let his arms drop to his sides. After spending a moment noticing the sensations of warmth and relaxation in his arms and hands, instruct him to tighten his abdomen and buttocks. Tightening these muscles is similar to straining to have a bowel movement. After counting to five, tell him to let all of those muscles relax, then concentrate on how they feel. Proceed by having him tense his upper chest, shoulders, and face. He should raise his shoulders as high as he can, clench his teeth, draw back his lips toward his ears, and squeeze his eyes shut. Once again, have him release all of the muscles and notice the sensations of relaxation. Finally, he tenses all of the muscles in his body at the same time, keeps them tight for five seconds, and releases and sinks into the chair. Tell him to sit for a moment and notice how it feels to be completely relaxed.

Meditation

Parents constantly tell hyperactive children to settle down, but that does not teach them how! The popular practice of sending rowdy children to time-out misses the point. Time-outs help by removing them from situations that are overly stimulating. They drive home the message that rowdy behavior is unacceptable and provide parents with respite. But there is no guarantee that a child will discover the key to calming down while sitting in time-out. One solution is to teach your child to meditate. Then have him sit down and practice in lieu of assigning a traditional time-out.

Meditating may lessen or solve other behavioral problems as well. EEGs and various brain imaging techniques have found some notable differences between the brain waves and blood flow, especially in the frontal lobes, of children diagnosed with ADD/ADHD (see Chapter 11, Cutting-Edge Treatments). Transcendental Meditation is a proven method for normalizing both, and this type of meditation can be readily taught to children. Research shows that meditating regularly produces a host of benefits, including improved impulse control, increased IQ, and enhanced cognitive functioning.

Alert!

Some people spend a lifetime studying meditation. They sit in the lotus position and practice for hours on end. However, parents can teach by providing a brief explanation, walking their child through the steps, and practicing together at home for brief periods each day.

Meditation classes abound. They are offered through continuing education programs at local colleges, Parks and Recreation Departments, yoga centers, Buddhist temples, and through private instructors. Parents can sign up for a class and then teach their youngster at home. Or they can read about the techniques and purchase instructional materials online. Meditating just ten minutes a day can yield substantial benefits. It is a much more effective way to relax than watching television! Put on Jim Malloy's CD, *The Complete Meditation Class,* available at ✍*www.meditationcenter.com*, and let his soothing voice guide you.

There are many approaches to meditation. One is to sit still in a comfortable chair in a quiet room with the eyes closed and tell your child to concentrate on breathing, so that his only awareness is the sensation of air entering and leaving his body. Tell him to imagine that he is inhaling peaceful feelings of tranquility and relaxation with each breath he takes, and that he is releasing worries, negative thoughts, and tension each time he exhales. It is a myth that people should try to turn off their thoughts or make their mind go blank. The mere act of trying increases tension. Suggest that when his mind wanders, he gently return his focus of attention to his breath.

Alert!

After learning to meditate, children can calm down by concentrating on their breathing for a moment whenever they feel scattered, restless, or "hyper." But emergency fixes may not be needed very often if they practice meditating ten minutes a day. They will probably be calmer, more alert, and more focused.

Different people prefer different ways of meditating. Instead of concentrating on breathing, some children find it more helpful to close their eyes and concentrate on the patterns of light behind their eyelids. The goal should not be to analyze or interpret them, but just to be aware of them. Others find it works better to keep their eyes open but unfocused as they relax their eyelids and gaze downward. If their mind wanders or they find themselves staring at an object, they should let their eyes go out of focus again and return their attention to their unfocused gaze.

The mere act of sitting still to meditate is not easy for anyone at first, and it is especially hard for hyperactive children. Restlessness and urges to shift about can be intense. Although youngsters should be encouraged to remain still, they obviously cannot relax while fighting the urge to move. If they need to wriggle or persist in swinging their leg, it is better for them to do it. Many children react to the novelty of the situation with silliness. It is usually better to ignore misbehavior. Continue to speak slowly in a soothing tone as you tell your youngster to note the sensation of air entering and leaving his nostrils, of his diaphragm opening and closing, of his chest rising and falling. Instruct him to imagine feelings of relaxation being inhaled with each breath and moving down to his toes and out into his fingers.

Panic Control

Three months after the car crash, Jillian continued to be whiny and clingy. She had frequent headaches, was fidgety and restless, and could not concentrate for more than a few minutes at a time. Jillian's parents took her for counseling and met with the therapist to discuss ways to work with her at home. The therapist taught them a particularly useful sensory focusing exercise for helping Jillian when she was turning molehills into problems the size of mountains. They had her sit in a comfortable chair, close her eyes, and breathe in and out slowly. Then they told her to spend about twenty seconds trying to detect sounds in the room—the noise of passing traffic, the knocking of pipes, the creaking of floors, music playing, or conversations from another room, etc.

The next step in the focusing exercise was for Jillian to spend about twenty seconds trying to see if she could detect any odors, such as the scent of her shampoo, of the chair she was sitting on, or the smell of food. Next, she focused on trying to detect tastes in her mouth for twenty seconds, then sensations on her skin: the feeling of her feet touching the floor, her back against the chair, hair on her neck, a slight breeze on her face. Finally, she was to open her eyes but keep them unfocused, noticing the blurry shapes and hazy colors directly in front of her. Then she closed her eyes and was told that on the count of ten, she would feel relaxed and refreshed and should open her eyes. As Jillian's parents did the exercise while guiding her through it, they were amazed at how relaxed they felt afterwards. They had not realized that they also felt tense and anxious a good deal of the time. Perhaps Jillian was reacting to their tension, just as they did to hers. They began doing the sensory focusing exercise as a family the first thing on arriving home and before leaving in the morning. Jillian shared that when she was angry with a classmate, she spent a few seconds calming herself by letting her eyes go out of focus and concentrating on the shapes and colors. Her father tried focusing on sounds the next time he was caught in traffic, and it worked for calming him, too!

CHAPTER 16

Classroom Coups

U nhappy employees can quit their jobs to seek work better suited to their personality and talents. School is a child's job, but students cannot quit—at least, not until they turn sixteen. Because children with ADD/ADHD symptoms have so much trouble in traditional classrooms, many mentally withdraw early on and drop out at the first opportunity. This is unfortunate, because some simple classroom changes, special education help, a change in schools, or homeschooling can make for a happy and successful educational career!

Sitting Still to Learn

All of John's relatives had gone to college, and his parents assumed that he would do the same. His grandparents opened a savings fund for him at birth, and his father made regular contributions each month. As an infant John's mother held him on her lap and they looked at picture books together. John was as enamored with Mother Goose as his brothers had been. However, John's interest in books waned shortly after he learned to walk. He still wanted a bedtime story, but he would not sit still to listen.

It was obvious early on that John was not interested in books. He fidgeted and kept interrupting when his parents read him bedtime stories. They feared he would have big problems in school, and they were right. In third grade the school psychologist diagnosed learning disabilities but said that John could attend college if he got the help he needed and buckled down. But John could not stand school and would not apply himself. He was only nine, but his parents were very worried about his future.

Alert!

To keep a hyperactive child's attention when reading stories, vary the pace, let her ask questions, and discuss the pictures. Let her stand or play nearby while listening. She may be perfectly capable of doing two things at once.

The Traditional Classroom

Modern textbooks have lots of color pictures, schools have computers, and in some classrooms students' desks are arranged in a circle instead of rows. Otherwise, education has changed little since the early 1800s, when the goal was to train factory workers. Although the industrial revolution ended a century ago, students still sit all day long, move to bells, and do mindless tasks. Their teacher-foremen try to insert information and then grade students like cuts of meat as they progress through the educational assembly line. On graduation, the prime cuts are transported to premium institutions of higher learning, while the lowest grades work in low paying jobs or languish in unemployment lines. The high tech information age needs employees who can think, reason, innovate, make decisions, work in groups, multitask, and cope with ever-changing job duties. The nation's outmoded educational factories need to be re-tooled, but most efforts at reform involve stricter quality control to lessen the number of defective products rolling into the workplace. Yet their numbers are growing. Some public school teachers are very flexible and work well with students who do not fit the mold. Many innovative private schools can accommodate special-needs students. Increasing numbers of parents have set up small shops and are homeschooling their youngsters. There are many good options, but parents need to be proactive to ensure that a child with ADD/ADHD symptoms gets a decent education.

Simple Solutions

If your child is having problems at school, the first step is to talk to your youngster to see what *she* thinks would help. Ask what the teacher could do to make it easier for her to understand the lessons, concentrate, and do her work. Next, ask your child's siblings and friends how they see the problem and what they would recommend. They often hear the inside scoop on a teacher's personality, expectations, and classroom problems through the schoolyard grapevine. They are aware of their siblings' or friends' strengths and challenges. Be tactful when broaching the subject so as not to cause embarrassment. Try some general questions such as, "How do you like Mrs. Brown as a teacher?" "Do a lot of the kids have trouble understanding the lessons and doing the work?" and "To be a really great teacher, what should she do differently?" Query your child's previous teachers to find out what worked and what did not.

The next step is to meet with the teacher to conduct a joint search for solutions. Moving a student away from a distracting classmate is often enough to produce a dramatic improvement. Reducing homework loads or providing remedial work can often cure what ails a student. Moving her desk to the front of the room can eliminate the visual distraction of other students. Donning headphones to listen to instrumental music when working on assignments can boost concentration by eliminating distracting sounds.

Kid-Friendly Classrooms

Many children learn better while moving and talking, and a second grade teacher at an exclusive private Dallas school demonstrated the benefits of allowing students to move at will. The rule was that some part of their body had to touch their desk or chair at all times. As long as one finger was on the desktop or a shoe made contact with a chair leg, the students could stand, sit, jump, run in place, or orbit around their seat. When they raised their hands, they could wiggle their fingers, wave their arms, and sway their bodies. Talking was encouraged. When the teacher asked a question, the students shouted, "I know! Pick me!" When they were disappointed that they had not been called on, they could yell, "Shucks!" "But I know the answer!" If a student correctly answered a question, everyone shouted, "Way to go!" or clapped. If the answer was wrong, students made a noise like a gong or a buzzer and called out, "Too bad!" Excitement ran high, and when it was time to work quietly, the students were ready for a break. The teacher never had to stop the lesson to reprimand bored students or remind them to stay on task.

 Essential

> Students with attention deficits are often sent to study carrels or their desks are turned to face a blank wall. That helps to reduce distractions, but most concentration problems stem from too little mental stimulation. The trick is to keep students' minds from wandering. If they do, their bodies often follow.

Educators need to be pressed to provide the opportunities for exercise every child needs to remain alert and healthy, and that especially active youngsters require. The trend in recent years has been to eliminate recess and gym to allow more time for academics. A few teachers allow students to go to the back of the classroom to stretch, run in place, or do jumping jacks whenever they need to. Some encourage it. "You look like you need some exercise," a teacher might say when a child is growing restless. "Would it help to stand and stretch?" Students quickly learn to take exercise breaks without having to be prompted.

Learning Style

Many college-educated adults value book-learning and have difficulty comprehending that people can learn in other ways. Although there has been a push in educational circles to present more hands-on lessons, most teachers continue to rely on reading, writing, and listening to lectures. It is no wonder that students who learn best by other methods only like gym, recess, and lunch! Visual students learn best through written language. Pictures, charts, and diagrams help them understand and process information. Auditory students prefer lectures, films, tapes, and learning through dialogue. Kinesthetic students learn best through hands-on activities. Trying to teach hands-on learners history through lectures is like trying to teach the piano by explaining what to do. Having them read history books is like assigning articles about piano playing. Giving them a written test is like asking them questions about a song to assess their ability to play it. If they can tape interviews with senior citizens, make digital movies, and create exhibits from poster board and clay, they can learn a lot of history and demonstrate how much they learned.

 *Fact*

The trend is to diagnose "kinesthetic" students with ADD/ADHD. Montessori and Waldorf schools are just what the educational psychologist ordered for hands-on learners. Individualized learning and self-paced instruction are commonly emphasized.

Because kinesthetic students learn best by touch and movement, simply clapping while repeating the multiplication tables can make memorizing them easier. These students grasp mathematical concepts and solve arithmetic problems more quickly by working with sets of specially designed educational blocks. These "manipulatives" come in various sizes, shapes, and colors. Many students learn more science by taking apart a broken video recorder or dissecting a flower than by listening to lectures and completing worksheets. Educational toys abound, but game playing is usually a classroom filler activity. Students learn that Park Place and the Boardwalk are expensive properties from endless Monopoly games but never learn which presidents presided over which wars. A good way to teach is to have them invent and play educational games.

 **Fact**

Moving seriously disrupts children's lives. According to a 2004 National Public Radio report, thirty-five percent fail their grade in school the year after moving, and seventy-seven percent develop serious behavior problems. Many executives are now declining to relocate, and eighty-three percent give "family considerations" as the reason.

The Gifted Child

Children with exceptionally high IQ scores are at risk for being diagnosed with ADD/ADHD. Boredom commonly drives their inattentiveness, and their personality quirks often strain relationships with parents, teachers, and classmates. Many thwart rules and evade consequences—or try to—by using their advanced verbal skills to talk circles around adults. When children sound like adults, people tend to expect them to behave with a similar level of maturity. "Act your age!" they admonish a very bright fourth grader who is in fact doing just that.

A gifted student is usually among the first to spot teacher errors and know the answer to questions. Having their mistakes duly noted and corrected in front of a group is unpleasant. Students who wave their hands and blurt answers are considered impulsive and annoying. Their usual intention is to help the teacher and speed the pace of boring lessons. Explain that teachers pose questions to find out if the class comprehends and is listening, not because they do not know the answer. Envy leads some teachers to overreact to minor problems. A few retaliate by dealing blows to gifted students' self-esteem. Gifted people are targets of envy throughout their lives. Strengthen your child by discussing the need to treat envious people with compassion.

Academically talented students are usually the first to finish in-class assignments. Keeping them challenged creates lots of extra work for their teachers. The short-cut solution is to assign busywork, punish them for misbehaving and daydreaming, or declare them learning disabled and send them to special education. The latter is easy since only a rare student is equally gifted in all areas. If your child's teacher cannot come up with enough meaningful learning activities, he may appreciate having you send enrichment materials to school. Educational stores offer a wealth of interesting workbooks, and materials can be downloaded from the Internet for free. An alternative is to help your child develop independent study projects to do in his spare time at school.

Alert!

If achievement tests indicate that your child is not progressing as expected based on her IQ test score, she is likely to be diagnosed with a learning disability. Special education can help, but so can a better mainstream classroom environment.

Special Educational Needs

Students with ADD/ADHD symptoms and learning disabilities may simply suffer from a lower tolerance for poor educational practices than their classmates! They do best in educational settings that reflect current wisdom about what *every* student needs.

- **Intellectual challenges geared to the student's skill level.** Lessons that are too easy are too boring to hold students' attention; lessons that are too hard cause undue frustration and cause students to give up.
- **Emphasis on understanding and applying concepts.** Most teachers place too much emphasis on acquiring information through rote memorization, which many students perceive as useless and tend to forget soon after they are tested on it.
- **Involvement in setting learning objectives.** Some students benefit more from the opportunity to learn a little about many subjects; some do better exploring a single subject in depth.
- **Opportunities to pursue individual interests.** Students are more motivated when they choose the topic they want to learn about. Virtually any topic can be investigated from the standpoint of any school subject. A project on frogs can incorporate reading and writing about them, studying the meaning of frogs in various cultures for social studies, and calculating population growth rates to learn math.
- **Self-paced learning.** Some students need more time to learn the material. They just do. That is not a reflection of how intelligent they are.
- **Instruction that incorporates the student's preferred learning style.** Lessons that engage all of the senses tend to be most effective at reaching the largest number of students.
- **Involvement in decisions about how they will be graded.** Many students learn more from producing a project than from taking a traditional classroom test.

Learning Disabilities

It is common for students diagnosed with ADD/ADHD to be diagnosed with one or more learning disabilities. Most involve language (especially speaking and understanding what is being said) or a specific academic subject (usually reading or math). A host of educational tests claim to be able to identify learning disabilities, yet many professionals have challenged the whole concept. Most learning difficulties, they maintain, are not disabilities but differences. There is certainly nothing to suggest that the average learning "disabled" student has brain damage. A few generations ago, almost every youngster mastered the basics. The research data suggests some simpler explanations to explain student's academic difficulties, including:

- Disinterest/poor motivation
- Poor tolerance for frustration
- Difficulties concentrating
- Poor persistence and difficulties remaining on task
- Personality differences
- Ineffective teaching
- Nutritional problems
- Sleep deprivation
- Inadequate exercise

Psychologists and educators talk about visual-motor deficits, sensory-integration problems, and dyslexia to explain why so many students do not line up their numbers in math, spell correctly, write neatly, understand their teacher's explanations, comprehend what they read, and produce error-free worksheets. A few generations ago, most every sixth grade student could read on a sixth grade level. Now reading deficits have reached epidemic proportions. Reading problems are commonly attributed to language-processing and sensory-integration deficits. Dyslexia, an especially severe reading problem, is believed to affect as many as seventeen percent of school children. Recent brain imaging studies have confirmed that the problems stem from the way sounds (not visual information) are processed. The problem is blamed on a hereditary brain malfunction. Yet, instead of reading, students watch television and play video games. Their busy parents do not work with them at home. Many dyslexic children have been found to be deficient in essential fatty acids (EFAs), and supplementing their diets is an effective treatment. It is ridiculous to say that nearly twenty percent of children cannot read because a genetic brain problem has disabled them. For most, the best cure is a healthier lifestyle and better teaching. Students need to read and play educational games at home. They need to eat properly, go outside to play, and get enough sleep so they can apply themselves in school. They also need to do their homework.

Essential

Having students do homework each day communicates the value that studying is important. To motivate them, read *The Homework Solution: Getting Kids to Do Their Homework* by Linda Sonna (Williamson Publishing, VT, 1990).

Special Education Services

If regular classroom teachers cannot accommodate your child's educational needs, special education help may be a good option. Special education services may involve going to a special classroom all day, getting extra help in a particular subject for an hour a week, or anything in between. It may mean having a specially trained teacher come to the regular classroom to work with your child. To qualify, a child's ADD/ADHD symptoms must cause significant learning or behavior problems at school. Section 504 of the Individual Education and Development Act legally obligates public schools to ensure that children with a disability have equal access to education. That includes children with "a physical or mental impairment that substantially limits one or more major life activities including learning and behavior." ADD/ADHD falls into this category. Students must receive "appropriate accommodations and modifications" to the regular classroom that is tailored to their individual needs.

To qualify to receive services under Section 504, a student must have a disability that "substantially limits one or more major life functions, including education, learning, and behavior." Only the school can determine if a child qualifies. If you think your child needs special services, the first step is to submit a written request for an evaluation via certified mail to the school. Special education classes are expensive due to the small classroom sizes and advanced degrees of the teachers. Parents may have to be assertive to see that evaluations are handled in a timely manner and that the recommendations are implemented. It is a good idea to request a copy of your school district's policies and procedures for complying with Section 504. It will list your rights and the district's responsibilities. If your complaints are not satisfied, you can call the Office of Civil Rights Hotline of the U.S. Department of Education at (800) 421-3481 for information about how to proceed.

With its individualized instruction and self-paced learning, special education can help any student. If the current trend continues, every child may someday qualify. Most students enjoy special education classes and like their teachers. But declaring students disabled can do more harm than good by sending such a negative message about their capabilities. Some students reap more benefits from developing their strengths and talents than from dedicating inordinate amounts of time to struggling to overcome their weaknesses. Fun activities such as gymnastics, Aikido, and piano lessons are good ways to help them develop better balance, coordination, and fine motor skills.

Homeschooling

Most people assume that homeschooling requires a stay-at-home parent with a teaching degree and a cooperative, highly motivated child. If you work full time, do not know the first thing about teaching, and have a hard time getting your child to pick up his socks, homeschooling can still be a very good option. Going to school is a source of misery for many students with ADD/ADHD. They learn too little about reading, writing, and arithmetic and too much about their own incompetence. Unless your ADD/ADHD child is a happy camper and is thriving in his current school environment, homeschooling should be investigated.

Parents as Teachers

Most parents are amazed to discover how little hands-on teaching time is required to equal what goes on in a typical 180-day school year. According to *The Everything® Homeschooling Book* by Sherri Linsenbach, parents do not need to devote much time to sitting down and working with their homeschooled student one-on-one.

- Preschool and kindergarten: ½ to 1 hour
- Elementary school: 1 to 1½ hours
- Middle school: 1½ to 3 hours
- High school: 2 to 4 hours

Homeschooled preschool children of working parents need childcare since little ones cannot be left alone. But being with a private babysitter in a home can be less stressful than spending long days in a room filled with other tots. If you are concerned about academics, devote thirty minutes to educational activities on weekday evenings and make up the rest of the time on the weekends. A playgroup, swimming lessons, free play at the park, or a couple of half-day sessions at a nursery can provide adequate time to socialize with peers.

 *Question?*

Can I just pull my child out of school and homeschool her?
Most states require parents to file an educational plan. Some districts monitor closely to ensure that compulsory education laws are being observed. Contact your local school district's central administration office or your State Board of Education.

To homeschool an elementary student, add an extra bedtime story and practice reading. Play an educational game each evening and review the assignments your child did while you were at work. Make up the rest of the time by sitting down to explain new material on the weekends. If your youngster needs more peer interaction than the neighborhood can provide, enroll him in an afterschool program or some extra-curricular activities. By middle school, your student can do assignments while you are at work. He may be able to get most of the individual help he needs online or, if he needs more structure, from a couple hours with a private tutor. Otherwise, spending thirty minutes to review his work, answer questions, and work out the next day's assignments should be sufficient on weekday evenings. Some public schools are quite hostile to homeschooling; others gladly allow the students to attend part time. If so, parents may arrange for their youngster to attend art, lunch, and P.E. so they can interact with youngsters their own age, or take a foreign language course. Since parents cannot teach all of the advanced high school subjects, teens usually get help from Web sites, online tutors, and chat groups. For social outlets, most communities have meetings and activities for parents, students, or both. Teens can attend community events with their parents. Homeschooled students tend to enjoy warmer relationships with their parents and are typically more mature than other children the same age.

 ## Essential

You obviously need to do your homework before deciding that homeschooling is for you! Research other parents' experiences by doing an online search for "ADHD homeschool discussion." For articles, materials, and curriculum guides, join the American Homeschool Association by calling ☎(800) 236-3278 or see ✍www.americanhome schoolassociation.org.

The Homeschool Curriculum

When John's mother was told that her hyperactive son had learning disabilities in math and reading and needed special education, she decided to try homeschooling him for the remainder of the academic year. She figured that if it was a disaster, he would return to public school and repeat the year. Being a bit more mature might help with his behavior, and anything he learned would give him an edge in the fall. She was relieved to find that all kinds of packaged educational programs were available online. Some were free, others cost several thousand dollars. She could purchase the services of a consultant to create an individualized study program and to provide feedback on John's e-mailed assignments. There were chat rooms so that John could talk online with homeschooled peers.

Alert!

Homeschooling children can actually make parents' lives much easier. Most youngsters help with everything from cooking to taxes. Homeschooled siblings bond while working on joint projects. Without peer pressure and long, stressful days in school, children are more relaxed. That makes for a happier family.

John did not like to read or write, but his mother was advised by the parents in the homeschool organization she joined to forget about study schedules and coercion. Instead, they suggested that she toss the video games, buy a device to restrict John's television-viewing to educational programs, and stock up on books and educational toys. They reassured her that children's natural curiosity motivated them to learn; her job was to support her son's desire to pursue his interests. She said that John's only interests were baseball and comic books, and they pointed out that by calculating percentages of home-game victories and RBIs, John might have fun learning math.

A woman in the homeschool support group said that a comic book fan was likely to be an avid reader. John did love to read, which made his reading disability diagnosis seem rather mysterious. His reading problems only seemed to appear during school assignments. Another homeschool parent suggested that John might like to read the science behind his favorite science fiction stories. That might give him some ideas for stories of his own. If he wanted to create a comic book, he could learn grammar and spelling in the process. He could also learn economics, business, and marketing by investigating how to print, advertise, and sell his wares. His mother was beginning to see how following John's interests could motivate him. As it turned out, John did well in his homeschool. He even decided that he wanted to learn Spanish and found a free online course. He loved his homeschool so much, he decided to give it a name. He wanted to hang a sign on the front of the house, but his parents protested and he settled on his bedroom door. "Superman Escuela" was named for John's favorite classic comic book hero and favorite homeschool course. "But that's just one meaning," he explained. "My school is for a super man, though I'm actually just a super boy." That was when his parents knew that their decision to homeschool John had been wise.

Chapter 17

From Defiance to Compliance

Every youngster needs to learn to comply with rules and follow instructions. Nagging is stressful, and many youngsters continue to drag their feet until their parents lower the boom. Providing clear, concise "do" and "don't" lists is a start, but to get your child to do what you say requires smore. You need to adopt a zero-tolerance policy and follow through with consequences designed to reinforce what you are trying to teach. Fortunately, getting your child to comply is easier than you may think.

Chronic Foot-Dragging

"I'll be there in a minute," Shea said when her mother called her to dinner each evening. "Just a second," Shea responded when her father told her it was time to get off the telephone and do her homework. Agreeing to do what they asked her "soon" was Shea's standard response to most everything. When her parents reminded her a few minutes or hours later of what she had promised, Shea would say, "Sorry, I forgot" or "Yes, I was just on my way" or "As soon as I finish this, I'll do it." Having to continually remind her made them feel like nags. When they finally lost patience and ended up yelling or threatening to ground her, Shea would adopt an indignant, self-righteous tone.

The cure for her foot-dragging was to present Shea with something she wanted to do. She moved with lightning speed when she needed to get ready to go to the mall or when they told her a friend wanted to talk to her and she needed to pick up the telephone. That made her seem hopelessly self-centered. Her parents wanted to set a good example for their daughter by being considerate and respectful of her. They did not expect her to drop whatever she was doing on the spot to do what they wanted. At the same time, it was obvious that Shea was taking advantage of them, and their good example was not teaching her to be considerate and respectful of them—or of her teachers or friends, for that matter.

 **Fact**

Saying, "You should know better!" when your child makes a behavioral blunder is like saying, "You should know better!" when he multiplied the fractions wrong. Telling him that he *should* know only serves to humiliate him. Your job is to teach what he needs to know.

Testing the Limits

When children persist in misbehaving, their parents often say that it is because they are "testing them" or are "testing the limits." Many therapists also say that persistently misbehaving children are testing their parents to see how much they can get away with. This suggests that youngsters are purposely trying to make things difficult for their parents on the one hand, or are actually begging to be controlled on the other. Both can happen but rarely do. Children continue jumping on the furniture after having been told to stop and do not turn off the television to start their homework when called because what they are doing at the moment is more enjoyable than what their parent is proposing. Their parent's patience may be sorely tested, but such children are not "testing the limits." They are simply ignoring their parent in the hopes that their mother or father will give up, forget, or have a change of heart. Wanting to do as they please does not mean children are lazy or bad; they are just young people following their druthers and having fun.

Alert!

Do not take your child's misbehavior personally. Just because he is getting to you does not mean he is out to get you. If you find yourself repeating, "Quit playing around," your child probably needs more time to play!

Children learn from experience that they do not have to do as they are told unless they feel like it—or until their parent begins counting to ten, dons a particular expression, or adopts a certain tone of voice. Then they know there will be an unpleasant scene. Still, many proceed to argue or debate. Even if they inevitably end up having to comply, they are able to express their feelings of displeasure by not complying right away. And once their parent's fit of temper is past, many youngsters know that they can resume doing as they please. Adults wear down much faster than children. After having corrected their youngster several times, many parents lack the energy to tackle the same problem yet again. Instead, they pretend not to notice what is happening.

When "No" Means "No"

When you ask your child to do you a favor, whether he consents or not should be up to him. But issuing instructions and then counting to three to give your youngster time to decide whether or not to obey is a serious mistake. The common practice of issuing the "three strikes and you're out" threat is a mistake as well, since it effectively allows youngsters to misbehave two more times. Parents delay taking action in an effort to be flexible, but there are better ways to cut your child some slack.

Providing additional time or chances for youngsters to comply after correcting them or issuing an instruction sends a confusing message. The end result is that they get a lot more practice doing things wrong than doing things right. Since indulging in forbidden activities and ignoring instructions is in some way rewarding for them, children are reinforced for misbehaving when parents fail to act immediately. When they finally take action, their message shifts from "You should not do that because it is wrong" to "You should not do that when I am really angry and have run out of patience."

 *Essential*

Saying, "Don't let me catch you doing that again, or you're going to get it" teaches children that their mistake is getting caught! Instead, teach values: "Jumping on furniture ruins it; you are not to destroy property. It is dangerous because you might fall off. You must not do it—not ever."

Communicating the New Plan

Children need to learn to refrain from forbidden behavior altogether. They need to do what their parents tell them the first time an instruction is issued. To teach your youngster, the first step is to discuss how you handled behavior problems and defiance in the past and how you will handle them in the future so that he understands the changes that will take place. Tell your child that in the past you sent some mixed messages by pointing out misbehavior or telling him what you expected, then nagging and giving him second, third, and fourth chances to comply. Explain that you thought his problem was lack of motivation, and that issuing repeated reminders would be enough to induce him to follow rules and instructions. Now you realize that motivation and obedience are not the issues; he needs to develop better self-control and self-discipline. Your failure to take action immediately when he broke a rule might have led him to believe that when you lacked the energy to control him, it was OK for him to misbehave or ignore you. Emphasize that misbehaving and ignoring you are definitely *not* acceptable. And whether an adult is present or absent, energetic or tired is not relevant. Each rule exists for a reason, and you will try to do a better job of explaining the rules and the reasons they are important. Your duty as a parent is not to control him; it is to teach him to control himself. Learning to do that will help him immensely at home, school, and in the neighborhood. It will make the rest of his life a lot more pleasant.

Question?

How can I tell if I am being too controlling and rigid?
If the only reason for a rule is a preference ("I always do it that way," "Everybody does it that way," or "I like it that way"), the rule may be unnecessary. Consider other family members' preferences, too.

List some of the specific household rules your child has trouble with and explain why each is important. Rule number one is that when you issue an instruction, such as announcing that it is time to come to the dinner table, get ready for bed, or to start on homework, etc., he is to comply immediately. That is important because the alternative is for you to nag and get angry. If he is arguing with his brother, blasting the stereo, or interrupting your telephone conversation and you tell him to stop, he is to stop immediately. Otherwise, there will be a consequence designed to teach him better self-control.

The "Zero Tolerance" Policy

The "zero tolerance" policy is not as severe as it sounds. Your youngster does need to learn to follow rules immediately and comply with instructions the first time he is told in order to end the arguments and nagging that make family life so stressful for everyone. But rather than expecting your child to jump to your every command, be flexible by providing advance notice. Announce that dinner will be served in ten minutes so your youngster can finish what he is doing or let you know in advance that he will have difficulty arriving on time. That encourages him to think ahead and bring up problems when there is still time to do something about them. Learning to follow instructions without argument and communicating problems before the deadline has arrived will save tremendous time and energy for years to come. But the benefits for your child are even greater. Mastering these critical life skills will serve your child well in school and eventually in the workplace. Teachers and employers expect workers to follow instructions without arguing and to observe deadlines. They need to comply or dedicate themselves to the project of bringing about change—and stamping their feet and swearing is not the way to go about it.

Parental Flexibility

Help your child to prepare for transitions. When it is nearing time for the fun to end at an amusement park or birthday party, or when you want him to be ready to leave the house on time, give the countdown: "We'll be leaving in fifteen minutes . . . in ten minutes . . . in five minutes . . . " That helps your youngster prepare psychologically. If he wants to lodge a protest, he needs to do it in advance, *before* you give the instruction that it is time to leave. When your child objects to an impending deadline, you might or might not decide to extend it. But once you have issued the instruction, "It's time to say good-bye. We are leaving," arguing about staying longer is merely an unproductive way to express anger. If you then allow additional time, your child has succeeded in defying your instruction. That small victory encourages most children to argue louder and longer next time. In many families, arguments about not wanting to leave ensure that virtually every outing starts and ends on a negative note.

Handling Protests

Give advance notice so your child understands that soon it will be time to eat dinner, do homework, etc., and can prepare. If your child proceeds to argue when the final moment arrives, there is no need to say anything. If it is time to leave the house, simply head for the door. Carry a young child or physically steer a tween toward the door. You may need to leave your teenager at home and let her find another way to get to school. If you must carry your child's shoes, hat, and coat so she can put them on in the car, so be it. If your youngster needs to fuss and fume, let her. Demonstrate by your behavior that she does not have to like rules; she does have to follow them. It takes two to have an argument. If you refuse to participate, there will not be one! And when she does settle down, congratulate her on her accomplishment. Being able to get over being angry about having to follow rules is a big step. Soon she will learn to follow them without so much upset.

Alert!

Transitions are hard for many children with ADD/ADHD. You can help by giving advance notice and by guiding her through the process: "It's time to start putting away the toys . . . time to get your coat . . . to say good-bye."

Improving Compliance

It is fine to call out or have your child set an alarm so he can prepare to do a chore or leave the house. You do not need to track your child down each time to announce that he has fifteen minutes, then ten minutes, then five minutes remaining. But when you announce that the moment has arrived for him to start the chore or get into the car, it is important to find him and tell him rather than yelling from across the house. In fact, whenever you are issuing instructions, avoid shouting. Most children resent being ordered about and treated in a manner they consider rude. Some children issue instructions of their own by saying, "You do not have to shout!" Others lodge a silent protest by foot-dragging. Be respectful, polite, and considerate. The time to be firm is when your child does not follow an instruction.

Clarifying Rules

Outline the rules so your child knows how you expect him to behave *before* he arrives at a destination, *before* company arrives, or *before* he starts doing a chore. To wait until he breaks rules to tell him what he did wrong sets him up to fail. Most children with ADD/ADHD have more than their share of failures as it is. When listing the rules, keep each one short and to the point. For instance, before going into the grocery store, remind your youngster that he is not to run in the aisles, not to swing on the rails, not to beg for toys or candy. You might say that he will be allowed to push the shopping cart as long as he can steer it and not bump into things.

Alert!

How many rules you present depends on your child's age and her current needs. You might focus on teaching a three-year-old just one rule she needs to follow at nursery school and work on it in the car as you drive her there every day for several weeks.

Present rule lists in a straightforward manner. There is no need to announce them as angry edicts or speak in threatening tones. If the response to your rule list is a disgusted, "I know, Mom! Gee— I'm not a baby!" refrain from defending yourself by pointing out all of the rules he broke and all of the babyish things he did when he was in that same situation last time. Instead, be proud: "You're right!

You are not a baby." Ask what rules he thinks he has mastered, and what he needs to work on. Before taking your child to soccer, consider the rules he needs to focus on:

- Do what the coach tells you.
- Get a schedule of practices and games.
- Do not blame others if you miss a goal.
- Thank the coach for volunteering his time.

After outlining the rules, remind your child of any successes he had the last time he was in that particular setting. Perhaps he only followed one small rule. There is no point in brow-beating your child by listing his failures. However, it is important to note past accomplishments so that he can build on them: "Last time I let you look at the toys while I shopped, and you stayed in that section of the store so I could find you, then you came right away when I called you." Pointing out what he did right reassures him that he can please you, boosts confidence, and pinpoints a concrete success he can build on.

Teaching Children to Follow Rules

Teachers dedicate a lot of time to creating lesson plans before they arrive at school. They consider what they want to teach, and their students' capabilities and readiness for particular types of lessons. Sometimes they put the new lesson on hold and devote time to reviewing old material first. They decide how to present the lesson. They plan what they will say so they can provide explanations in language the students can understand. Teachers also decide what kinds of sample problems to present, whether to go over examples or have students look at them by themselves, and whether to assign homework for additional practice. The same procedures are effective for teaching children to comply with rules. Whether you are taking your three-year-old to daycare or your eleven-year-old to see fireworks at the local park, consider the rules your child is likely to forget and prepare a mini-lesson to present in the car.

Lesson Plan: "You are not to fight with the other children."

- **Reasons:** You might get hurt. You might hurt another child. Or you might hurt their feelings. Fighting is not fun. The children won't want to play with you if you fight with them. The teacher will get mad if you fight.
- **Example:** If Mary takes your toy, you need to say, "No, Mary! That is my toy! You have to ask me nicely."
- **Problem 1:** If Mary grabs your doll, what should you say?
- **Reinforcement:** Yes, you say, "Mary, you need to ask me nicely."
- **Problem 2:** If Mary takes your doll and won't give it back, what should you do? Remember that you must not hit her.
- **Discussion:** You could let her keep your doll. Or you could tell her she can only play with it for five minutes and then she has to give it back. Or you could tell the teacher. You could say, "Teacher, Mary took my doll! She won't give it back. Could you please help me?"
- **Quiz:** Pretend I'm Mary. "Andrea, give me that doll! There! I've got your doll, and I'm not giving it back!" What should you do?
- **Feedback:** That's right. You could ask the teacher for help.

The Punishment Problem

Punishments may help parents vent some of their anger and frustration and can improve children's behavior in the short run. Hence, punishing misdeeds can be satisfying and create the illusion that the efforts to discipline are working. But research shows that over time, harsh punishments are associated with worse behavior. That is undoubtedly because punishment involves controlling through force and intimidation. As youngsters get older, they become harder to intimidate. Once they are old enough to escape out a window, it is impossible to use force to control them. They must be willing to comply.

Consequences Versus Punishment

For consequences that are designed to correct misbehavior to be of value, they must help children master particular rules. Your youngster may *feel* punished if he dislikes a consequence, just as it is common for well-nourished children to *feel* angry and claim they are being deprived if they want cookies and are only allowed to have vegetable slices. But that does not mean their parents are depriving them. Anger is anger; deprivation is deprivation. Since it is easier to avoid or end an unpleasant scene by handing a child a cookie, and since enduring tantrums wherein a raging youngster screams and hurls vegetable slices across the floor is so trying, it is understandable that parents so often seek to appease their youngster. But it is important not lose sight of what your youngster needs most at such moments: to learn to control himself. It is natural to hurt when your child is hurting. But because he feels bad does not mean you are a bad parent! It may mean that you are a very good one!

Setting Consequences

The first step to getting your child to comply with your instructions is to discover what needs are being fulfilled by certain persistent problematic behaviors. Next, try to work out alternative ways for your child to meet his needs. Jumping on the furniture usually indicates the need for exercise, and there are less destructive ways to get it. Accordingly, tell your child that sedentary pastimes such as television and video games will be forbidden in the evenings to free up time for playing outside or in the basement.

 *Essential*

Parents overuse and misuse time-out. Sending a child away can provide time to calm down but does not usually solve problems. Give your youngster a specific assignment to work on. Afterwards, discuss what transpired with an eye toward avoiding similar difficulties in the future.

Rowdiness before bedtime may signal that your youngster is overtired, so setting an earlier bedtime is often the best consequence.

Rowdiness can stem from boredom, too. You might have your child sit down and make a list of ways to entertain himself. Some children become rowdy when they are excited, so meditating for a few minutes can calm them (see Chapter 15, Calming Young Worry Warts). Some children become rowdy when they are angry with their parent but cannot say what is on their mind. In that case, they may need to sit down and write out their feelings in a letter, pound a pillow to discharge tension, or bring up their complaints in a family therapy session. The hyperactivity that drives rowdiness may be the result of having eaten foods to which the child is sensitive. The consequence may be stricter control of pocket money so that forbidden snacks cannot be purchased at school.

No More Criticism!

Many youngsters with ADD/ADHD are so hard on themselves and so sensitive that criticism of any kind beats them down rather than helping them to improve. Point out an error on a school paper, and they tear it up or suddenly become distracted and cannot finish. Play a game with them, and they cheat or quit the moment their opponent is a tiny bit ahead. Suggest that they did not do a good job cleaning up their bedroom, and they blame someone else or maintain that they are always being picked on. Their egos are simply too fragile to manage any hint that they might be less than perfect. It seems that children would need constructive criticism—how else are they to learn? Some parents try pretending that a child's imperfect effort or completely botched job was a great success. They pour on the praise hoping to shore up self-confidence and instill that can-do attitude that causes people to try harder. But phony praise is dishonest. It gives children an over-blown view of their competence. Or, because the rest of the world lets them know they are not nearly as wonderful as they had hoped, they lose trust in their parents' accolades. Instead of criticizing on the one hand or showering a very sensitive child with undeserved praise on the other, try giving gentle but honest feedback that instills pride in small accomplishments and points the way to improved performance in the future.

- "You remembered to put away your toys and you cleared your desk. Your room is looking good. Call me when you make your bed, and I'll bring a star to put on your star chart."
- "You got along with your brother for the first eight minutes we were in the car. I think that comes close to setting a record. Soon we'll make it all the way to school without an argument."
- "You did these three homework problems right! Congratulations!"
- "You remembered to hang up your coat! A lot of teenagers can't even do that. I used to lose lots of gloves, but then I realized that if I stuck them in the pockets, they would be there the next time I went out."
- (Speaking loudly enough to be overheard.) "What do I see here? The towels are hung up! And the cap was put back on the toothpaste! If you also start rinsing out the tub after you take baths, the bathroom will be so sparkly, I'll be squinting when I walk in."

When reviewing your youngster's homework assignments, mark the items or the portions of questions he got right with a plus sign or smiley face. Then, if he corrects errors, you can add more marks. When everything is correct, you can marvel over his perfect paper. Similarly, create checklists for what needs to be done when your youngster straightens his room, does the dinner dishes, or handles another chore. Have him call you when he finishes so you can congratulate him on the things he accomplished. Many children with ADD/ADHD symptoms are convinced that they cannot succeed at anything or ever please their parents. List the behaviors you are concerned about, note your youngster's successes, and celebrate by discussing what you liked or appreciated. List areas for improvement under goals, but if you have already addressed misbehavior at the time it happened, do not go over it again.

Target Behavior Checklist		
Behavior	**Behavior Successes**	**Goals**
Brush your teeth.	Did not argue.	Will not have to be reminded.
Get ready for school.	Was ready on time.	Will remember to take his lunch.
Be considerate.	Helped set the table.	Will not tease the baby.
Be respectful.	Stayed seated during dinner.	Will not make gross sounds.
Control temper.	Said what he was mad about.	Will not slam doors.

Enforcing Consequences

Change, even change for the better, is stressful, Shea's parents learned. When they began tackling her foot-dragging and defiance head-on, her behavior worsened and the power struggles turned into open warfare. "Make me," she said when they sent her to her room. She was sixteen years old, and they realized they could not. They had to work hard to come up with consequences they could enforce.

Kiddy Crimes and Consequences	
Problem Behavior	**Consequence**
Continues arguing when told to stop.	Parents do not respond until child can speak calmly.
Not ready in time for school.	Leave her at home and call the truant officer.
Does not clean room.	Does her own laundry.
Abuses telephone privileges.	No talking on the phone for a week.

Despite the storms that followed, Shea's parents were careful to point out when she was cooperative. When she raged, they comforted her by saying that learning to follow rules would get easier with practice—and that it was critical that she learn. "Soon you'll have a roommate or husband and a job. We are helping you to prepare for adult life." Shea's attitude softened sooner than they had expected, and she became much more pleasant and cooperative. They wished they had started being firmer years ago. But they were trying not to be too hard on themselves, either. They were learning to focus on Shea's successes and not berate her for the things she had handled poorly, and they realized that they needed to be similarly patient with themselves. "Congratulations to us! We're finally getting through to her," Shea's mother told her father. "She's sixteen, and we're finally learning."

CHAPTER 18

Building Social Savvy

F riends are important for youngsters' mental and physical well-being. Stress born of social isolation and peer conflict suppresses the immune system and increases vulnerability to illness and depression. For your child to master the art of getting along with others, making friends, and maintaining healthy relationships, you will need to teach a number of essential social skills. Casual comments like, "Play nicely," and "Ignore them and they'll leave you alone" barely scratch the surface of what youngsters need to learn. Get ready to serve as your child's social director!

Befriending Trouble

The memory of having been ganged up on by a group of preschool classmates remained painful for Meredith a dozen years later. "I was sobbing when the teacher pulled the kids off of me. The teacher shook me hard and said that's what I got for being so bossy and mean. I was just four, and she was blaming me!" In fact, Meredith's mother said that coming on too strong and being bossy had been problems since she was a toddler. She did not improve as she got older. The neighborhood children let Meredith tag along when they played outside, but they often teased her mercilessly. They did not play at her house or invite her to theirs. Having to find a partner on the bus or when lining up at school was humiliating because no one wanted to sit or stand next to Meredith.

Meredith recalled her father blowing up at her when they were playing cards. "This is why no one wants to play with you!" he exclaimed. "You're too bossy!" Meredith feared people would try to run right over her if she did not put them in their place. Still, hearing her father say that made her feel terrible. She tried being nicer by giving some classmates her lunch money, but it did not help her make friends.

 **Question?**

How can I help my child make friends at school?
Perhaps the teacher would ask a classmate to mentor your child and provide tips for getting along with others. Research indicates that simply having a well-liked student and an unpopular one do a project together provides an enduring social boost.

Finding a Niche

In eighth grade Meredith found a group to hang out with. They were outcasts like her, but they accepted her. Having people to chat with before school and to sit with at lunch felt like the answer to her prayers. Her parents disliked her new friends and kept grilling her about whether they drank or took drugs. They did, but Meredith said that her parents had no right to judge people they did not even know. She just wished her parents would be glad for her. They forbade her to see them, but they did not know what she did at school. And if she wanted to see her friends on weekends, her parents were easy to fool.

Peer Power

Peer relationships are now a big factor in children's happiness, but that has not always been the case. A century ago, youngsters' lives centered on the family. Relatives doubled as playmates and friends. In some subcultures, that is still the case. But most youngsters growing up today have only one or two siblings, and many have none. Sibling bonds have weakened to the point that many relate more like enemies than friends. Divorce, parents' long working hours, and separation from extended family members have separated children from their parents and other relatives.

Alert!

Family members can fulfill your child's need for companionship. Once your youngster behaves without having to be nagged (see Chapter 17, From Defiance to Compliance), he will probably prefer spending time with you. To pass the time in ways you both enjoy, see Chapter 8, Family Fixes.

Between daycare, school, afterschool programs, and extra-curricular activities, children are constantly surrounded by peers. Peers fill the family gap, and not having friends leaves many youngsters with no one. Suicides and school shooting sprees demonstrate the tragic results of social alienation. Because children with ADD/ADHD tend to have poor social skills and behave in ways that alienate others, they have a harder time making and keeping friends.

Young Loners

Although research shows that loners have more adjustment problems than the social butterflies of the world, that is a group average and is *not* true for everyone. Some junior technicians would rather build model airplanes, work on the computer, or put together a short-wave radio than trade baseball cards or skateboard with neighbors. Many aspiring musicians dedicate every spare moment to practicing their instrument and have no interest in chatting with peers about rock stars and getting together to watch MTV. Dedicated swimmers may be happiest when doing solitary laps, and some junior activists are too immersed in their political projects to think about scout meetings and playing with dolls. Many youngsters do not want to put time and energy into peers unless they share their interests. Being alone and feeling lonely are very different. It is a mistake to try to cure a child of what does *not* ail him! If he is happy, that is all that counts.

Alert!

The staff at therapeutic nurseries teaches troubled tots age three through six how to relate to other children. Individual play therapy and family counseling are also available. Many government programs have closed due to spending cuts. Contact your local child guidance clinic to see if one is available in your area.

The best solution for a child who is suffering because he lacks friends is to find an activity he likes that he can really get involved in. Like adults, children often bond around shared experiences. Peers with a common interest are more willing to overlook one another's personality quirks. But before searching for ways to fill your child's social calendar, you do need to help your youngster learn some basic social skills.

Parents as Social Directors

To teach your youngster how to get along with others, focus on the "do's" rather than the "don'ts." Saying "Don't!" is fine when your youngster has balled his hand into a fist and is about to punch a peer. But telling your child not to hit does not teach him how to handle himself when he is angry. Telling him not to take another youngster's toy or making him give it back does not teach him how to approach a peer and politely ask if he can play with it.

Etiquette Mini-Lessons

Before taking your child to the playground, dropping her off at school, or having other children to the house, provide a short list of instructions for getting along with other children. Younger children may need a lot of hands-on help as well. To a shy four-year-old who is planning to play in the sandbox at the park you might say, "See that little girl playing by herself? Sit down next to her and play with your sand pail for a few minutes. Then tell her your name and ask if she wants to play. If she says 'no,' tell her to let you know if she changes her mind. Can you do that?" If your child says she cannot, help her out by introducing her to the other child so she can see how to handle this type of situation. On your way home, discuss her successes in interacting with the other child. For some very shy youngsters, smiling and nodding at someone they do not know is a very difficult social skill.

 Essential

Children are often hesitant to reach out to make friends for fear of being rejected. This is as true for four-year-olds as for fourteen-year-olds. Tell your child how to save face if he makes a friendly overture and is rejected. Perhaps he can say, "If you want to play later, let me know."

When dropping off your tween at school, list a few of the social rules you think he needs to work on. "If a group of classmates is talking at recess and you want to join in, listen to the conversation for a while before speaking. Like adults, children do not appreciate having someone come in during the middle of a conversation and change the subject. Do not interrupt when someone else is talking. They think it is rude. And if you do interrupt, be sure to say, 'Sorry,' as soon as you realize your mistake. Then back off and listen carefully—*really* listen rather than thinking about what you want to say. People like good listeners. They do not like to have their conversations hijacked."

Teenagers also benefit from being given the words they can use in difficult social situations. Before your teen leaves for a party, tell him how to respond to antisocial pressures: "If someone asks if you want a cigarette, you can say, 'No, I don't smoke.' If you need an excuse, you can say, 'I can't, I'm trying out for track,' or 'No, but blow it in my direction. I'm an addict and I'm trying to quit,' or 'My parents have noses like beagles and will ground me for life if I come home smelling of smoke.'" Do not bombard your teen with a dozen lectures before he gets together with friends. Tackling one issue per outing is plenty.

Modeling

When you observe your youngster making a social blunder, such as being rude, bossy, selfish, or inconsiderate, be careful about how you intervene. Embarrassing your child in front of his peers almost always does more harm than good. That goes for toddlers as well as for teens. To teach your child to be considerate and respectful of peers, you need to demonstrate appropriate behavior. Call your youngster aside and speak with him privately if you need to make a correction. That is what your youngster needs to do if he is upset with someone. If he criticizes another child in front of a group, he is likely to find himself being shunned or challenged to fight the person he humiliated.

Teaching Without Preaching

Your child will be more willing to heed your advice about social matters if you have a close relationship and if he believes that you understand the social dilemmas he is facing. An excellent way to achieve a closer relationship and demonstrate that you understand what he is up against is to share stories from your past. Sharing how you felt about being teased when you were growing up lets your child know that you empathize and have grappled with the similar problems.

Telling what you did to try to win friends and influence enemies can give your youngster ideas about new things to try and mistakes to avoid while helping him to consider his situation more objectively. Recounting personal stories is especially effective with adolescents.

Essential

Making negative comments about your teen's friends may cause her to rebel and cling to them more tightly. Describe how relationships with troublemakers ended up hurting you, and she may at least be more alert to the need to protect herself.

Developing People Skills

There is an art to finding friends and sustaining relationships, but many aspects of getting along with others can be taught. Your child must be considerate of others, and command respectful treatment by being sufficiently assertive to hold his own with peers. Some children are very kind and compassionate toward others but can't stand up for themselves. They serve as handy targets for bullies, as well as for anyone else who happens to be in a bad mood. Some children are not naturally empathetic. They miss peers' subtle cues about how to behave and end up alienating others by committing social errors. Both types of children benefit from group therapy or a social skills training group, but such groups are few and far between. You may need to serve as your youngster's teacher.

You need to teach your child how to approach other children, join a game or conversation, and extend invitations to people she would like to get to know better. To sustain friendships, she needs to learn to give positive feedback, to share, to compromise, and to solve interpersonal problems. She needs to be able to respond assertively and defend against aggressors. See Chapter 9, Medication Maze, for suggestions for teaching your child how to fend off bullies.

Making Friends

For children to get along with one another, maturity level is more important than age. If your youngster's social skills are very poor, she may have fewer conflicts and more in common with younger children. And since older children tend to make allowances for younger ones, they are often more tolerant of immature behavior. Hence, your child may do better with playmates who are younger or older than with people her same age. Parents are understandably concerned if a student in middle school spends time with a group of teenagers. There is a risk that she will be exposed to too much too soon, but it really depends on the personalities of the children involved. Some teens are very protective of the middle school "child" in their midst. They go back and forth between relating like peers and like surrogate parents.

 **Essential**

The new kid on the block is likely to be especially open to friendship, and welcoming newcomers is a common courtesy. Walk your child on over to meet the new neighbor. If going with Mom is too embarrassing, have him deliver the casserole by himself.

To help a young child learn to initiate friendships, you may need to take him by the hand and walk him over to meet another child, introduce them, and suggest they play together. Teach a tween by giving him a mini-lesson en route to a social gathering. On the way to his first soccer practice, instruct him to say, "Hi, my name is Jim. What's yours?" Give him a conversation opener, too. "This is my first time playing soccer. How about you?" If your child thinks your suggestions are "dumb," tell him to watch to see how other people start conversations and report back to you. Afterwards, ask him what he noticed. The best way to learn social skills is to watch how other people interact. Many children with ADD/ADHD symptoms have poor social skills because they do not tune into the subtleties of social interactions or misread social cues. They benefit from reminders to pay attention, and they can often be more objective when watching how peers interact with one another.

An adolescent may pretend that your recommendations are too old fashioned to be of use. Nevertheless, your teen may re-fashion your ideas to fit his social group's slang and use them. When he's leaving for a dance, you might suggest, "Go up to someone you recognize, and say, 'Hi. Aren't you in Dr. Bob's third period English class?' or whatever. Whether or not you are right, you can start a conversation about your English teachers by asking how she likes her class.'" Even teens with good social skills can be lost when approaching members of the opposite sex. The idea of holding a normal conversation never occurs to them.

Keeping Friends

Use common courtesy expressions at home so your child develops the habit of saying them. If your youngster is having trouble keeping friends, remind her to use them with peers when you give a mini-lesson en route to a social gathering.

- Please.
- Thank you.
- I'm sorry.
- Excuse me.
- Would you mind . . . ?
- I'd appreciate it if . . .

Direct your child to give positive feedback to her friends by letting them know something that she likes or appreciates about them. She can tell a classmate that she liked her oral report, compliment her on her new haircut, or say something positive about her expertise at jump rope, long division, or anything else. She of course needs to be sincere and to keep her comments simple. Very needy children make peers uncomfortable by piling on the praise, so stress the importance of confining herself to one positive comment per day. Model this important social behavior by giving your child positive feedback, but aim for one positive comment per hour when interacting with your youngster.

Sharing and compromising can be hard for children with low self-esteem, so lots of children with ADD/ADHD symptoms need help in this area. Youngsters who are constantly on the defensive commonly fear that if they give an inch, they will end up having everything taken from them. Explain the miracle of sharing: by giving up something, they stand to keep a friend. At the same time, it is not possible to buy friends. They must be able to give without expecting anything in return. The point of compromising is to create a win/win situation. If your child and a friend cannot agree, he needs to toss out some suggestions that he thinks both of them might feel OK about. Role-play and/or give your child examples: "If you want to play one video game and your friend wants to play a different one, offer to play his game for ten minutes if he will then play yours for ten minutes." To teach your child the art of interpersonal problem-solving, use the techniques in Chapter 13, Tempering Temper, and role-play conflicts he is having with friends.

Finding Social Outlets

Most children with ADD/ADHD are unhappy at school and feel unsuccessful a good deal of the time. Finding an activity they enjoy that helps him feel successful can go a long way to improving the quality of their lives. For extra-curricular activities to be positive social outlets, your youngster needs to be able to handle himself in a group setting. When choosing activities, your child's interests need to be taken into account.

Organized Sports

When trying to find an extra-curricular activity for their child, many parents automatically think about soccer, baseball, and other team sports. They hope that playing a sport will improve coordination and provide good exercise, and that being on a team will instill discipline, teach sportsmanship, and provide a positive social outlet. Some youngsters are very physical, and their happiest times are spent in little league practices, at hockey tournaments, and playing in volleyball matches. But many children diagnosed with ADD/ADHD are clumsy and inattentive. They are regarded as liabilities by team members and coaches who are more concerned about bringing home a trophy than about having fun. A teammate who does not follow rules and instructions, stay on task, control his temper, and hold his own athletically is a source of frustration for everyone. The intense stimulation and stress of games can easily undo sensitive, insecure children. Their difficult behavior upsets everyone.

 ## *Essential*

"I made bad grades, had no friends—I was miserable. But then I started swimming. I was on the town team and the school team. I had teammates and something I could do well. Swimming saved me," one adult with ADHD remembered. Find an activity your child can enjoy.

It depends on the child, but team sports are not good choices for many youngsters with ADD/ADHD. Individual sports are another matter altogether. The emphasis on personal development can lessen the pressure to perform while providing healthful exercise and sensory-motor training. Possibilities include swimming, gymnastics, tennis, Aikido, Karate, bicycling, skiing, ice skating, and skateboarding. Dance is not a sport, but the emphasis on rhythm and body awareness can be good physical therapy for physically awkward youngsters.

Community Centers and Clubs

From puppet making to pottery, from judo to jewelry making, from basketball to basket weaving, town Parks and Recreation

Departments, youth centers, YMCAs, YWCAs, and many health clubs and fitness centers offer a wealth of fun activities for children. Open courts give them the chance to shoot baskets without the pressure to show up for scheduled practices and to perform for spectators catcalling from the bleachers. During the summer, check to see if they offer day camps, nature hikes, trips to swimming pools and museums, and other community outings. Youngsters can meet new people without having to worry that their negative reputation at school will interfere. Urge your child to take the opportunity to practice new skills.

Alert!

If your child is not ready for the intense peer contact of an over-night camp, try a day camp instead. Alternatively, find a camp for children with behavior problems and for at-risk youth at the American Camping Association Web site at ✑*www.acacamps.org.*

Churches and synagogues often have youth groups that are especially kid-friendly. Parents do not have to be members for their children to be welcome. Meetings usually begin and end with a prayer, but the emphasis is on fellowship and fun. Like scouting troops, youth groups sponsored by religious organizations tend to be less structured than school classrooms but more closely supervised than neighborhood free-for-alls. Hence, they can be especially good choices for special-needs children.

Positive Peers

When Meredith's parents discovered that she had been hanging out at the mall with the friends they had forbidden her to see, they had a heated confrontation. As Meredith defended her friends, her parents learned that she thought it was cool that one friend was going to have a baby and supported another friend's plans to drop out of school.

"School's a waste," Meredith maintained. "They don't teach us any-thing worth knowing." Her parents felt that they could not influence her, but her friends were influencing her in the wrong direction. They decided to try another approach. They apologized to Meredith for trying to control her, admitted that she was old enough to decide who to associate with, and suggested she invite her friends over for dinner. Meredith was delighted.

Kim and Wanda arrived wearing tight skirts, too much make-up, and sporting a dozen tattoos. Still, they were pleasant enough, and making conversation was easier than Meredith's parents had expected. When the evening ended and Meredith's mother said they should come again, Kim hugged her. "Your Mom's way cool," Wanda told Meredith. After they left, Meredith was friendlier than usual. The girls started hanging out at their house, and Meredith's parents supposed that was better than having them hang out else-where unsupervised. In fact, it turned out to be ever so much bet-ter. When Meredith's parents asked, "How's Kim?" or "What's Wanda up to?" Meredith would fill them in. They ended up discussing how scary it must be for Kim to face raising a baby alone even though she said she was not worried. They talked about how Wanda could not find a decent job since dropping out of school, so she watched soaps all day and had started taking drugs. Meredith's parents real-ized that their conversations with their daughter were causing her to see her friends more objectively. She had stopped glamorizing their lives. When Meredith said she was determined to stay in school, stay off drugs, and not to have a baby until she was much older, her words rang true. Her parents had not thought that inviting trouble into their home would help harden their daughter's determination to stay away from it. But it had.

CHAPTER 19

Daring to Discipline

T
he saying, "Sticks and stones may break my bones but names can never hurt me" is wrong. Name-calling may not break bones, but it can do some very real physical damage. Stress affects brain chemistry and alters the structure of the brain. ADD/ADHD symptoms worsen over time. Firmer discipline can often break destructive relationship patterns that drive chronic conflict at home. If you are struggling with the same problems day in and day out, punishing your child may help. It is less extreme than medication, but to be effective, your child must be capable of controlling himself.

Dialogue Disasters

When Philippe's mother asked him to go to the corner store to pick up a gallon of milk or do a chore around the house, a dreadful scene usually followed. Unless her son happened to need a favor, such as money or a ride, he would inevitably say, "In a minute." But when she checked on him half an hour later, he still had not started. When she pressed him, he would mutter rude comments, drag his feet, and do a very slipshod job. Often he would simply refuse to do as she asked. The same scenario often sensued when she told him to do his homework. As a result, his grades were not what they should be. He was often wild and rowdy in the house. At best, he settled down for five minutes. Getting him to do anything he did not want to do was impossible. When she tried, Philippe could be horribly disrespectful.

Despite Philippe's stubborn refusal to do as he was told, his mother knew he was at heart a good kid. He was openly affectionate toward her. When he sensed that she was especially tired or unhappy, he might massage her shoulders or tell a joke to cheer her up. He presented her with birthday cards he had made himself, and on Mother's Day she could count on breakfast in bed. Other parents commented that she was lucky to have such a polite, respectful son, so obviously he did not display the unpleasant side of his personality to others. He often got in trouble at school for getting out of his seat and not paying attention. But he also had some very good days. She was hesitant to be too strict because he had been diagnosed with ADD/ADHD and oppositional/defiant disorder. Supposedly Philippe could not control his rowdy, inattentive behavior. Yet he usually managed to do so when his father was at home. Unfortunately, her husband worked long hours and often traveled.

 **Fact**

Absent fathers and chauvinistic television role models have been blamed for boys' tendency to be disrespectful toward their mothers, but parenting style is undoubtedly central.

Identifying Your Parenting Approach

How parents discipline and communicate with their child depends on which of the three main parenting approaches they use. Most parents lean in one direction or another rather than using one exclusively.

- **Permissive: The "Hands-Off Approach."** Children make most of their own decisions, and parents limit themselves to suggesting, advising, guiding, and recommending. They assume that happy children will be motivated to behave correctly and believe that youngsters should be allowed to develop in their own way. They focus on building a positive relationship rather than dealing with misbehavior directly.

- **Strict: The Authoritative Approach.** Parents make most of the decisions but take their youngsters' opinions into account. They ask for their children's input, listen to their objections, and then make the final decisions. They assume that children need rules and limits and should be taught how to behave correctly. They teach by explaining and enforcing consequences.

- **Harsh: The Authoritarian Approach.** Parents make unilateral decisions. They lay down the rules and communicate by commanding, issuing orders, and by announcing what their youngster must and must not do. They view misbehavior as disobedience and believe a rule-breaker should be punished. To that end, they may take away privileges or spank.

Alert!

If lots of punishments are not working, try talking to and reasoning with your youngster instead. If you have tried to talk and reason, try enforcing consequences. If consequences have not worked, try punishment. Or see a family therapist to get professional recommendations.

Most parents automatically discipline their child the same way that they were disciplined when growing up. Until about 1955, the authoritarian approach was in vogue. The permissive approach became popular in the 1960s. For the last twenty years, the authoritative approach has been favored. Most child guidance experts now recommend it. Parenting books, articles, and classes teach parents how to communicate authoritatively and apply the concepts to combat behavior problems. While the approach is sound, you need to consider your child's personal capabilities and individual needs when disciplining. The approach that worked for you may not work with your child. The approach that works for most children may not work for yours. And you need to be flexible. The approach that works sometimes may not have an effect at others.

Most children being treated for ADD/ADHD are not psychologically disturbed. Most are not even unhappy, although their parents are suffering greatly. They administer medication because they do not know how to manage a youngster who would rather play than sit still, study, and do chores. Many college-educated parents hope that amphetamines will improve their youngster's study habits to increase her chances of getting into a top college and decrease rowdiness at home. They have talked until they are blue in the face and assigned endless time-outs and other consequences without effect. It is cruel to drug uninspired students and children who are too active for their parents' taste. By comparison, authoritarian parenting methods seem far less harsh, even though they sometimes involve spanking and other punishments.

Many youngsters steal from their parents because they want money to buy toys and candy. They lie to conceal their misdeeds, not because they fear punishment, but so as not to displease their parents. When asked what will happen if their parents catch them, it is clear that the consequences designed to deter them from misbehaving are unpleasant but ineffective. Most children say they will "just" be grounded, lose television privileges, or have to listen to a lecture. When asked how they manage to behave themselves in certain classrooms or at their father's house but not their mother's, the typical response is that they are afraid of "getting in trouble." For some that means having a teacher or parent get mad at them. For others it means having their name put on the chalkboard or being grounded. Still others fear being sent to the principal or being spanked. Clearly, many children are able to settle down, pay attention, and do a good job on homework and chores when being supervised by someone they consider very strict. Their ADD/ADHD symptoms improve dramatically. Too many are diagnosed with oppositional/defiant disorder as if something were wrong with them. Some are diagnosed with a conduct disorder and viewed as budding criminals. But they are not bad, although they are often very naughty.

Alert!

"Bad" children lack a conscience, are unconcerned about hurting others, and are only remorseful when caught. "Naughty" children know the difference between right and wrong. They want to please their parents but want to please themselves, too. They may misbehave when they cannot do both.

Parental Permissiveness

Some children do best with a basically hands-off approach. They are anxious to do the right thing, need little discipline, and make good decisions with little guidance. Many (but not all!) children diagnosed with ADD fall into this category. When they whine and argue or are irresponsible, mild consequences such as having to take a time-out may be enough to get them back on track. For serious misbehavior, consequences can relieve their guilty conscience. But in general, many parents find that clear rules and respectful explanations often work like magic for shoring up relationships and for getting youngsters to settle down, pay attention, and behave.

The permissive approach works best with all children some of the time. Youngsters need their parents to be sensitive and responsive to their desires. When youngsters understand *why* rules are important and *why* they need to apply themselves in school, study, contribute to upkeep of the household, and participate in family life, their behavior sometimes improves. But children are children, and the best among them can at times be self-centered, thoughtless, irresponsible, and disobedient. Toddlers and teens tend to be especially contrary.

If the current generation of youngsters is less well behaved, that is partly because many parents are permissive at times when their youngsters need more structure. Too many youngsters are given choices about most everything before they can hope to make good decisions. On visits to the ice cream parlor, even toddlers are asked whether they want a vanilla or chocolate cone. When they realize that they dislike the flavor they chose, their parent is likely to turn around and buy a different one. Children come to expect to be consulted about everything, to have their choices honored, and to be allowed to change their minds at will. They do not feel obligated to keep their commitments or adhere to their promises. When parents violate the unwritten rules they have unwittingly established, their children protest. "That's not fair!" they say. "Nobody asked for *my* opinion!"

Alert!

Shouting at your youngster sets a bad example for her. Yelling at her in public disturbs others. Raising your voice will not encourage her to do what you say. Be respectful when setting limits, and hold firm so your child will learn that you mean what you say.

Many parents believe in a permissive approach but cannot successfully pull it off. They say things they do not mean when they are upset or tired. Their children learn to discount their words and tell themselves, "Dad is just mad now" or "Mom's only saying this because she's in a bad mood." Negative communication patterns can quickly become entrenched. A parent addresses her youngster politely, and her child does not respond. The parent bridles at the lack of respect, becomes angry, raises her voice, and begins yelling, "Look at me when I'm talking to you!" "When I speak to you, I expect an answer!" Offended youngsters sound rude when they shoot back, "OK! I heard you! You don't have to shout!" Soon a sort of verbal shorthand develops. Parents who are accustomed to being ignored begin conversations by issuing orders and making threats. They sound authoritarian but do not follow up with punishments or even consequences. Many strong-willed children simply refuse to do as they are told. Many bossy, disrespectful youngsters learned to try to bend others to their will at home.

Visitors to the U.S. are often shocked to hear how rude and disrespectful American parents are toward their children. Most parents are polite when dealing with other people's youngsters, but when correcting their own offspring, they sound as though they are issuing commands to dogs. "Shut up!" parents shout when their youngster whines and begs for candy bars in the grocery store. "Do that again and you're going to get smacked!" they scream when their child bangs silverware on a restaurant table. Yet many parents turn around and buy the item their youngster wanted or pretend not to notice when she resumes banging the restaurant silverware a minute later. The result is that they literally train their youngster to ignore their admonishments while encouraging the very behaviors they want to eliminate.

Communication Coups

Permissive parents can have more success getting their youngsters to pay attention by varying how they talk. Instead of following a predictable course from irritated to irate as you repeat instructions and issue reminders, try going from silly to hilarious. Sing your instructions or use the strategy elementary school teachers find so effective: lower your voice to a whisper. When making corrections, speak firmly but do not raise your voice. Explain what your child is to do and why. This is standard practice among Japanese parents, and their children tend to be much more respectful and compliant than the average American youngster. Explaining, "No, you must not touch the candy. It belongs to the store, and candy is not good for you" conveys the rule, teaches that it is wrong to touch items that one is not planning to purchase, and explains why you are declining to buy candy. Adding, "I'll fix you something to eat when we get home" affirms your willingness to meet your child's needs, if not every momentary want and passing desire.

Toddlers may not understand verbal explanations, and no one likes to be told "no." Regardless of their age, upset children need to be comforted, not shouted at or indulged. A hug and some kind words, such as, "I know you want candy right now. I wish it weren't bad for your teeth" or "It's fun to bang the silverware. You love that noise, don't you?" helps many children to settle down. If your youngster is too angry or upset to accept comfort, try distraction. Have her help you empty the grocery cart in the store or hand her something else to play with in the restaurant. If distraction does not calm her, she may just need to cry or carry on for a bit. Depending on her temperament and how you have dealt with similar misbehavior in the past, the protests may be brief and mild or loud and long. Either way, they will eventually end.

Question?

How can I tell if I'm being too strict with my son?
Ask your child what he thinks he needs in the way of discipline, and how he would handle various situations if given more privileges. If his answers seem sensible, you might want to give them a try.

When your youngster is upset about a rule or chore, it is important to remain focused on the issue at hand. A verbal child can easily sidetrack his parents. For instance, a youngster may complain that too much is expected of him and too little of his brother. Instead of allowing yourself to be diverted, say that you will be glad to discuss other issues when the task at hand is completed. Or, if you are comfortable with using firmer discipline, say that while he is completing the task, you will decide on a consequence to teach respectful behavior or a punishment to convince him that rudeness is unacceptable.

When Talking Fails

When talking fails, many parents assume they have not used the right words. They keep explaining their position in hopes of finally getting through to their youngster. But some children do not respond well to words. Moreover, some youngsters refuse to participate in family meetings or to abide by the consequences even though they chose them. They would rather sit in time-out, be grounded, or lose privileges. They need more structure and firmer discipline. Their parents may have inadvertently taught them that they need not do as they are told or be responsible. Once destructive patterns have been established they are very difficult to change.

 **Fact**

ADD/ADHD is supposedly a psychiatric disorder. Yet few with this diagnosis jump on the furniture, torment their siblings, play with matches, and are cruel to animals because a voice in their head urges them to do bad things. Instead, they say that they do such things for fun.

Authoritative Parenting

The authoritative approach does not work for every child all of the time. But it is the most effective parenting method for most children most of the time. It involves providing clear structure, teaching, and enforcing consequences to improve behavior (see Chapter 17, From Defiance to Compliance). The consequences used by authoritative parents may be unpleasant but are not intended to punish. Instead, they are carefully designed to "fit the crime," to teach, and to solve a specific behavior problem. For instance, parents may revoke television privileges to ensure that a child who made poor grades has adequate time to devote to his studies. For stealing, the consequence might be requiring a young thief to apologize to his victim and return the stolen item or compensate him. Money to pay restitution might come from his allowance or be earned from doing chores. If a youngster strongly objects to a rule or consequence, parents consider his wishes before making a final decision. To communicate that a youngster's desire for candy has been considered, a father might say, "I understand that you want candy, but I will not buy it because it will ruin your appetite for dinner." Alternatively, he could say, "All right, since you missed lunch, I have decided to buy it for you." Either way, the parent makes it clear that he is in charge.

A good time to solicit children's input about family rules, discuss behavior problems, divvy up chores, and determine what consequences will motivate youngsters to comply and cooperate is during a family meeting. Create an agenda, set up a time, and do not try to cover too much at once. For negotiable items, write up agreements and have your youngster sign them. Written contracts can make an amazing difference to a child who is accustomed to being allowed to wriggle out of oral agreements. Agree to disagree when necessary and set up another time to tackle unresolved issues. Or say that you will inform your child as to your decision once you make it.

Alert!

"But what if your Mom finds out?" children ask when planning to do something that they know is wrong. "Oh, she'll just get mad and ground me. No big deal," many reply. Others say, "I'd better not. She'll get mad and I'll be grounded." Different things motivate different children.

Harsh Discipline

Rather than consequences, an authoritarian parent's goal is for her youngster to learn to behave out of fear of being punished. Such a mother may ground her child, assign unpleasant chores, shame, or spank. Some children with ADD/ADHD symptoms seem to need strong displays of parental firmness but do not actually benefit from them. Instead, their disobedience intensifies, and they become sneaky and deceitful or rebel. It is often better to use an authoritative approach for tackling one or two issues at a time and adopt a hands-off approach for everything else.

Even though shaming and spanking are controversial, they are sometimes beneficial. Most parents do both, even while maintaining that such tactics are tantamount to bullying, and are cruel and immoral. Most experts see many abused youngsters and traumatized adults still struggling to recover from childhood traumas inflicted by parents who thought they were merely being strict. It is understandable that they consider harsh methods too dangerous to recommend. Yet in Asian cultures, shame is commonly used and is considered necessary for children to develop consciences. Their youngsters tend to be better behaved and have fewer psychological and behavioral problems than U.S. children. In the animal kingdom, adult mammals swipe at misbehaving cubs, pups, and kittens to settle them down or to stop misbehavior, but they do not hurt their young. Many adults maintain that childhood spankings motivated them to behave. Although children dislike spankings, many report that they are sometimes more helpful than lectures and other consequences.

Alert!

Strong-arm parental methods inspire children to feel afraid, not respectful. Nevertheless, punishment can sometimes motivate them at least to *behave* respectfully. Too many children order, command, threaten, shame, and punish their parents. Parents do not deserve to be abused, either.

Some of the problems with punishment are described elsewhere (see Chapter 17, From Defiance to Compliance). There are other problems as well. Many parents try to shame their youngsters by humiliating them, which is traumatic and can have serious emotional repercussions. Instead of developing consciences, children become hard and conscienceless. Some parents lose control when spanking. They injure or abuse their child. Even if they do not spank hard, a very sensitive child can be seriously traumatized. Many parents claim they administer spankings to teach their child a lesson but are too out of touch with their own emotions to realize they are hitting out of anger. Because the short-term improvement in behavior is often dramatic, many parents spank too often. The predictable result is that their child's behavior becomes much worse than if they had not been so harsh.

A Michigan child care center was sanctioned for punishing an eighteen-month-old by "hot saucing" him for biting other children in 2002, although his mother had given permission. The technique of putting a drop of Tabasco sauce on a child's tongue has been used in the south for some time. In 2004, a parent was charged with child abuse for using this technique. When interviewed, some youngsters say it helps them behave and is better than time-out. As previously discussed, children with particular temperaments and personality characteristics think time-out is far worse (see Chapter 7, Hyperactive Heroes). Others happily serve their sentences playing in their rooms. Parents and professionals need to accept that abuse is not a black-and-white issue; the sensitivities of the individual child must be considered. To identify useful punishments, begin by asking your child what she thinks would help. Avoid punishments that local officials and your youngster view as cruel and abusive.

If a child truly feels that he did nothing wrong, a spanking will not convince him otherwise. It will trigger resentment and alienation. To have a positive effect, a youngster must agree that a spanking is warranted. Shaming a child is an attempt to convince him that he misbehaved. If the attempt fails, the result will also be resentment and alienation. To be beneficial, a youngster must have learned something useful. When children perceive their parents as unduly harsh, they are motivated to sneak and lie. Rather than deterring bad behavior, harsh treatment is more likely to prompt a criminal mentality. Teens should never be spanked, and parents need to avoid harshness when disciplining them. If adolescents perceive their parents as unduly harsh, they are likely to flee the house altogether. Many prefer living on the streets to putting up with a tyrannical parent. Many parents are afraid to shame or spank a child diagnosed with ADD/ADHD, because they have been told that he cannot control his hyperactive, inattentive behavior. If that is the case, punishing him is cruel, will be ineffective, and may well create far more serious behavior problems. But some can control themselves and simply choose not to.

Young and Developmentally Delayed Children

For spanking to be effective, a child must understand what he did wrong. Therefore, toddlers, preschool children, and developmentally delayed youngsters of any age should not be spanked. Swats can deter misbehavior by startling a tot and communicating displeasure. They can be effective for controlling dangerous behavior, such as running into the street or persistently reaching for a stove burner. A toddler will only associate a swat with his action when he is in the midst of misbehaving. If you delay, it will seem as though you are suddenly hitting him for no reason. That can destroy trust and cause serious emotional trauma that leaves lasting scars. But many parents need to delay until they are calm. If they swat when they are angry, they lose control, hit too hard, or cannot stop. The result is emotional trauma, physical injury, and a child abuse conviction. If there is any possibility that you will lose control and injure or traumatize your child, do not swat him! Do not remove your child's clothes, and only use an open hand. More than three swats at a time is abusive, and swatting once a day should be a maximum. Consult a therapist to investigate other disciplinary options if you feel the need to swat more often.

Spanking

Spanking entails inflicting a few short bursts of pain. It is cruel and abusive to spank children for things they cannot control, such as bedwetting, dropping and spilling things, and fidgeting. Instead, impose consequences designed to teach, such as requiring your youngster to change soiled sheets, wipe up spilled milk, and find other outlets for physical energy. If you are considering spanking your child, the first step is to discuss what your youngster has done wrong and verify that he agrees that he misbehaved. Announce your intention to spank him as punishment, and tell him what he must do to avoid being spanked in the future. Send him to his room to wait until you are calm. Hitting when angry is too dangerous. Do not remove your child's clothes when spanking. Only use an open hand, not a paddle, belt, or other object. Only strike the buttocks. Injuring a youngster by leaving bruises, welts, and red marks constitutes child abuse. See a therapist if your youngster seems to need to be spanked more than once a month. Do not spank a pubescent child. The sensations and emotional reactions can create sexual confusions and problems down the road.

 Essential

Try the opposite of what you have been doing. If talking about rules has not worked, use time-outs and other consequences. If imposing consequences has not worked, try explaining the rules and discussing their importance.

Rethinking Discipline

Philippe's mother held a family meeting to discuss his behavior. "What do you think I should do when you are disrespectful?" she asked. She was shocked to hear him reply, "You should spank me." She asked how that would help. He shrugged, and then said, "It would teach me to behave." Her husband agreed, but that seemed like a barbaric solution to his mother, and she could not imagine it would help anything. She scheduled an appointment to discuss the matter with Philippe's doctor, and was amazed when he agreed it was probably something to try. The next time Philippe was blatantly disrespectful, she did. It was a terrible experience for her, and she was sure that it hurt her more than Philippe. It turned out that she was right. When she asked if he thought he would be more respectful in the future, Philippe shook his head. She asked why, and he smiled. "Because it did not even hurt." That sounded nonsensical. She asked if he actually wanted her to hurt him. He shrugged, and said, "When you yell, it hurts my heart. That's worse than when Dad spanks."

 **Fact**

> The goal should be for youngsters to learn to control themselves, not for their parents to control them. When children reach adolescence and are big enough to fight back or run away, parents can no longer control them. Too often, jailors and prison guards have to take over.

Since the alternative was to medicate Philippe, the next time she spanked him she used more force. He cried and apologized for having been rude and disrespectful. She felt terrible, but it made a huge difference in his behavior. Afterwards, threatening to spank was enough to garner an apology and settle him down. If not, a consequence worked. His bouts of nastiness and rudeness declined dramatically, and there were fewer arguments. A year passed, and then he was too old for spankings. But his mother discovered that speaking more forcefully and enforcing consequences consistently were enough to keep him in line. Family life was less stressful, and because she was no longer afraid that if she gave an inch Philippe would take a mile, she was not so guarded. They had a lot more fun. She had always loved her son but had sometimes felt that she did not like him. Now she really liked him, too.

CHAPTER 20

Ending Bedtime Battles

merican children share an intense dislike of bedtime, and many parents have given up trying to force the issue. Yet sleep deprivation causes all of the major ADD/ADHD symptoms: inattentiveness, poor concentration, memory problems, disorganization, impulsiveness, and learning problems. Lost sleep cannot be made up. Once it is gone, it is gone forever. Toddlers, tweens, and teens have different sleep needs and issues. There are solutions for every child. You need to do your part to ensure that your youngster gets a good night's rest.

Sleep Deprivation

Even as an infant Larry had resisted bedtime. He did not sleep through the night reliably until he was five months old. His desperate parents sometimes put him in the car and drove him around the block to get him to sleep, but often the howling started again as soon as he was back in his crib. The only way to settle Larry down was to let him sleep in their bed with them. As a toddler, he often napped there as well. In nursery school Larry's parents tried to be patient with his requests for one more story, one more drink of water, and one more goodnight kiss. In primary school he was still calling to them an hour after he had been put to bed, usually because he was sure there were snakes under his bed. He begged to have his closet light turned on and the bedroom door left open a crack, then a little wider still. In third through sixth grades, Larry begged to be allowed to watch one more television show or to play one more video game even though his parents almost always said no. He insisted he was not sleepy, though prying him out of bed and dealing with his moodiness in the morning was a misery.

Question?

Is it wrong to allow children to sleep with their parents?
In most cultures, parents and children sleep together, and youngsters do not resist bedtime. The fear of sleeping alone that propels children into their parents' bed may have had survival value in prehistoric times.

In seventh grade Larry often stayed up past his bedtime to study. In high school he stayed up later than his parents and would have slept all day without them to drag him out of bed for school. They wondered how Larry would pass his college courses or hold down a job, but it was too late to do anything for him now. However, they had custody of their grandson. He was a lot like Larry, and they could not bear to fight the bedtime battles for another eighteen years. As young parents, they had survived with little sleep, but now they needed a full eight hours to function. Something had to give. They only hoped it would not be their sanity.

Reading Sleep Signals

If your child is generally relaxed, content, alert, and has no special problems with hyperactivity, attentiveness, or memory, it's safe to assume he is getting enough shut eye. Signs of sleep-deprivation include falling asleep in the car, being hard to awaken in the morning and after naps, crankiness and irritability during the day, and hyperactivity, especially in the evening. Being sleepy and being tired are very different, and learning to tell them apart is an important piece of the puzzle for getting your child to bed at night. Once children have crossed the line from being sleepy to tired, they have a harder time falling asleep because muscular tension increases. It is hard to be mentally relaxed enough to drift off when the body is physically primed for action. When children are sleepy, their bodies as well as their minds are relaxed, and slipping off to sleep is easier.

Essential

Children may not be in touch enough with their bodies to realize when they are tired. Pointing out, "You are cranky/hyperactive because you are tired; try to notice how your muscles feel," can help them start to recognize the symptoms that signal the need for sleep.

Watch for the subtle changes in appearance that signal whether your child is rested, sleepy, or tired. When sleepy, the face usually looks a bit softer, even puffy. The muscles around the lips and chin typically droop. Movement slows and youngsters lose energy, so they seem lethargic. There may be some yawns. Tired children, on the other hand, appear tense. The muscles around the eyes are tighter. Their eyes may appear sunken, and their faces show signs of strain. Activity level increases, but their movements are more random and their play is less organized. Moodiness usually increases as well, so children become sillier, crankier, and cry more easily. Pointing out, "You look sleepy now" or "I think you're unhappy because you're tired" upsets children because they expect that the order to go to bed will soon follow. Nevertheless, children who resist going to bed deny what they are feeling and may not notice, so parents should not be deterred from sharing their observations.

Sleep Apnea and ADD/ADHD

If your child snores, there is a good chance that he is not getting enough sleep due to a condition called obstructive sleep apnea. Children age two through five are at special risk, but people of any age can have it whether or not they snore. Sufferers go through repetitive cycles: they typically snore, choke, or gasp due to blocked airways. The airways eventually collapse, preventing them from breathing. Sleepers rouse as they struggle for oxygen, sometimes hundreds of times a night. But they do not awaken and do not realize that their sleep is being interrupted.

Common Symptoms of Sleep Apnea	
Physical Symptoms	**Behaviorial Symptoms**
Snoring	Inattentiveness
Awakening from snoring	Reduced intellectual functioning
Gasping or choking while sleeping	Poor academic performance
Awakening with a dry mouth or sore throat	Oppositional behavior
Falling asleep during the day	Defiance
Feeling tired during the day	Restlessness
Having high blood pressure	Depression and anxiety

Usually the cause of sleep apnea is unknown. Sometimes an obstruction is caused by fat or from having a small or receding jaw. Fat narrows the air passage and the shape of the jaw affects the position of the tongue in the mouth. Because children with sleep apnea do not get sufficient oxygen at night and have such poor quality sleep, their intellectual functioning and behavior are seriously affected. Sleep apnea is commonly overlooked and diagnosed as ADD/ADHD.

Alert!

Any sleep disorder or problem puts children at risk for an ADD/ADHD diagnosis. Sleepwalking, narcolepsy, insomnia, early morning awakening, and problems that stem from staying up too late and getting insufficient sleep are commonly misdiagnosed as ADD/ADHD. Depression changes sleep patterns, too, so sleep quality is usually poor.

Help for Young Insomniacs

The secret to falling asleep is being able to relax, so anything that aids relaxation helps to combat insomnia. "Trying" to fall asleep is the wrong strategy because it increases tension. If your youngster complains that she cannot sleep, anything that induces relaxation can help. That is why a warm bath and a gentle backrub can help. Reassure her that just relaxing in bed will ensure that she at least gets some rest. Counting sheep or engaging in a similarly boring mental exercise works for some youngsters but does not lure the sandman into every child's bedroom. Auditory children learn best by listening, and many find that falling asleep to music works by distracting them from the chatter in their minds. For visual children who learn by seeing, imagining a restful scene such as lying on the beach or gazing at stars (or actually opening the curtains and looking at the night sky) can be especially helpful. Tactile children learn best by touching. Concentrating on the physical sensation of breathing can make it easier for them to fall asleep.

There are a number of solutions for insomniacs of all ages. Number one is to set and enforce a regular bedtime. Allowing your youngster to stay up later will not teach the skills he needs to fall asleep. Rather, by going to bed at the same time each night, children become programmed to respond by feeling sleepy as the time approaches. Awaken your youngster at the same time each morning even if he stayed up very late the night before, and do not try to make up for missed sleep by allowing naps for older children or by lengthening toddlers' naps. Some youngsters have biological clocks that do not keep pace with the rest of the world. Such night owls cannot fall asleep at a reasonable hour despite a regular wake/sleep schedule, so they end up chronically sleep-deprived. Discuss the problem with your child's health care provider to see if a short course of melatonin might be helpful.

Be sure your child gets good exercise. Besides draining off excess energy, exercise relieves stress and anxiety. Help your youngster wind down with regular bedtime rituals that follow the same schedule each night. For example, follow a bedtime snack with a warm bath, bedtime story, prayers, a good-night kiss, and lights out.

 Essential

To help your child fall asleep, choose books that are soothing, not exciting. Be cautious about discussing problems before bedtime. Doing so is fine if it helps your child relax. Otherwise, set aside a time earlier in the evening to talk one-on-one.

Putting on some soft music in your child's room can serve as white noise and mask the sounds of television and conversation in other parts of the house. Anticipate your youngster's needs and eliminate excuses to get out of bed by having him use the bathroom before you tuck him in, putting a glass of water by his bed, and leaving a light on when you leave the room. Provide fearful children with a magic wand to keep the monsters away. Sometimes a flashlight works even better. Mean it when you say he is only to get out of bed if he is ill or has an emergency. Respond to manipulative bids for attention by refusing to respond other than to say, "You are supposed to be in bed."

Aromatherapy

Aromatherapy works! Lavender essential oil dispersed in the air enabled geriatric patients to sleep as well as when they had been on prescription medication. A more workable alternative is to buy lavender oil (the real thing, not a chemical imitation), mix a drop in vegetable oil, and use as a lotion. Try dabbing some under your child's nose so he can inhale it. Or purchase lavender-scented lotion from a health food store.

Teatime

Some herbs have sedative, tranquilizing, and hypnotic properties.

- Bugleweed
- Calamus
- Catnip
- Celery
- Chamomile
- Couchgrass
- Elecampane
- Feverfew
- Ginseng
- Goldenseal
- Hawthorne
- Hops Hydrocotyle
- Jamaica Dogwood
- Lavender
- Lemon balm
- Lemon verbena
- Mugwort
- Mullein
- Nettle
- Oats
- Passion flower
- Peppermint
- Rauwolfa
- Sage
- Scullcap
- Shepherd's Purse
- St. John's wort
- Valerian
- Verbena
- Wild Carrot
- Wild Lettuce

For a soothing bedtime drink, brew calming herbs to make tea. Use heat-resistant glass or a ceramic mug. Use two tablespoons of fresh herbs or one tablespoon of dried herbs and fresh distilled water. Just before the water begins to boil, pour it over the tea and steep for ten to fifteen minutes. Keep the tea covered to keep volatile oils from escaping.

Bedtime Snacks

There is a reason that people feel so sleepy after Thanksgiving dinner. Turkey is rich in tryptophan, a chemical that induces sleepiness, according to the National Institute of Mental Health. The body uses tryptophan to help make serotonin. Serotonin is a neurotransmitter that seems to be important for sleep and mood. Stuffing, a complex carbohydrate, facilitates the absorption of tryptophan. A bedtime snack that combines food high in tryptophan with a complex carbohydrate slows brain activity. Besides turkey, tryptophan is found in chicken, milk, cheese, fish, eggs, tofu, soy, nuts, and peanuts. Complex carbohydrates are found in whole grains (including whole grain breads and cereals), starchy vegetables, and legumes (peas, beans, and lentils). That makes chicken sandwiches, eggs and toast, pasta and cheese, and tuna fish with whole wheat crackers much better choices for bedtime snacks than chips and ice cream. Or try a warm glass of milk and a piece of toast. If your child turns up his nose at healthy choices, he is not actually hungry!

Essential

Oats (*Avena sativa*), lemon balm, and scullcap nourish and normalize the nervous system. Hawthorne is used to calm the mind in Chinese medicine. Because chamomile is in the ragweed family, allergic children should not drink it.

Best Bedtime Solutions

Beware of sending your youngster to his bedroom for time-outs when he misbehaves during the day. He will come to associate his room with punishment and upset. Going to his room at bedtime will evoke the same negative emotions. Try another location for time-out. One option is to have him sit near where you are working, have him follow you around the house as you vacuum and do other chores, or require him to hunker down in the hall. Avoid roughhousing, tickling, exciting stories, and emotional conversations that evoke strong emotion before bedtime. Caffeine is generally to be avoided after dinner, although consuming it in the late afternoon keeps some youngsters awake at night. For a list of foods and beverages containing caffeine, see Chapter 10, Over-the-Counter Remedies. Some cold and headache remedies also contain caffeine. Obviously amphetamines and other stimulant medications need to be avoided in the evenings.

Many parents work hard to ensure the day ends on a happy, upbeat note. To avoid arguments about bedtime, they try to sell their child on the idea of going to bed instead of enforcing strict limits. For most children, that is a very hard sell. The end result is nagging that lasts for hours and negativity that goes on for years. Teach your child to relax using the methods in Chapter 15, Calming Young Worry Warts, and in Chapter 7, Hyperactive Heroes. Learn how to get your child to follow your instructions the first time you announce that it is time for bed by following the recommendations in Chapter 17, From Defiance to Compliance. Use the suggestions in Chapter 12, Behavior Management, and focus on small accomplishments as you move your child toward the goal of going to bed without an argument. Once your child learns that you never agree to postpone bedtime on school nights, he may still not like to go to bed. But he will go.

Toddler Sleep Problems

The best cure for toddler sleep problems is to let your youngster sleep with you. Be sure to create a barrier so she cannot fall off of the bed. If you are not up for a wiggly, wet bedmate, try putting her in her crib with an article of clothing or a blanket that smells like you to add to her comfort.

Co-sleeping Safety

Although most of the world's children sleep with their parents, U.S. pediatricians warn that co-sleeping can be dangerous. If you push your bed up against your toddler's, check to be sure he cannot become wedged between the mattresses, or between his mattress and the wall. Co-sleepers, which are three-sided cribs designed to attach to the parent's bed, are supposed to be safer. Do not use a slatted headboard, or railings that could trap your child's head. Do not sleep together in a water bed. Never sleep together when you are under the influence of drugs or alcohol. You might roll on top of your toddler and not know it. Check areas within your youngster's reach for strangling hazards, such as dangling curtain cords. If you are not up for co-sleeping, move your child's crib or toddler's bed into your bedroom. This can cure sleep problems by enhancing the feeling of security that comes with having a parent close by. If she can tolerate having a curtain used to separate her sleeping area, light will not awaken her when you go to bed.

Toddler Sleep Patterns

Toddlers' sleep needs vary. Nine- to twelve-month-old babies average two naps per day. The average is one nap per day from age fifteen months to twenty-five months. Most children continue napping until age four. Although the quantities of caffeine in breast milk are small, be careful to avoid it when nursing your toddler. Avoid putting sugary juices in your baby's bottle. Doctors say that sugar does not affect hyperactivity, but parents say it does. The research suggests that the parents are correct.

Age	Total Sleep	Naps	Night Sleep
12 months	13¾ hours	2½ hours	11¼ hours
18 months	13½ hours	2¼ hours	11¼ hours
24 months	13 hours	2 hours	11 hours
36 months	12 hours	1½ hours	10½ hours

Some overly active tots simply will not stay in bed. They crawl over the top railing of the crib and fall and must be switched to a regular bed, and that makes them even harder to contain. It is dangerous for toddlers to roam the house alone, and some persist after their parents explain that they could get hurt and need to stay in bed. In that case, the only way to prevent late-night expeditions is to carefully childproof your toddler's bedroom and install a gate in the doorway to keep him inside. Leave out some toys he can safely play with and instruct him to call if he needs you.

Tweens and Sleep

The recommended sleep for eight-year-olds is 10¼ to 10¾ hours. For age nine it is 10 to 10⅓ hours, and for age ten it is 9¾ to 10 hours. Insufficient sleep suppresses the immune system and makes children more vulnerable to viruses. It also makes children less able to tolerate frustration and more impulsive. Many youngsters in this age group are sleep deprived because they lay awake at night worrying about personal and family problems. However, the most common impediment to sleep is their unwillingness to turn off the television, and put aside their video and computer games. To overcome that barrier, the simplest solution is for a parent to enforce lights out. If your tween receives overly taxing homework loads, hold firm about bedtime. Tell the teacher how long your child spent studying, and ask for a recommendation about what to do. Your youngster may need to work on assignments when given time in class or may need extra help. Many teachers do not realize that the assignments are so time consuming and shorten them on discovering there is a problem.

Teens and Sleep

The recommended amount of sleep for teens is 9.2 hours per night. Teens may not feel sleepy at bedtime because their biological clocks run on a 24.6-hour day. If it were up to them, they would stay up a half hour later each night and sleep in longer in the morning until they were staying up all night and sleeping all day. Some districts have seen improvements in both attendance and achievement by changing the school schedule to start later in the morning. Expect to have to set limits to get your teen to go to bed at night. Research shows that sleep deprived teens score lower on tests involving intellectual tasks, effort, memory, and concentration than when they get proper rest. However, teenagers do not realize how their lack of sleep is affecting them. They rate their performance on tests the same as their rested counterparts, even though it is much lower. Insufficient sleep is also associated with crankiness and irritability.

Reduced sleep has been linked to poorer grades, higher drug use, more frequent driving errors, and more moodiness. High school students who are concerned about doing well on a test should study over several days and turn in early the night before. Staying up late to study the night before may help her get a better score than if she did not study at all. But by insisting that she observe her regular bedtime, you teach the more important lesson: She needs to plan ahead and manage her time wisely. Rather than encouraging her to procrastinate, be firm about bedtime rules!

Explaining ADD/ADHD to Your Child

Q: What Is ADD?

A: "ADD" stands for attention deficit disorder. It is the term doctors give to children who have a hard time listening and paying attention. Many people do not believe they have a disorder but simply have a different personality, because many are especially creative.

Q: What are the symptoms of ADD?

A: At times children with ADD concentrate so deeply, they lose track of what is happening around them. At other times, every little thing distracts them and they have a hard time getting through a chore, school assignment, or project. They tend to look at the big picture and have trouble keeping track of and remembering details.

Q: What kind of problems do people with ADD symptoms have?

A: When students do not listen and pay attention in school, they miss a lot and their grades suffer. Missing parts of conversations can cause them to make unrelated comments that sound strange to others. Children with ADD can have a lot of conflicts if they do not pay attention when their parents speak to them. People with ADD have a hard time organizing their rooms, desks, and notebooks, so they tend to lose and misplace things. They do not naturally keep track of time, which can cause them to be late. Because they tend not to notice and remember details, they make more errors when doing schoolwork and chores.

Q: What can I do about ADD symptoms?

A: For most children, eating a healthier diet, getting enough sleep, and reducing stress improve their concentration and memory, and help them to think clearly. Develop creative talents, and be proud of them. Try to be patient with people who are not very creative and have a hard time appreciating how creative people think.

Q: Is there anything good about ADD?

A: Many people with ADD like being able to concentrate so deeply on a book, movie, video game, or project that time seems to stop and the rest of the world disappears. When they concentrate so intensely, they can get a lot done. Many children with ADD are able to get the main idea and to see the big picture more easily than people who are careful about details. And many children with ADD are intuitive, which means they often have hunches that turn out to be correct. They know a lot of things without knowing how they know them.

Many children with ADD are especially creative and inventive. Some are drawn to art, music, and poetry. Others are especially fascinated by ideas or inventions. Since people can be creative doing most anything, creative children excel at many different hobbies and jobs. Most people are not very creative, and they admire people who are. At the same time, most people believe it is better to follow directions and instructions than to invent new ways to do things.

Q: What is ADHD?

A: It stands for "attention-deficit/hyperactivity disorder." It is the term doctors give to children who are especially active. They may act or talk without pausing to think. Many have a hard time listening and paying attention. Not everyone agrees that ADHD is a disorder. Some think it is a different type of personality that is hard for most people to understand.

Q: What are the symptoms of ADHD?

A: Hyperactive children are restless and have a hard time sitting still. They constantly need to move. They need lots of excitement and action to keep from becoming bored.

Q: What kind of problems do people with ADHD symptoms have?

A: Hyperactive students get into a lot of trouble if they keep getting up from their desks or the dinner table without permission. Most adults get upset when children are rowdy indoors. Rowdiness annoys other children as well, so making and keeping friends can be hard. Unless children with ADHD symptoms pause to think before they do something, they can place themselves in danger. They may run into the street without looking both ways or hurt themselves when playing. They may touch things without first asking permission, which gets them in trouble in stores, upsets family members, and makes other children angry. They blurt comments, annoy others by interrupting their conversations, and hurt their feelings by making thoughtless comments. Boredom is often a big problem for them.

Q: What can I do about ADHD symptoms?

A: Getting more exercise and eating a healthier diet are what helps the most with troublesome symptoms. That can make it easier to sit still in school, be less rowdy in the house, and to feel less cranky. Although it has not been definitely proven, watching a lot of television and playing a lot of video games may make the symptoms worse. Most people advise children with ADHD symptoms to slow down so they will make fewer mistakes on schoolwork and chores. But the minds of children with ADHD tend to work very quickly. Some children actually concentrate better, make fewer errors, and do better work when they speed up.

Q: Is there anything good about ADHD?

A: Having a lot of energy is great! Energetic people can do a lot. Because their minds work very quickly, children with ADHD may be able to do several things at once and make fast decisions.

Q: Does anybody famous have ADD/ADHD?

A: Yes! Many well-known people have it. Historical records and biographical accounts suggest that if many successful people were growing up today, they would be diagnosed with ADD/ADHD. Some have achieved enduring fame, including:

Ansel Adams, Photographer
Alexander Graham Bell, Telephone Inventor
Hans Christian Anderson, Author
Beethoven, Composer
Terry Bradshaw, Football Quarterback
George Burns, Actor
Sir Richard Francis Burton, Explorer, Linguist, Scholar, Writer
Andrew Carnegie, Industrialist
Lewis Carroll, Author
Prince Charles, Prince of England
Cher, Actress/Singer
Agatha Christie, Author
Winston Churchill, Statesman
Bill Cosby, Actor
Tom Cruise, Actor
Harvey Cushing, M.D., Neurosurgeon
Salvador Dali, Artist
Leonardo da Vinci, Inventor, Artist
John Denver, Musician
Walt Disney, Filmmaker, Founder of Disneyland
Thomas Edison, Inventor
Albert Einstein, Physicist
Dwight D. Eisenhower, U.S. President
Malcolm Forbes, Magazine Publisher
Henry Ford, Innovator, Businessman
Benjamin Franklin, Politician, Elder Statesman
Galileo, Mathematician, Astronomer
Bill Gates, Computer Software Developer, President of Microsoft
Danny Glover, Actor

Whoopi Goldberg, Actress
George Frideric Handel, Composer
William Randolph Hearst, Newspaper Magnate
Ernest Hemingway, Author
Alfred Hitchcock, Filmmaker
Bruce Jenner, Athlete
"Magic" Johnson, Athlete
Michael Jordan, Athlete
John F. Kennedy, U.S. President
Jason Kidd, Athlete
Bill Lear, Founder of Learjet
John Lennon, Musician
Jay Leno, Comedian
Frederick Carlton (Carl) Lewis, Athlete
Meriwether Lewis (Lewis and Clark), Explorer
Abraham Lincoln, U.S. President
Wolfgang Amadeus Mozart, Composer
Napoleon Bonaparte, Emperor
Sir Isaac Newton, Scientist, Mathematician
Jack Nicholson, Actor
Nostradamus, Physician, Prophet
Louis Pasteur, Scientist
General George Patton, Military Officer
Pablo Picasso, Artist
Elvis Presley, Singer
Dan Rather, News Anchor
John D. Rockefeller, Founder of Standard Oil Company
Nelson Rockefeller, U.S. Vice President
Anna Eleanor Roosevelt, U.S. First Lady
Babe Ruth, Baseball Player
Muhammad Anwar al-Sadat, Nobel Peace Prize Winner
Will Smith, Rapper, Entertainer
Socrates, Philosopher
Steven Spielberg, Filmmaker
Henry David Thoreau, Author

Leo Tolstoy, Russian Author
Jules Verne, Author
Gen. William C. Westmoreland, Military
Robin Williams, Comedian, Actor
Woodrow Wilson, U.S. President
Walt Whitman, Poet
F. W. Woolworth, Department Store Innovator
Frank Lloyd Wright, Architect
Orville and Wilbur Wright, Airplane Developers
William Wrigley, Jr., Chewing Gum Maker

. . . To name just a few. Pursue your passion, and *your* name may be added to the list!

Appendix B
Resources

Books

A Symphony in the Brain: The Evolution of the New Brain Wave Biofeedback by Jim Robbins (Grove Press: New York, NY, 2000).

Beyond Ritalin: Facts about Medication and Other Strategies for Helping Children, Adolescents, and Adults with Attention Deficit Disorders by Stephen Garber, Marianne Garber, and Robyn Freedman Spizman (Villard: New York, NY, 1996).

Driven to Distraction: Recognizing and Coping with Attention Deficit Disorder from Childhood through Adulthood by Edward Hallowell and John Ratey (Simon and Schuster: New York, NY, 1994).

Peer Rejection in Childhood by Steven R. Asher and John D. Cole, editors (Cambridge University Press: New York, NY, 1990).

The Anxiety Cure for Kids by Elizabeth DuPont Spencer, Robert L. DuPont, and Caroline M. DuPont (Wiley: Hoboken, NJ, 2003).

12 Effective Ways to Help Your ADD/ADHD Child: Drug-Free Alternatives for Attention-Deficit Disorders by Laura J. Stevens (Avery Books: New York, NY, 2000).

The Everything® Homeschooling Book by Sherri Linsenbach (Adams Media: Avon, MA, 2003).

The Everything® Toddler Book, The Everything® Tween Book, and *The Everything® Parenting a Teenager Book* by Linda Sonna, Ph.D. (Adams Media: Avon, MA, 2002, 2003, and 2004).

The Diagnostic and Statistical Manual of Mental Disorders, Fourth Edition, Text Revision (American Psychiatric Association: Washington D.C., 2000).

Pocket Guide for the Textbook of Pharmacotherapy for Child and Adolescent Psychiatric Disorders by David R. Rosenberg, John Holtum, Neal Ryan, and Samuel Gershon (Brunner/Mazel: Washington, D.C., 1998).

PDR Nurse's Drug Handbook by George R. Spratto and Adrienne L. Woods (Delmar Learning: Clifton Park, NY, 2004).

The Feingold Cookbook for Hyperactive Children by Ben F. and Helene S. Feingold (Random House: New York, NY, 1979).

Ritalin Free Kids: Safe and Effective Homeopathic Medicine for ADHD and Other Behavioral and Learning Problems by Judyth Reichenberg-Ullman and Robert Ullman (PrimaPublishing: Roseville, CA, 2000).

Please Understand Me: Character and Temperament Types by David Keirsey and Marilyn Bates (Prometheus Nemesis Book Company: Del Mar, CA, 1978).

Talking Back to Ritalin: What Doctors Aren't Telling You About Stimulants for Children by Peter R. Breggin (Common Courage Press: Monroe, ME, 1998).

ADD/ADHD Behavior-Change Resource Kit by Gary Flick (Jossey-Bass: San Francisco, CA, 1998).

Without Ritalin: A Natural Approach to ADD by Samuel Berne (Keats Publishing: New York, NY, 2002).

Nurture by Nature by Paul and Barbara Tieger (Little, Brown: New York, NY, 1997).

Web Resources

✍*www.meditationcenter.com*
Lots of information and tapes to help you teach your child to meditate.

✍*www.chadd.org*
Children and Adults with Attention-Deficit/Hyperactivity Disorder (CHADD)
✍*www.504idea.org*
Council of Educators for Students with Disabilities

✍*www.nimh.nih.gov*
National Institute of Mental Health

✍*www.feingold.org*
The Feingold Diet

✍*www.ritalinfreekids.com*
Information about homeopathic treatments.

Videos

Don't Pick on Me! (Sunburst Communications: Pleasantville, NY)

Index

THE *EVERYTHING®* PARENT'S GUIDES SERIES

Expert Advice for Parents in Need of Answers

ISBN: 1-59337-043-1

How do I make sure my child is successful? What defines a successful child? Is my child already "successful"?

As parents struggle with these questions on a daily basis, *The Everything® Parent's Guide to Raising a Successful Child* helps put their fears to rest, providing them with professional, reassuring advice on how to raise a "successful" child according to their own standards.

This title walks parents through all emotional, intellectual, and physical aspects of development, including: building character, choosing—and limiting—extracurricular activities, disciplining effectively, ensuring a quality education, and instilling morals and values.

For parents of children with autism, daily activities such as grocery shopping or getting dressed can become extremely challenging. *The Everything® Parent's Guide to Children with Autism* offers practical advice, gentle reassurance, and real-life scenarios to help your family get through each day. Written by Adelle Jameson Tilton, the About.com Guide to Autism, this sensitive work helps you:

- Communicate effectively with your child
- Deal with meltdowns—public or private
- Keep your family together as one unit
- Find a school that suits your child's needs—integration vs. special education
- Learn about assistive devices, such as computers and picture boards
- Find intervention and support groups

ISBN: 1-59337-041-5

All titles are trade paperback, 6" x 9", $14.95

Help, hope, and guidance

William Stillman

ISBN: 1-59337-153-5

While children with Asperger's are generally of average or above average intelligence, they experience challenges with social skills, communication, and coordination, among other issues.

The Everything® Parent's Guide to Children with Asperger's Syndrome is an informative resource that helps parents recognize areas in which their child needs support. Filled with helpful hints and practical guidance, this authoritative work is designed to provide parents with the latest information on the best treatments and therapies available, education options, and ways to make life easier for parent and child on a day-to-day basis.

Also including information on resources, and vetted for accuracy by Diane Twachtman-Cullen, Ph.D., this title is a must-read for parents of children affected by ASD.

The Everything® Parent's Guide to Children with Dyslexia by Abigail Marshall—manager of www.dyslexia.com—gives you a complete understanding of what dyslexia is, how to identify the signs, and what you can do to help your child. This authoritative book seeks to alert parents to the special needs associated with this learning disability and offers practical suggestions for getting involved in the classroom. You will learn how to:

- Select the right treatment programs for your child
- Secure an IEP
- Choose a school and reduce homework struggles
- Develop your child's skills with the use of assistive technology
- Maintain open communication and offer support

All you need to ensure your child's success

Abigail Marshall

ISBN: 1-59337-135-7

A child's tantrum can happen at virtually any time—but whenever or wherever one occurs, it's always inconvenient, frustrating, and embarrassing for a parent and sometimes dangerous for the child herself. *The Everything® Parent's Guide to Tantrums* teaches parents to identify various triggers that provoke extreme reactions and helps them strategize ways to calm down their children and minimize any long-term effect.

Child care specialist Joni Levine, M.Ed., also helps parents to:
- Identify warning signs of a tantrum
- Cool off the child before the tantrum escalates
- Develop strategies and interventions to redirect the behavior
- Handle the outbursts without losing your own cool

R ising ⋯ Amer⋯ children. *⋯ Child* gives ⋯ develop th⋯ title includ⋯

- Prepar⋯
- Find ways to encourage more exercise and outdoor activity
- Maintain a child's positive self-esteem

Filled with vital information that can positively influence a child's future, *The Everything® Parent's Guide to the Overweight Child* is a parent's must-have reference for preventing and combating a child's obesity.

The Everything® Parent's Guide to Positive Discipline gives you all you need to help you cope with behavior issues. Written by noted psychologist Dr. Carl E. Pickhardt, this authoritative, practical book provides you with professional advice on dealing with everything from getting your kids to do their homework to teaching them to respect their elders. This title also shows parents how to:

- Set priorities
- Promote communication
- Establish the connection between choice and consequence
- Enforce punishment
- Change discipline style to reflect the age of the child
- Work with your partner as a team